Best Friends

OTHER BOOKS BY TERRI APTER

WORKING WOMEN DON'T HAVE
WIVES: PROFESSIONAL SUCCESS IN THE 1990S

THE CONFIDENT CHILD

SECRET PATHS: WOMEN IN THE NEW
MIDLIFE

ALTERED LOVES: MOTHERS AND
DAUGHTERS DURING ADOLESCENCE

OTHER BOOKS BY RUTHELLEN JOSSELSON

REVISING HERSELF: THE STORY OF
WOMEN'S IDENTITY FROM COLLEGE TO MIDLIFE

THE SPACE BETWEEN US: EXPLORING
THE DIMENSIONS OF HUMAN RELATIONSHIPS

FINDING HERSELF: PATHWAYS TO
IDENTITY DEVELOPMENT IN WOMEN

Best Friends

The Pleasures and Perils of Girls' and Women's Friendships

TERRI APTER, Ph.D., and RUTHELLEN JOSSELSON, Ph.D.

Crown Publishers, Inc. / NEW YORK

Best Friends
The Pleasures and Perils
of Girls' and Women's
Friendships
Apter & Josselson

To all who have been our best friends

Copyright © 1998 by Terri Apter and Ruthellen Josselson

Published by Crown Publishers, Inc., 201 East 50th Street, New York, New York 10022. Member of the Crown Publishing Group.

Random House, Inc. New York, Toronto, London, Sydney, Auckland
www.randomhouse.com

CROWN and colophon are trademarks of Crown Publishers, Inc.

Printed in the United States of America

DESIGN BY LYNNE AMFT

Library of Congress Cataloging-in-Publication Data
Apter, T. E.
    Best friends : the pleasures and perils of girls' and women's
friendships / Terri Apter, Ruthellen Josselson. — 1st ed.
    Includes bibliographical references.
    1. Female friendship. 2. Teenage girls—psychology. 3. Women—
psychology. 4. Interpersonal relations. I. Josselson, Ruthellen.
II. Title.
BF575.F66A68   1998
158.2'5'082—dc21   98-5661
                                              CIP

ISBN 0-609-60116-4

10 9 8 7 6 5 4 3 2 1
First Edition

ACKNOWLEDGMENTS

We are deeply grateful to all the girls and women who so candidly shared their experiences with us. To protect people's privacy, we don't name them here, but several people we can thank publicly. We are grateful to Cornelia Donner, Silvia Garnsey, Lee Hendler, and Dee Noonberg for their special contributions to our project. Many, many other people, however, told or wrote us their stories, and we learned from all of them.

Jaimie Baron's insightfulness was critical to our confidence in the way we represent girls' experience. Not yet out of adolescence herself, she gathered the stories of what we were missing in earlier drafts and helped us gain a perspective on the teenage years that is perhaps only available to one who is in them. She commented on the material, edited drafts, added and interpreted stories. An accomplished writer, she also helped us with the organization and presentation of our work.

Annie Rogers was an important contributor to early discussions of the project, and helped us formulate chapters long before they were written. Meg Ruley, our agent, gave us an insistent enthusiasm that ensured that the original idea would be fulfilled. Our editor, Karen Rinaldi, offered what every writer needs: a critical but appreciative response, as well as some of her own stories.

We also here thank each other for making the writing of this book such a pleasurable experience. There were no perils: working together was a joyous and enriching collaboration through which we became friends.

CONTENTS

Contents

PREFACE

Having spent years studying girls and women, we became aware of a disturbing lack of attention to girls' friendships. We have followed the growing scholarly and public interest in how girls develop and why adolescent girls are experiencing so much depression and anorexia and so many other disorders. We have puzzled over the fact that so many psychologists have located the storm centers of girls' experiences in families that don't understand them; in patriarchal society, which objectifies them; in schools that ignore them; and in the media, which encourages them to hold to impossible standards of beauty and behavior. But girls' emotional lives are lived with their girlfriends, and it is through their friendships that much of developmental significance comes to them. Why, we asked each other, isn't anyone writing about this?

Mothers of adolescent girls are particularly chagrined when they see their daughters, whose lives they could pretty well manage before early adolescence, in great distress because of events with their girlfriends—events mothers can neither see clearly nor control. Dealing with the cries of a hungry infant seems, in retrospect, like easy work compared to finding a way to respond to a daughter who was not invited to a party or whose best friend suddenly drops her. How can a mother counsel a daughter whose heart is set on that most elusive of prizes—popularity? Often, mothers attempt to minimize these problems, thinking, "Oh, well, she'll get over it." Girls then conclude, "She doesn't understand," and become unable to talk to their mothers. But mothers do understand, all too well. They understand from their own adolescence, even though these are painful experiences they would just as soon not remember.

Moreover, as women work together in companies, schools, and hospitals, these old dilemmas appear in new guises. Many women we interviewed described their workplaces as having much in common with junior high, as subgroups and shifting alliances with female coworkers, where issues of loyalty and betrayal, become the emotional center of the workday. Even as grown-up women, we don't "get over" the dilemmas of friendship; we carry our adolescent selves around with us.

We began this project working as like-minded colleagues; we met through our work. Our plan to write the book first emerged early in 1993 when Terri, at Ruthellen's invitation, gave a paper to the Harvard Colloquium on Human Development, presenting her research on girls' cliques in primary school. A brief conversation gave us the sense of homecoming: A book about girls' and women's friendships was an idea that would stick. Modern technology allowed us to work together with an ocean between us. Both of us wrote from the information and insights gleaned from years of interviews with girls and women, and we conducted yet more interviews specifically for this project. Terri observed girls on the playground of a British state (i.e., public) school while Ruthellen wrote from her experience as a therapist to adolescent girls and women. We also talked to guidance counselors and principals, who fervently told us that it was about time someone talked about this. Middle-school counselors, in particular, told us that the majority of their time is spent trying to console or advise girls in the throes of friendship problems. We were invited to come and listen to worried parents (primarily mothers) anxious and uncertain about how to handle their adolescent daughters' anguish at the hands of friends. We also drew from our own experiences, and the deeply personal nature of our writing convinced us that we should adhere to, when appropriate, the first-person singular of the narratives. The "I" in many vignettes refers sometimes to Ruthellen, sometimes to Terri. But the entire book was written together, layered by each author, each contributing to the authorial voice.

We have talked to girls and women in three countries and across race and social class, but this book does not investigate differences that may be culturally based. Instead, we were in search of commonalities across cultural divides. We try to represent experiences that seem universal, even though we recognize that we skim over interesting questions about differences. We speak primarily of the experiences of heterosexuals: Though we do discuss the special dilemmas of lesbian girls, we recognize that this subject is so broad that it merits a separate book. Undoubtedly, there are other experiences that we overlook—those of disabled girls, for one—and, while we expect that most girls and women will find some of their experiences accurately represented here, there will be others who will say, "But that's not how it is/was for me."

We wanted to write this book for both girls and women, but partway into the project, we became uncomfortable in the position of being two women writing a book (in part) for girls about *their* experience. Though girls' voices are ever-present in the text, and emerged in the very first drafts, we wanted to ensure their immediacy and freshness—after all, we hope this book will be read not only by women strengthened by maturity, looking back at their own friendships or trying to coach their daughters through their early friendship days, but also by teenagers and very young women who are still in the thick of these raw experiences. We therefore invited Jaimie Baron, a college freshman, to join us, because of both her writing talent and her greater proximity to the adolescent experience. Jaimie, who is also Ruthellen's daughter, added the voice of the younger generation, enriching and deepening our understanding of the world of teenage girls today.

Our aim in writing this book was to encourage a dialogue about what happens in girls' and women's friendships and how this affects their development. While we celebrate these friendships, that is not all we do, nor is that the book's point and purpose. Instead, we try to take an honest look at the perils and dangers inherent in them, the pitfalls and places where girls and women can stumble and lose faith in themselves and in relationships. We believe that friendship is a place where girls and women learn about relationships—about their pleasures and their anguish. We struggled with the problem of whether we had any advice to give to solve these enduring dilemmas, and so we asked adolescent girls what advice they had ever been given that was useful to them in dealing with their friends. The response was unanimous: "That's ridiculous. No one can give advice. It's something you just have to talk about with your friends." We were struck by the wisdom of this.

We offer no simple how-tos in this book; rather, we describe women's and girls' friendship experiences in order to try to understand them better, in the hope that our analysis will enable everyone to learn more from those experiences—and suffer less. The problems are inevitably ongoing, with each dilemma arising within a very particular relationship, between highly individual people. We don't believe that there is any simple advice, but we do believe in dialogue and conversation as the only way for girls and women to make sense of their relationships; therefore, we hope that mothers and daughters—and girlfriends of all ages—will use this book as a springboard for talking together, honestly, about their relationships. The more we understand about these relationships, the more we will be able to "be there" for our daughters and our friends—for each other.

Chapter One

"WHAT ARE FRIENDS FOR?"

There is a passion felt by girls and women that is so common, so routinely satisfied and frustrated, that it often fades into the taken-for-granted fabric of our lives. Girls' and women's craving for female friends, the work they do to construct and maintain these friendships, the pleasure and support they gain from them, the loneliness they feel when a friendship ends, are seen everywhere but seldom taken very seriously by psychologists—or even, sometimes, by other friends. Yet the ways in which girls and women negotiate these relationships play a crucial role in their happiness and their development.[1]

Each friendship makes its mark on an individual's psychology, and at each phase of development, friendships are molded to our changing needs. Girls at the mall are not just shopping. Women chatting over coffee are not just sharing news. Instead, they are involved in intricate patternings of love and conflict that inexorably shape and change who they are.

Within female friendship we satisfy our psychological hunger to explore different thoughts and feelings, to expand our understanding of our social and emotional worlds, and to exchange insights born out of that understanding. Because we are of the same gender, cultural norms about how we should look, how we should act, what we should say, when we should smile—and even how and when we can be sexual—are transmitted and enforced. Girls, however unwittingly and indirectly, teach other girls how to "be nice." They also teach other girls how to be streetwise or stuck-up. They build one another's confidence or tear it down. And it is only within the inner recesses of girls' society that these norms can be changed.

During the last two decades, as awareness of girls' and women's special developmental patterns has grown, attention has focused on girls' capacity for interpersonal skills, including their ability to empathize with others, to express their own feelings, and to cooperate with others.[2] What has been ignored is how frightening and frustrating it sometimes is to manage the closeness and conflict that are inherent in these relationships. This book explores the dynamics of these difficult and valuable relationships, their danger points, and their strong potential for growth.

No matter how many times girls suffer on behalf of friendship, they continue to pursue it. Again and again, girls return to a friend who teases, taunts, or betrays. Time and again, girls reveal themselves to a "best friend" whose heart, they should know from experience, will soon change. Over and over, girls trust an alliance that now protects them but, they should know from experience, will soon wound them. Nevertheless, these friendships remain important—and too valuable to give up, despite the fact that they sometimes hurt.

As girls mature into women and their sense of self becomes more stable, friendship often becomes less fraught on a day-to-day basis with anxiety and distress, but the earlier dilemmas of bonds with friends nevertheless come to the fore from time to time, causing anguish. Particularly as women increasingly work together in organizations, old ways of scuffling for place and recognition, for love and loyalty, seem to pervade the experience of life at work. How are we to understand this, we wondered, when the female of the species in our society, in contrast to the male, is currently depicted as relational, collaborative, and nurturing? The closeness and connection aren't shams. The meanness isn't more real than the caring. But how, we wondered, are these different aspects distinguished—or joined? Where can we find an account of female friendships that neither idealizes nor denigrates them?

We have been talking to girls and women in order to understand the private, screened-off world of girlfriends. We have discovered that this world is much less ideal—and also much richer—than we had imagined.

Friends are never "just friends." They also serve a variety of emotional and developmental needs. And, as in all relationships that are catalysts of growth, the changes they instigate can either push us forward or pull us back. In childhood and adolescence, having a girlfriend protects a girl from feeling isolated. If a girl has a best friend, she knows that she is special to someone outside her family, and she can take pride in being a person able to make friends. At the same time, some girls may sacrifice themselves to a friend, doing more than they want and saying less than they mean, for fear that she is the only friend they will ever have.

As girls experience their dependence on other girls, they become aware of profound inequalities, even among their "peers"; as they feel their way around the emerging rules and regulations of friendship, some girls feel inferior and powerless. Awareness of her difference from her friends is played out many times in a girl's life. Through friends, girls encounter values and expectations beyond those they learned in their families. As they discover their ability to make a wide range of friends, they learn more about what may be possible in their own lives. Admiration of a friend may lead to new life possibilities but may also mire a girl or woman in the swamps of envy.

As girls talk to friends, they learn that their inner worlds are neither crazy nor ridiculous. They discover that even their peculiarities are shared by others, and this gives them the comfort of common experience. And as they learn to listen to their friends in turn, they develop their ability to understand others. Girls use this sharing of selves to see themselves in new ways and to gain deeper self-knowledge. In adolescence, girls may create different persona and try them out on their friends. Later in life, women, too, when they are poised for change, try out new ways of being with their friends. Throughout life, as a girl or a woman searches for what is genuine and authentic in herself, she looks in the mirror of her girlfriend's gaze. She hopes to find a confirming and comforting reflection. If she sees criticism or rejection, she can be struck with panic, so accustomed is she to trust what she sees through a friend's eyes.

Over time, as change occurs within a friendship, girls may lose trust in others as they have to cope with betrayal, envy, and competitiveness. The quest is for security and stability in friendship, and girls may be willing to make all manner of transformations in themselves to ensure it. They may hide those aspects of themselves that they think a friend will disapprove of, or may give up certain activities and ambitions—or even other friends—under pressure from a friend's disdain. At an extreme, some may lose touch with who they really are or what they really want as they focus on what their friends expect of them.

Recently, friendships among girls and women have been portrayed in idealized terms, as though good friendships involve only good feelings.[3] These powerful relationships should, indeed, be celebrated, but if we lose sight of the rough learning processes within them, we simplify and distort what we need to understand. Girls' and women's friendships become laboratories for experiencing and resolving conflict. How is she to manage betrayals—secrets revealed, gossip spread? How can she voice her problems and feelings when she fears that a friend won't understand? Can she learn to argue with a friend without risking the loss of the relationship? Many women avoid speaking their minds to other women for fear of a dirty or destructive fight. Sometimes a valued friendship ends because a girl feels unprepared for the conflicts that arise. She sees an argument as an ending, a sign that someone is not a friend, when in fact she is simply unprepared to negotiate a flashpoint.

In addition, girls learn that networks of friendships can set up minefields of jealousies. Whose friend are you? they ask one another as they monitor their precious alliances for any signs of change. Later, in the midst of mapping out loyalties to girlfriends, they also have to work out how to keep up with their friends as romance and sex become part of their lives. Some women complain that girlfriends drop them as boyfriends take precedence, yet many women grow increasingly certain that bonds to girlfriends outlast the comings and goings of husbands and lovers. Far from being merely competitors in the search for a partner, other women help by assessing the character and value of a potential suitor and analyzing the progress of the relationship. Later, girlfriends may fill in the emotional gaps in couple relationships, and may even help stabilize marriages.

Though it is generally accepted that we develop our sense of who we are through "significant others," psychologists usually focus on the ways in which our parents put their stamp on us. Behind the most confident and powerful adult, we are reminded, lurks a baby screaming for her mother and a child wanting to please her parents. What is seldom understood is that behind the most confident and powerful woman is a girl who wants a friend, and a girl who has learned to be terrified of a friend's abandonment and betrayal.

Taking Friendship Seriously

In talking to girls, in reading their diaries, in seeing how they behave, we heard loud and clear how important their friendships are. Yet adults often look at friendships as the icing on the more important substances of a girl's psychological life.

Sidrian, in the course of her own therapy, expressed concern about Holly, her otherwise docile, good-natured fifteen-year-old daughter. Holly's grades had been falling. She'd been moody and uncommunicative. A crisis occurred when, one night, Holly stayed out all night without letting Sidrian know where she was. Sidrian thought she knew where the problem lay. Holly's father had recently remarried and Sidrian was herself about to remarry. She assumed that Holly was upset about these changes. She desperately sought counsel about what she could do to ease the transition. She tried to talk to Holly about it, but Holly angrily proclaimed that talking was no use, her mother just wouldn't understand. Finally Sidrian insisted that Holly see a therapist. Several months later, in consultation with Holly's therapist, I learned that Holly's distress had little to do with anything that her parents were doing or not doing. In fact, what was troubling her was a breakup with her best friend. Sidrian knew about this but hadn't accorded it any real emotional importance. Although otherwise psychologically astute and sensitive, she hadn't classed this friend trouble as anything serious enough to cause the changes in her daughter. "I guess if it had been a boyfriend, it would have been more apparent to me," Sidrian later said.

Only with more work in therapy was Sidrian able to remember that she, too, had once had a cherished girlfriend who turned against her, leaving her shattered and alone. She had forgotten that the pain of seeing her former best friend laughing with other friends was much like seeing her ex-husband with another woman. The echoes of lost intimacy, the sharp pangs of betrayal, the howling emptiness of being without a person who had been so central to her life—all these came back to her and she was able to tell Holly—now in a new way—that she understood.

Mothers of adolescent girls often dread the advent of the friend-ship wars. "Uh-oh, here it is," a woman may think as she sees her daughter come home crying from school for the first time because another girl called her "a name." Most mothers don't want to remember the pain of those years, so they try to minimize it for their daughters. "So what?" they may say. "What do you care what she says? Don't let it bother you." Yet mothers find themselves often quite helpless in this situation—it's one of the first signs that they cannot control the world for their growing daughters. "Should I call the mother of the offending girl?" they may consider. And, among their friends, they may ask, "What should I do when my daughter is not invited to the party she thinks everyone else has been invited to?" or "What do I do if my daughter chooses girls who I think are pressuring her into doing bad things?" These dilemmas occupy mothers as they see their daughters encounter the threshing floor of friendship.

For mothers of girls, problems of inclusion and rejection create complicated psychological conundrums. Briana told of her anguish over her daughter Lilli's birthday party. Lilli, age nine, was planning the party and wanted to invite all seven girls in her class except one. This girl, Kimmy, was, as Lilli described her, "always making trouble, not going along with anything, crying and being a pain." Lilli didn't want her there. Briana knew Kimmy and recognized that she was probably mildly impaired in some way—she was clearly different from the other girls—but told Lilli, "You can't just not invite her. She'll find out about the party and feel terrible." Lilli began to cry and scream. "But it's my party," she said. "Why can't I invite who I want?" This put Briana in what she felt was a hopeless position. "What am I teaching her?" she wondered. "If I make her invite Kimmy, I'm teaching her you have to put other people's interests before your own—to be 'nice'—when I've spent years learning not to spend all my life taking care of other people rather than doing what's good for me. On the other hand, I don't want to teach her to disregard other people's feelings and that it's okay to hurt others deliberately. If I would tell her to try to see it from Kimmy's point of view, I'd feel hypocritical, and anyway, I don't think she could really understand what I meant. She just felt that Kimmy would ruin the party." In the end, Briana did insist that Lilli invite Kimmy and Kimmy behaved just as Lilli had predicted, insisting on her way, crying inconsolably when she didn't get it. But Lilli thought it was a good party anyway. Briana, though, continued to worry about what she had taught her daughter. "I guess there's no right way here," she said. "Either way there's a price to pay."

Teachers and school counselors also note that much of their nonacademic work with adolescent girls is about friendship struggles—dilemmas that they also feel perplexed about how to handle. "Girls are in my office all day complaining about each other," said one middle-school principal. "One day one's feelings are hurt. The next day it's another. I wish I knew how to make this easier for them." One high-school counselor remarked, "The girls aren't violent as often as boys, but they take their fights more personally, and argue more, and come to us constantly about their problems with other girls. It's really hard to help them."

One reason women are so puzzled as to how to help girls with their friend troubles is that they sometimes miss the fact that these issues stay with them, too. As we worry about our daughters' obsession about weight and appearance, for example, we might notice that it is we ourselves as women who carry this social preoccupation—and that we practice it among our friends. Just observe women greeting each other: "You look terrific," says one. "Did you lose weight?" And the other laughs, unwilling to accept the compliment: "I wish!" The greeting ritual continues with more discussion of looks and weight before other topics are broached—news of job and family and other friends, painting pictures of success or failure. Similarly, adolescent girls begin to diet when their friends do. They are quick to notice who has gained or lost a few pounds. Boys seldom notice—it is girls who are most critical of one another. Boys don't read *Seventeen* and scrutinize the models in order to judge who has the "perfect face," the "nicest hair," or who "isn't really pretty." Girls do—and they do it together.

What keeps women from asserting themselves and taking more risks? What causes girls to mute themselves and their voices? While other writers have located the causes of girls' lowered self-esteem in the family, in the tyranny of men, and in the exploitation of Western culture, we here suggest that the worst anguish, that which women strive most to avoid, is learned in the neglected but indelible doings with girlfriends. Yet in these relationships, too, lie the paths to authenticity and confidence. The challenge is to tolerate the tension within these relationships so that we can make good use of them—and thrive.

But how can women perform that essential double act of understanding the formative experiences of our own lives while supporting our daughters so that they can learn from their own experiences? If grown-up women can remember their own adolescent experiences of friendship, if they can understand how they feared (and probably still do) a friend's harsh judgment, if they can recall their own panic at a friend's rejection, they can support their daughters by understanding them. But remembering is sometimes hard. It is hard because the early experiences of friendship are so raw with emotion, so fraught with contradiction. They are the crucial dilemmas of human relationships writ large: the longing for attachment versus the need to protect oneself from loss, the need to be liked for oneself versus the need to please, the wish for someone to understand perfectly versus the need for privacy, the longing to be like an idealized other person and the awareness of oneself with all one's limitations.

My adult life is peppered with responses that are not too different from what my adolescent daughter experiences, moments with friends that make me worry about whether I have misunderstood the nature of my relationships, whether I have trusted too much and am about to get clobbered. Janice, a close friend, rushes in to share some news: "Lydia has invited me to present a paper at the conference she is organizing in Paris. I hope she invites you, too." Immediately I am plunged back to my eighth-grade self. The popular girl has invited my best friend to a party and hasn't invited me. I hear the note of guilt and fear in Janice's voice—she wants to go, but doesn't want me to feel bad. If I am invited, too, she can rest easy. If I am not, she must fear my envy and worry that I will think her disloyal. And I am struck with a momentary pang of terror. Is Janice a little pleased that she's been singled out, and me not? What, then, does that say for our friendship? What if Janice now pulls closer to Lydia than she is to me? After all, Lydia has more to offer her—she is the queen; everyone does her bidding.

As adults, we may look back ruefully at the struggles of adolescent friendships, yet we fool ourselves to think we have ever really escaped them. The dilemmas remain, and what we learned about friendship in those trying years forever after colors our sense of self and our responses to others.

I am in my editor's New York office and her colleague comes in to tell her about the people who will be coming for cocktails that evening. I recognize the names, all famous—Jack Nicholson, Naomi Wolf, Amy Tan—and immediately I am back in the seventh grade listening to two girls talk about the party they are giving that weekend and who is coming. They name all the "popular" kids—the pretty girls, the athletic, good-looking boys. It's not only that I am not invited—it's that no one would even consider inviting me. I sit and smile pleasantly, pretending I'm not really listening. I want to feel, "I can accept this. These people have lives and interests apart from my own, and such well-known names arouse excitement that I do not. This is just how life is." But as an adult woman, I find the feeling (or the memory of the feeling) is powerful enough to make me want to run away. I'm not really an author, I feel, I don't belong here. I feel close to making a fool of myself.

Later, when I recount this story to Clara, my close friend, she points out indignantly how rude these women were to me. I should have gotten up and walked out, she counsels me. I laugh, remembering so many conversations like this, calling a "best friend" to assuage my humiliation and counting on a best friend to take my side and make me feel worthwhile. With her, my idiosyncrasies and merits have a sharp focus. With her, I feel as interesting as anyone.

As I hold on to these memories, I can assess my daughter's friends in a new light. Her long chats on the phone are not always "time wasting," and when she suffers a disappointment, or when she seems down in the dumps, I won't feel offended or shut out when she just wants to be with a friend. But when she is wounded in the friendship wars, I can treat her broken heart with the respect such pain deserves.

A woman's understanding of her own emotional journey through friendship is a valuable asset. Only by coming to terms with our own growth through friendship can we better recognize the role of friends in our current lives as well as be able to support our daughters, younger sisters, students, and patients through the maze of these relationships.

Friends — and Other Friends

Aware of friends' essential roles in their lives, girls and women construct a variety of different friendships for different purposes, which are regulated according to different rules: best friends, good friends, work friends, holiday friends—each is owed her special level of confidence, trust, affection. The rules, or codes of behavior appropriate to different friends, stay with us. When we are familiar with them we think, "I am a person who can understand others and fit in with them." When these rules escape us, we feel, "I'm out of it. I always say the wrong thing. I don't fit into this world."

That painful feeling of not belonging, a very particular agony, haunts us throughout life. We may defend against it by not venturing where we may not be welcome, by staying with those with whom we feel safe. To protect ourselves from exclusion, we ponder the meaning and nature of friendship. What does it mean to be or to have a good friend? What is expected of a relationship that is so ambiguously defined?[4]

Tanya spent the summer after high-school graduation seeing her friends every minute she was not working. Before they left for college, she and her three closest friends got together and solemnly swore together that they would be "friends forever." But when Tanya returned from her first year of college, she called none of them.

> I think I changed when I realized it was like a fake friendship. I realized in college that I didn't want to be like them. At the time, they knew everything about me. We always laughed, had fun, went out to lunch, went out at night. But in college it was a whole different experience. When I came back, I thought of them differently. I don't want to say they're immature—I would say they aren't as nice as my friends in college. And it seemed like other people's friendships sounded much more real. I used to look up to my friends here and then I realized that they are just interested in popularity and status. Sometimes in high school I would wonder about if they were true friends, but I didn't know any different. If I was upset, they'd cheer me up or listen to my problems or whatever. But they'd drop you in a minute if something else came up. And so much of our friendship was kissing up to Jane and doing everything she said because she had all the power. I can see that now. And there were plenty of times when I wasn't that good of a friend—if Jane called me up, then I'd forget Suzanne. I have a better idea of what friend-

ship is—and those are my college friends. Now my friends in college won't let me get away with that. They really care.

Here Tanya is trying to work out what makes a real friend, as opposed to a fake friend. She attended an urban high school in a city that seemed to seethe with movement and change, yet her friends had been her friends since middle school, and the stable enclaves of the other friendship groups in her class had made her own seem natural, safe, and satisfying. But her college experiences led her to rethink her high-school friendships, to experience and understand them in a new way. And she will continue, as she gets older, to think about friendship in many different ways.

The label "friend" is a slippery one, and girls and women continue to puzzle over what makes a "real friend." Friendship ranges from deep, abiding love to temporary companionship, from soul-searing intimacy to momentary shared laughter. Some women consider the neighbor with whom they exchange pleasantries and garden tools a "friend"; others reserve this word for people they have known for years and with whom they have shared important milestones. Friendships can be situational, bonds that grow from a shared activity and wither when our interests change. In other cases, friends transcend situations and become people whom we keep in our lives no matter where we are or what activities we may pursue. Women discover that friendships can take many shapes, and they have friends for quite different purposes—and struggle with the linguistic problem of calling both their most intimate confidante and their tennis partner a "friend."

As we brood upon these matters, so important to us, we are often led astray by the cliché that a good friend is always supportive—certainly never mean, never envious. If a friend isn't reliable or consistent—the assumption is—then she's not a good friend and we should get rid of her. But with friends, as with parents and lovers, we form complex relationships that involve both good and bad elements, moments of joy and closeness alternating with times of misunderstanding and disappointment.

Recently, I had a phone call from a friend of mine, Roz, who is fifty-four. She was distraught because a woman whom she considered one of her best friends wrote her to say that she thought their relationship had disintegrated into mere acquaintanceship and she did not wish it to continue. Roz, who's a confident, thriving artist with three teenage daughters, said that she could not have been more deeply hurt had she been sixteen and dumped by a boy she adored. And yet she rejected my attempt to comfort her by condemning her friend's behavior. "Don't think she's not a nice person," Roz pleaded with me. "She's nice and intelligent and really wonderful. And that's what makes it so awful." Roz wants to mend the relationship, but even if it can be mended, she will mourn the loss of what they once had. "I'll have to be careful now about what I say, and always check up on how she's responding to what I do. So even if I apologize for whatever I've done to hurt her, and she accepts, it just won't be the same."

Like Tanya, Roz is still working out what it means to be a friend. And, in part because there is no clear socially shared definition of friendship, each girl and woman has the opportunity to be creative in sculpting the purpose and quality of her own friendships. But in doing so she must constantly revise her understanding of what she can expect from others.

"She's my close friend," says Evelyn, age fifteen, "but I'm not sure we really like each other. We do almost everything together, but I don't think she's really interested in me, really wants to know me. I don't know what it is. It's like we're friends, but there's no real love there." Evelyn is in mid-adolescence, but she could be any age, trying to make sense of her emotional experience in relationships. What is love in friendship? she wonders. What can—and does—she expect? These issues, of course, seem much more familiar when they are expressed in the context of an intimate partner relationship. But we also practice and ponder these problems in friendship, where we first wrestle (in our social, noninfantile experiences) with the fact that people can give you some things emotionally but not other things, not everything.

Friends Through the Ages

Whatever we learn about ourselves in our families is only a prelude to testing who we are in the larger world. Through our efforts at friendships with other girls we form an indelible sense of our value in the world of others. At first friendship is relatively easy—we play with whoever is available. Soon friendships begin to put their stamp on our identity. As we talk and play and fight with girlfriends, we begin to ask: Are we like the sporty girls, the popular girls? Are we easily liked? Are we valued? What are we valued for?

Around the age of eight or nine, girls discover new meanings in their relationships, and new power to include and exclude friends from the magic circles of their affection. Suddenly it dawns on us that girls who we have known for years choose to play together and don't ask us to take part. Or the girl we have always lent our math homework to viciously mocks the clothes we are wearing. The world, which had been an accepting place, begins to appear cold, unpredictable, and hurtful. "Isabel sat and talked to me for an hour today!!!" I wrote exuberantly in my eighth-grade diary. "Maybe I could get in with her and her friends," I continued hopefully. Then, two days later, I wrote, "Isabel passed me today in the hall and wouldn't even say hello. What a snob she is! I hate her!"

The tragedy of this time is that we never really understand what goes into being accepted or rejected. We study the qualities of those who seem to us to be "in." Is it that they are prettier, have better

clothes, make jokes, act tough, smile a lot? What is it that draws others to them but not to us? I look in the mirror: I have nice eyes and
spend hours on my hair, which will never flip up the way the other
girls' hair does, but it doesn't look bad. I take care only to wear colors
that match and I try to have a "good personality" even though I am
not sure just what that is. But it doesn't work for me. The "popular"
girls don't want to be with me. They won't talk to me if I try to sit
with them at lunch. For no apparent reason, I am an outcast, and oh,
how I want to belong . . . When I have a brief fling with "being
popular" in the ninth grade, I know my status is precarious. Wonderful phrases are whispered back to me: "Amy thinks you've got the
nicest clothes" and "Jay thinks you're cute" and "What a nice laugh
you have." I want to believe that the real me is now being discovered.

Throughout adolescence, girls make intensive use of friends as
mirrors and models. They work hard to express themselves so that
they can see their newly emerging selves in their friends' eyes. So,
too, they try to become what an admired friend already is, or choose
as a friend the person they wish they were. Learning to negotiate the
pitfalls of friendship begins to seem the core of existence to the growing girl: In friendship she discovers what she believes to be the final
verdict on her true worth. The center of life is one's girlfriends—the
ups and downs, the loves and hates. And the injuries from the battle-
field of friendship remain as sensitive scars to be reopened—and
healed—again and again.

By the time girls reach womanhood, they have had myriad relationships with girlfriends, each of which has provided an element of
emotional knowledge. There is always the friend who needs too
much of you—and the girl has to learn how to erect boundaries of
self-protection and to do this with tact. There is inevitably the competitive friend, the one who can always top your story—and if she
decides to put up with it, the girl has to learn to recognize this trait as
an aspect of her friend and not lose her own self-respect. There is also

the friend who is capricious, loving one moment and indifferent the next—and the girl must learn to tolerate the fluctuations in the emotional weather. The intimacy and enigmas of friendship create the proving ground for a girl's being a person connected to others, and they provide those centrally important negotiations for finding a place for both self and other that will occupy the woman for the rest of her life.

As life unfolds, girlfriends continue to structure the social world, defining the boundaries of what is possible and desirable. As young women step into the spheres of work and family life, they learn from one another about the choices of adulthood: They see one friend racing ahead in her career, another developing a hobby into a profession, another absorbed by family life. They may experience self-doubt through these connections, but as friends they also share excitement with, and gain confidence from, one another. In the workplace, women colleagues may experience working together in terms of the rules of friendship. Discussing an idea or strategy, women may take it personally when their suggestion is rejected. Even modification of a proposal may be taken as though it were a disloyal or critical response of a friend. Repeatedly, we heard women speak about the ways they could be troubled by their own responses to their female colleagues, or shocked by a hostile response to something they did, yet we also heard about the pleasure women felt in working well alongside one another. There was a generally expressed wish to understand the difficulties within these relationships, and to make sense of the persistent echoes of past friend troubles.

At midlife, women often find friendship at a different level, experiencing maturity and discovering together new, unformed aspects of themselves. The friendships between older women are no less important: "My friends keep the youth inside me alive," eighty-year-old Joyce said. "They remind me how sharp and funny I am." Through friendships, girls and women of all ages develop individual and independent selves: Their route to individuality is through these connections.

The camaraderie and fun of friendship make it a major source of joy. We can get immersed in it, pulled along by its currents. We have to be somewhere, do something, we mean to end the engagement with a friend, but each remark leads inexplicably to another topic, each a fishhook for our attention. There is the volley of information, the rising curiosity, the sudden eruption of humor. We feel better, see things more clearly, gain strength to face a challenge—or we see our former resolve crumbling and our former sense of clarity grow confused. As we go about our daily lives, making the small and crucial decisions that shape our fate, the voices and visions of our friends stay with us. As Kirsten, in her thirties, reflected during an interview, "The bond is so strong and wonderful—it saves your life sometimes. With all the judgments and difficulties and fear, friendship is as deep as any tie in life."

Chapter Two

"IF ONLY I HAD A REAL FRIEND"

I knew a variety of unhappiness long before I reached middle childhood, but I can date my awareness of one particular brand of distress from the age of eight, when first I experienced a new bliss of close friendship—some girls clearly wanted to be with me, took heart from my company, found interest in my games, and felt no party or team was complete without me—and then, just as suddenly, just as inexplicably, I was cast out, while other girls huddled together, whispered about me, and found me wanting. The issues, even then, seemed both minute and devastating. I kicked a ball at recess, and someone said I "let the boys see my underpants." I said my mother was going to New York, and my girlfriends later concurred that I was "always boasting." I asked whether someone could come to my house on a certain day, and one girl nodded knowingly to another: I was angling for an invitation to the party they were holding on that very day. Notes passed from one girl to another during class; they were both obvious and secret. I was meant to see that a note was exchanged, but there were gasps and looks of hilarious horror if it got so close to me that I might read it.

This was more than an experience of rejection. I was now aware that I could undergo, at other girls' call, a terrible transformation. One minute I was liked, I was valued, and the next minute I became something quite different—the focus of their criticism, the butt of their jokes. In this position I was powerless: Anything I said or did was proof that I deserved their criticism and derision. If only I had a real friend, I often thought, I would be safe.

In the seventh grade, I met Jenny. Her name followed mine in the alphabet in the days when we sat alphabetically in school, so she was next to me most of the time. We began writing furtive notes to each other during class, talked on the phone, then began going to each other's houses after school. We seemed to have the same outlook on things and we protected each other. We always made a place for each other—saved a seat for each other at lunch or in school assemblies. We laughed together and made up cutting stories about people who were mean to either of us.

By the eighth grade, I wrote in my diary, "If anything happened to Jenny, I would die." I took my parents for granted—they had to love me, I reasoned. But my best friend, Jenny, was the first to love me freely, to be loyal to me for no reason other than that she chose to be. She marked my first experience of a different kind of love.

The intensity of friendship is equal to that of any romance. Some girls experience early friendships like a crush. At age twenty, Tamara told us, "The first time my best friend, Allison, told me that she loved me, it hit me like a runaway truck. We'd talked on and on about how close we felt, how different our friendship was from all others, and when she said the word *love,* it all suddenly made sense. The idea that we loved each other had honestly never occurred to me before."

From an early age, girls begin to bond together to survive in the larger social world. In childhood, girls' friendships seem easy, placid, and interchangeable. A friend is someone to play with. But as a girl's world enlarges, a friend becomes someone to "be" with. Friendship evolves into a context in which to define oneself; each friend offers shifting norms and endless possibilities for reflecting on and discovering who we are. And as intimacy evolves in friendship, issues of loving and becoming intertwine and interact. We come to know ourselves only in a context of love.

As girls grow and their emotional experience becomes more complex and differentiated, they become aware of a range of responses to one another—there are girls they love and girls they hate, girls they long to be like and girls they despise. Girls are drawn powerfully to one another because they can see themselves in the other—an awareness that can arouse both comfort and anxiety.

Whatever intimacy women experience with men—either as partners, lovers, or friends—most say there is a different quality to their friendships with women.[1] Girls' and women's friendships offer the experience of talking "from the heart" and discovering the relief, pleasure, and humor of someone who we experience as fundamentally like us sharing experiences and opinions with us. Alice, fourteen, says her best friend understands even "the silliest things about me. I told her I liked the bath so hot I had to inch down in it real slowly, and she said she did, too, and her legs went red as lobsters, and I said mine did, too. And we eat our apples exactly the same way." We can catch Alice's feeling of warmth as she discovers how idiosyncrasies are shared. The ideal of sharing everything, understanding everything, and never arguing has staying power because it is so often—nearly—achieved in these friendships.

From infancy, girls show marked awareness of human responses: They scan facial expressions far more intently than do male infants. So, too, it is now thought, do girls emerge from infancy with a special capacity for empathy built into their sense of self. Their psychological legacy stems from their early family history: Because of the way families tend to be structured, both girls and boys, as infants, usually form their first, most primitive attachment to their mothers. Through this attachment, infants gain interpersonal experiences that build up an early sense of self: "This is the kind of being I am." As they grow, children establish a sense of a more or less separate and gendered self. As girls learn what it means to be a girl like their mothers, they retain their needs to connect closely, intimately with her, such that being close to someone and being like them feels part of an unbroken whole. For boys, however, the crystallization of a gendered self ("I'm a boy. I'm not a girl.") involves a radical shift away from their initial identification with their mothers and so they often defend their gender identities with strong self boundaries.

Girls form their distinct and gendered selves without the need for such sturdily defended self boundaries, and in fact girls often confirm their sense of self through connecting to others.[2] With this emotional readiness, they enter the arena of friendship with other girls, quick to talk, inquire, and empathize. But a girl's psychological penchant to blend with a friend doesn't mean she'll always feel sympathy for her, or always like her, or always be glad for her successes and displeased by her misfortunes, for girls' extra push toward feeling connected to others—which all humans have—also arouses envy and anxiety. And so she comes to the social cauldron of girls' friendships with a rich sensitivity to the meanings of even minor interactions. What does her smile say about me? If she turns away, what is she turning away from? Am I like that girl over there, who seems so confident and centered? Am I like that other girl, who's not likely to be liked by other girls?

The earliest female friendships try to re-create the unbounded harmony and closeness that girls once experienced with their mothers. This plays itself out in the joys of touching and exploring—much like the little girl enjoys snuggling with her mother, playing with her hair or jewelry, or trying on her clothes. Young girls walk to school arm in arm, stroking one another's hair, admiring its texture or color. Even a friend's clothes can be exciting. Lydia wants to borrow Sita's top or get shoes just like Callie's. Her borrowing and copying are proof of just how closely they are joined. How thrilling to be matched to such a wonderful person: "There's something so . . . well, it's sort of perfect about her. I can't believe how pretty her face is—and when she wears her yellow sweater . . . I don't know, there's just something about her . . ." Lydia gropes toward an explanation of the "crush" she has on Callie. This quartet of eleven-year-olds—Sita, Surinder, Lydia, and Callie—huddles together, speaking in voices too low for anyone else to hear, and touching one another as they talk. "Your hair is so silky!" Callie remarks, and rubs a strand against her cheek. Callie and Surinder style Sita's hair, enjoy the new look, and then put it back like it was.

Though these elfin-looking eleven-year-olds, in a suburban school plagued by neither crime nor wealth, are not yet concerned with glamour or fashion, their bond is reinforced through grooming. Their attention to one another is intense and full of wonder. Caresses and compliments are commonly exchanged. Many psychologists view this behavior as a practice run for later romantic attachments, as though the feelings between girls are mere shadows of future love. But as girls perform the rites and rituals of friendship, they are not simply rehearsing for the important stuff of subsequent sexual relationships. Instead they are both carrying forward the close bond with their mothers and beginning the long story of attachments to girls and women that will shape their identity and outlook throughout their lives. And, in doing so, they are learning about close relationships of all kinds. For the dynamics of girls' friendships are the dynamics of all relationships, and the process of learning about friendships, which begins before adolescence—the feelings of wholeness, homecoming, and delight, as well as the pain and confusion—continues into and through adult life.

When Anyone Will Do

A young girl's entrance into the larger social setting of school is frightening and threatening. Having someone to be with is a basic need, and the first element in friendship, and so initially, a girl may simply need someone to pair up with in order to prevent that awful feeling of being alone while in a large group. Without a friend, life is simply no fun. In the process of researching girls' friendships,[3] Alison Tamplin discovered these poems by two six-year-olds, which express the distress of isolation:

> *Bell's gone*
> *All out*
> *I'm lonely in the playground*
> *No one to play with*
> *people come and pull you about*
> *I tell the teacher*
> *but she says ignore them*
> *I stand near the wall*
> *people staring at me*
> *I feel sad*
> *I hate people staring at me*
> *Whistle goes*
> *All in*
> *I'm happy now.*

> *In the playground*
> *some shout and scream*
> *some moan and tease*
> *some grab and punch*
> *some growl and cry*
> *some kick and shoot*
> *some rush and fall*
> *and some*
> *like me*
> *just stand*
> *and stare.*

These situations arouse immediate empathy for the poor, lonely children. But why are we so quick to understand their pain? What are they feeling, and how can these feelings be explained? And how do these feelings echo in us throughout our lives?

We immediately understand the excruciating discomfort of being an outsider. "Nobody likes you. Nobody wants to play with you," is the cruelest thing one girl can say to another. Much of what happens with our friends involves a staving off of this fear. Though the playground setting is one we leave behind, the terror of being the unconnected one in a larger group returns at many points throughout life. Here is Tanya at eighteen, the confidence in her new maturity knocked out of her as she enters her first year in college:

> I thought I was grown up and ready to be on my own. I was itching to leave home! There would be no homesick phone calls from me. But the first day I walked into the dorm and I saw the other girls, and every other girl seemed so pretty and smart and so together . . . I'd just look at a girl and think, "Will she be my friend? Will she? Will she?" And if nothing clicked between us, I'd think, "Well, that's it, she doesn't want to be my friend." I'd walk down the corridor and feel like I was sticking out like a sore thumb because I was alone. I was so lonely I didn't want to go anywhere.

Tanya sees herself as "grown up," but the transition to college awakens old fears. As she begins her college life, her doubts about whether she is really smart and whether she can really be independent from her parents magnify doubts about whether she can attract friends. In the pressure to succeed, Tanya feels "unwanted and out of place, and I really wonder whether I'm going to make the grade." Nothing can banish this feeling as easily as being welcomed into a group of friends, or having a special "best" friend. Nothing reinforces this cold isolation as much as being alone and seeing others sharing talk and laughter, with the inevitable unease that she might be the one laughed at. At some point in every girl's life, friendship comes to signify who she is and what she is worth: "I don't have anyone to play with—I'm lonely" branches into something like "I don't have anyone to play with—I'm worthless."

I am fourteen years old and downtown shopping in a department store with my mother. Across the aisles I spot some girls from my school and immediately duck behind the racks of clothes, my heart beating fast, afraid they will see me. I know that if they do see me, they will immediately try to spot who I am with, and I will be utterly humiliated to be seen with my mother. Not that I don't love my mother or enjoy her company—I do. But I know the code: If you are with your mother on a Saturday afternoon, it means you had no friend to be with and that you are, therefore, the worst possible thing—an outcast.

This fear, ingrained in us on the playground, that being alone signifies a personal defect, persists throughout life. Even usually confident adult women may hesitate to go to a movie alone for fear that someone they know will see them and think they have no friends. There is shame that attaches to aloneness—the fear that others will think that being alone implies that one was unchosen, rejected by all. At such times, being with any girlfriend will do.

But Not *Just Anyone* Will Do

The need for a friend, however, goes beyond the fear and shame of being alone. Girls, from early adolescence on, have a deep need to find someone who experiences life as they do—a person who faces challenges and problems that no other people in their world are dealing with in the same ways. In order for a girl to find the emotional resonance she craves with a friend, the friend must share the same social climate and know how it feels to have a "bad hair day." A true friend knows about guys a girl likes who don't smile at her but seem to smile at everyone else. She knows about grumpy teachers who "pick on" her friend. A friend, with her knowledge of the significant minutiae of her life, can support her in ways her family can't, for too often her problems seem small, even funny, to those who have passed them by and entered into another age.

And then comes the dawning awareness that our friends reflect who we are. Our choice of friends—and who chooses us—helps to mark out our place in the social world and give us a reading on who we ourselves are. Inevitably the growing girl comes to learn about the tyranny of popularity and the pangs of status.

Although we may aspire to equality in relationships, we learn early on that it's very hard to achieve. Status constantly changes and is constantly renegotiated, and the safe haven promised by friendship is often found and often lost.[4] Reciprocity—the give-and-take that friends count on—is unstable. The idea that children of the same age are "peers" comes from outside, not from inside children's own experience. Girls of the same age, living in the same neighborhood, and going to the same school may seem "equal" in all important respects to parents and teachers who are outside their magic circle of knowledge, but the girls themselves are excruciatingly aware of inequalities among them. Callie knows that Sita's mother is available for chauffeuring and chatting during the day in a way hers isn't. Sita knows Surinder's dad is a well-respected doctor and can help Surinder with homework, whereas if she, Sita, has trouble in math, she has no one at home to turn to. Surinder knows she has a weekly allowance that would make her friends' eyes widen "if they knew—but I'd rather they didn't." And over and above the differences among their families, they are highly sensitive to who's prettier, smarter, more popular.

I remember how uneasy I felt at fifteen about my place in the pecking order. Am I more like Lizzie, I wondered, who has thin hair, whose skin has a strange tinge, whose voice squeaks, whose shape is "not right"? Or am I more like Pam, who is long and lean, who has an infectious laugh and a talent for writing poems? Am I anything like Kathy, who is so smart and self-contained, or Mary, who is worldly and friendly and has such nice eyes? These three girls have an importance and definition I lack. I want to be like them, and I don't want to be like Lizzie. Maybe I can be like those I most admire by befriending them. But when I do so, I learn that because I think they are so much better than I am, and because I am afraid of who I will have to be with if I can't be with them, I have no grounds for complaint, no thrill of self-righteousness, when they give me a hard time. I work to please them because the line between Lizzie and me is very fine. I touch a network of dilemmas in my attachment to others: What do I do to avoid being alone and still have the friends I want for friends?

Girls evaluate themselves in terms of who they can attract as friends. Their decisions about how to behave within a friendship are shadowed by their assessment of their own options within the friendship market. Erica, a soft-spoken, petite brunette, aged twelve, explains to me that she is reluctant to complain about Gail's bossiness: If she does, and Gail takes offense, then who will be her friend? Anna, her stocky, athletic classmate, also tells me that Gail sometimes annoys her. She solves the problem by spending more time with Iris. Anna explains:

> Gail can get so possessive, so you have to step away for a while. She says, "We're going to do this," and then gets mad if I don't want to. She even tells me where to sit at lunch. So I'm going around with Iris now. You can't just talk to Gail about it. She'll say, "How can you say I'm bossy? I'm not bossy. Go do what you want. I don't care."

Anna, because she is willing to walk away when things don't feel right with Gail, has more control in the friendship with Gail than Erica does. She has another friend to turn to. But such "contingency friends" are hard to come by.[5] Who wants to be picked up and put down at another girl's whim? Probably someone who is simply grateful not to have to be alone—like Erica, who worries about offending a friend and having no one to be with. Erica's strategy, based on her belief that she isn't good at attracting friends, is to put up and shut up. The fear of being lonely outside the friendship constrains what she can say or do within it.

We can never be sure we have left these insecurities behind. Tanya, during her freshman year in college, decided to pledge a sorority when her closest friends decided to do so. "They were so important to me and they were all going to do it. I didn't really want to pledge and they did, so I thought, 'What am I going to do? I'll be alone next semester.' So I had to, because I knew that they'd get closer and I'd never see them." Tanya's insecurities can be located, in part, within her family: She is fearful of disappointing her parents and worries about being overshadowed by her sister. These family dynamics set the scene for the paradoxes and compromises of human relationships that she reworks in the context of her friendships: Tanya needs her friends for support, but what real support can they offer if she does something she doesn't really want to do just so she won't lose them?

"Don't do something just because a friend does," mothers frequently tell their daughters. "You can always make other friends." But such parental wisdom doesn't acknowledge the depth and tenacity of very particular friendships, which may feel like keystones on which the whole social order depends. And so it may be that mothers, forgetting (or denying) their own turbulent friendship histories, give the same worn and useless advice that convinces a daughter that her mother doesn't understand or doesn't listen.

Girls need to be with girls they like and admire, rather than merely someone who will "do," someone who is "just company." The sociologist Barrie Thorne recalls the failure of her own strategy when she fell out with her best friend. The solution was easy—or so she thought at first. All she had to do was get another friend. This turned out to be tricky—especially if she wanted to like the replacement:

> I . . . remember a time in the fourth grade when Kitty, my best friend, and I had a falling-out. Feeling like an outcast, I took a pencil and paper and mapped the alliances then in place among the girls. My diagram indicated that Marlene was also without a best friend and hence the logical girl with whom to pair up. My problem was that I didn't like Marlene very much and couldn't force my feelings to abide by the logic.[6]

A substitute friend isn't easy to find—at least for a girl. Boys' friendships tend to center on activities, on doing things together,[7] and if one friend isn't available to go skate-boarding, then another friend can easily substitute.[8] But, as Barrie Thorne discovered, girls don't simply look for a stand-in when they look for a friend. When a young boy describes a friend, he speaks about his skill at sports, or his bravery, or maybe his sense of humor or adventure. Girls, long aware of the importance of closeness and intimacy, describe a friend's character in depth and detail. In making a friend, a girl will make all sorts of judgments about her: She has guts, she's daring, she is pretty, she listens to the same music as I do, she gets my jokes, she has a nice laugh, she can be depended upon to wait for me while I change for gym, or save me a seat in assembly. Girls also have a special sense of being understood when they are with a friend. Anybody will simply not do.

Friendship is a form of love, of attachment to a special person, and this increases girls' vulnerability and the potential for heartache. As Lillian Rubin notes in her book *Just Friends,* because the emotional promises implicit in friendships are often unfulfilled, there is "a particular urgency between best friends . . . that seems to seek constant reassurance—a tension that has no easy resolution."[9] The way we handle this tension affects us throughout our lives. Is the memory or fear of loneliness so striking that we do anything to attract a friend or sustain a friendship? Do we reach out to anyone who is willing to pair up with us, so as not to be alone, or do we exercise our judgment of who is a good friend and who is not, even when we crave company? Are we panicked into placating a friend when conflict is threatened, or are we able to stand by our own beliefs and values even when this means asserting our difference from a friend? Are we able to choose friends, or are we stuck with those who choose us—or whom no one else wants?

Our own sense of value is formed as we experience ourselves as having—or not having—the ability to choose friends, to choose as friends people we really like and want to connect ourselves to, as opposed to having to merely accept someone who will be with us. Much as girls may later learn to regard themselves as potential marriage material ("I could never get a guy like that!"), they first learn to evaluate their assets in being able to attract friends. This doesn't go away—it remains part of our day-to-day life, and how we handle it affects the ongoing variations in our sense of who we are.

It still takes guts for me to make friends. I feel an instant attraction, a shudder of interest, but am slow to make the first move. I remember old rejections, former disappointments. "Does she like me as much as I like her?" I wonder. "Does she really want to be with me?" I want to wait and see, test the waters, but as I do so, I can see how hesitation makes me seem reluctant and cold. Or I initially feel a connection working and then pick up on the fact that she is not focusing on me. Her warmth now seems mere politeness: I don't catch her attention, her notice doesn't linger. I am hurt by her disregard. When I listen to young girls talk about their sense of themselves as they make friends, I not only recall my past, but see what I often ignore in the present.

For twelve-year-old Mona, the girls she admires most are girls who are "beyond her" as friends:

> The girls I really like best—I just don't go near them. When they walk by, like in the dining room or somewhere, I kind of freeze. I'm super aware of them, but I know they don't see me. I have really nice friends, but I'll never have a friend like Gloria. I don't think I'd know what to say to her. I try, like I know I'm supposed to, but when I say something and she just looks right through me, it's the worst feeling, like you're worse than nothing, because you've tried to be friendly and she's not interested.

Our interactions with friends, our successes and failures with friendships, continue to batter us. As we grow older and our sense of self becomes more stable, we become less vulnerable to slights and rejections from people we might approach. But, as teenagers, an overture toward another girl can seem to put all our worth on the line, and how she responds—or doesn't—can feel like a final judgment on who we would ever be capable of being. Mona has not yet learned that although Gloria may not be interested in her, others will be. Gloria, who is esteemed by others, at this point seems to be the ultimate authority on who is and is not interesting, and so for now Mona will have to find a way to live as an "unpopular" girl.

How can we urge this learning process along, either in ourselves or in our daughters? We can't solve the problems once and for all— for ourselves or for others. "It's not just me," we can say to ourselves, or "It's not just you" to our friends and our daughters who seek comfort for the swings and reversals in friend fortune. This may not be much wisdom to offer, but if we understand these risks as part of the inevitable process of making friends, we are better equipped to meet the constant challenges and not feel so bewildered or battered or obsessed. As Bruno Bettelheim said, we can put up with almost anything, as long as we see a reason for it.

Best Friends

In any preteen boutique in any mall, there will be a large rack of broken necklaces sold together, two halves of a heart etched with letters that spell out "best friends." For girls just entering adolescence, having one half of one of these hearts means that she has a best friend, that she has been chosen by somebody as most important. This is an early introduction to the idea of the best friend as a protector, an ultimate security against being alone. "Who has the other half?" girls ask, and the wearer will name her partner, her double. For this is the stage in which most girls need a friend as ballast against the swift social changes that occur between childhood and adolescence. Feeling the overwhelming importance of friendship, girls constantly define and redefine it.

The role of the "best friend" is never finally scripted. There are no limits to the ways in which girls can entwine themselves with one another. Thea, fifteen, seeks constant interaction. At five-thirty she faxes news to her best friend, whom she has last seen at three-thirty, and last spoken to at four o'clock. She E-mails her midnight thoughts, and awaits a response before setting off to school in the morning. "I need someone I can share my thoughts with," she explains. "You think it's funny? My mom thinks it is. But that's just what being friends is—knowing what someone else is thinking. And you're thinking all the time. I can't think in a vacuum. I need a friend to think with." For Thea, a friend completes her thoughts, responds to them, evaluates them. Thoughts are about "all kinds of stuff, like what someone wears on a TV show, or what a good story line is for something I'm working on. And then, if something happens at home, like Mom will say something really stupid, I'll just have to tell her right away. It's not the same if you have to wait." A friend is someone who receives hot-off-the-press news and reads the small details like a main headline. For Thea, instant and constant communication centers a relationship.

Each friend forms a reference point for what a relationship should be. Early ideals of what a close relationship is can be knocked down or shattered, yet they stay with us. As in any form of love, there are always new vistas to explore and closeness beyond that which has yet been experienced. Therefore, we are always revising our ideas about what a "real" friend is or does.

At all ages, "best" friendship seems to imply certain additional obligations—and perhaps a greater amount of love—than other friendships.[10] Sometimes a best friend is the person with whom a girl or woman shares the most time and the most secrets. Above all, though, a best friend is the one who is expected to "be there for you," to meet whatever intense emotional or physical need may arise. But how much love is enough? And what is a good enough friend? Judy, a forty-year-old therapist, relates:

> I was listening to a patient tell about how, weeks after her husband left her, she was upset one night at three in the morning and called her best friend in tears. Her friend listened to her for hours and then brought her breakfast a few hours later. And I remember thinking that I always think of myself as having wonderful friends, but I don't think there is anyone I could call at three in the morning who would welcome me, let alone bring me breakfast.

As women will later wonder about how much they can expect in intimate relationships with a partner, girls and women, through trial and error, sort through what sorts of actions reflect love in friendship. "What do I want from a friend?" girls may wonder. "What can I expect from a friend?" and "What do I have to tolerate from a friend?" At all ages, women's and girls' main longing in friendship harkens back to an idealized bond: What girls and women say they want is for someone who is "always there" for them. A true best friend is someone who is ready to console you when you are upset, to listen to you when you need to talk, to take your side in any dispute, to try to meet your needs. A best friend looks out for you.

But while singling out a friend for special status offers some degree of emotional security, especially among teenage and early-adult girls and women, it can create dilemmas with other friends. Tamara recalls sharing a broken necklace in seventh grade with Allison:

> In fact, Allison and I rarely wore our necklaces. They were like lucky charms for when we needed someone else to know we had each other. But at other times, when each of us was with our other friends, the necklaces were left on our dressers. We agreed that we didn't want to hurt other people's feelings. Really, we wanted to be each other's best friend, but didn't want to keep other people from getting close. When dangerous, snobby girls stalked by, the necklaces could ward off an attack. When other friends came around, Allison and I each hid our necklaces so as not to be marked as "taken."
>
> Eventually, I lost my half of the necklace. Even though at times I continued, and still continue, to want to be loved best, the phrase "best friend" slowly lost its unearthly music. Not only did it seem childish, but it became a code for being possessive and controlling. Much later, at the beginning of junior year in high school, Allison told me she didn't want to

call anyone her best friend anymore. It cut me, cleaved my heart like the jagged halves of those necklaces. Really, I had been learning that best friendship was a children's fiction for a long time.

Many adult women still name someone as their "best" friend, while others name several close friends but don't feel that any qualify as a "best friend," seeing each friend within a wider network.[11] And even as they think in "best friend" terms, girls often form friendships in threesomes and foursomes, and establish a circle, a culture, with its own values and rituals. A cluster of girls can be "best friends." As Mara notes:

I have the best friends in the world. There are four of us, and we've been friends for years—we all went into junior high together and I don't know where I'd be without them. We've all gone in different directions, will go to different colleges, but we'll stand by one another forever. I can't stand the thought that we'd ever be jealous of anyone, or that one of us wouldn't stick up for another, or that we'd fall out.

Of Love and Disappointment

As we hear Mara say that she "can't stand the thought that we'd ever fall out," we see how vulnerable she may be to possible disappointment. One thing we, as women and mothers and psychologists, know is that girls' friendships are often not stable. And yet most girls we talked to told us that their friendships were secure and permanent—and, indeed, that's what they valued most about them.

But mothers or counselors of any sort cannot really prepare girls for the bumps and chasms of friendship. Each girl has to learn for herself about the delights of constancy and the heartbreak of splitting up. In getting close to someone, in learning when to trust and when not to trust, girls find that friendship becomes an arena for puzzling out the vagaries of love. Girls seek through friendship the closeness, care, and security once sought primarily within a family, and to be sought later with a partner and children. But these new attachments are not mere reworkings of those baby/parent relationships. Rather, they bear the distinctive mark of a girl's seeking protection, validation, and a sense of identity from someone whose sense of past, present, and future, whose sense of the world, is in sync with her own.

The growing girl tries to understand her relationships, but the shifting sands of her friendships create pleasures and perils that are beyond easy comprehension, and so the girl must learn to develop an emotional knowledge that goes beyond her reason. Again and again, middle-school girls expressed to us their distress and bafflement about what forces govern their friendships. Driving the middle-school carpool, I overhear the following conversation.

CHERYL: You're so lucky, Courtney. Everyone likes you.
COURTNEY (thoughtfully): Yes, everyone likes me. But no one really loves me. I walk into a room and people go, "Oh, there's Courtney."

What Courtney seems to be trying to express is her awareness of the range of emotional connection in friendship. She is aware that she is accepted and included, but senses a different quality of response and welcome than other girls seem to engender—a quality she calls "love." But if Courtney were to ask herself what she means by "love," she would be hard-pressed to articulate what she senses, that she is longing to see more enthusiasm and engagement from the other girls, to see this in the way they smile at her when she enters a room.

Older girls and women, more adept at naming their needs, also wonder about how much they really mean to their friends. However grown up they may be, insecurity about friends stays with them. If they are unable to deal with the inevitable flux of friendships, they may arrange moments in which to test friendships. Tanya tells us that she knew her friend was a "real" friend when she gave up going out on a Saturday night to spend the night with her when she was upset. Jane, age sixteen, tells us that her best friend is a "real" friend because she lent her her new sweater even before she wore it herself. We heard about friends who call regularly, or save seats at lunch reliably. We heard about women who can be called on to step in for a late or ill baby-sitter, or who listen to their friend's troubles for hours. All of these are the rites of friendship that are savored as sure signs of love.

But friend ideals translate differently into practice. No one can always be "always there," so the challenge becomes one of finding a good-enough friend—and keeping her.

Silvia, thirteen, reflecting about friendships, writes, "At eleven I met my current best friend, and ever since I have not felt whole without her." Through her, I remember my own adolescent attachment to my best friend, Jenny, who felt as necessary to me as air. For girls, these connections are as much a part of their sense of personal wholeness as parents and siblings. For Silvia, her best friend is not only as important as her family, but of paramount importance. This treasured relationship must be handled with care: Silvia stresses that her best friend is someone with whom she "never argues" and with whom she spends "ages talking; we don't have to be doing anything in particular."

Talking for ages but never arguing outlines one ideal of friendship—that there will be constant intimacy without any conflict. But this ideal frequently fails or is betrayed. Silvia wants to keep it safe, wrapped in fine tissue, set apart from the rough-and-tumble of ordinary life: Her best friend does not go to her school, does not share her teachers, does not see her with her everyday friends. She craves security for this precious friendship but is shadowed by the possibility of loss: "I've seen other friendships end, but it would be too awful if this did. I couldn't bear it." This first experience of passion marks both the potential intensity of her attachment to people outside her family and her awareness of passion's fragility.

For the promises of empathy, support, and equality implicit in friendship are often unfulfilled. We are criticized, snubbed, bossed around. Or a friend belittles us, or gossips about us, and the relationship that we hoped would protect us leaves us even more deeply exposed to social abuse, ridicule, and rejection. Or we just "go off" someone, cease to like her, find her annoying rather than amusing. Now in her late twenties, Kim traces problems of closeness and disillusion in her friendships:

> At twelve I felt safe with Rose. Like me she was critical of a lot of the other kids, and I really liked having this support. It didn't matter what others thought of us, because they didn't matter. It didn't matter that I was so-so at school, but I had big plans in life. Rose didn't laugh at my plans. But she eventually got on my nerves. And I could see I was annoying her, too. I'd try, but the conversation just palled. And then she started mocking me. "She wants to be this great writer," she told someone—right in front of me, after I got a C in English. And the same sort of thing happened when I was nineteen. There was this girl in college who was like me, kind of an outsider. We were both frustrated with the way most people saw us. And for a while it was great. We really believed in each other. Then she seemed to think her dreams were more important than mine, and she kept dropping these hints about how much more special she was. You know, I'd say I had this really interesting take on a text, and she'd shrug and say, "Oh, some critic already said that

and was debunked by someone else." I'd expect her to be impressed, but she'd put me down. This left me with a bad aftertaste for friendships with girls. I didn't like myself soliciting approval—and I sure didn't like being one-upped when I did! I need women friends. I'm sick with loneliness without them. But I'm always on the lookout for a sour turn.

Early disappointments, when not integrated into a realistic and positive view of attachment, can fester. Often we heard, "No one can be trusted to understand everything" or "No one can be trusted to keep her mouth shut" or "Everyone gets annoying after a while." But revision of expectations can be for the better, too: "Now, this is a real friend," we think as someone reads our mood right away, or understands just the point we are making about a parent or partner. Sometimes we discover that our friends love us more than we thought they did. Like someone in love who has "never felt this before," girls and women continue to redefine a real friend, and have their first "real" friend at the age of twelve and then again at fourteen or eighteen— or even at thirty-five. Candy, age thirty, has had many friends in her life, but not until after her divorce did she feel she found the friendship she had always yearned for.

I fell in love with her and we tell each other everything. We have been growing in this friendship and the friendship has been growing, and what I cherish most is that she really sees me and what I need, not just as a projection of her needs and what she wants. If I would say something about my ex-husband, she'd see him in his relationship with me and not the fact that she was having a hard time with her husband. She was the first person in my life who loved me for what I was and not for what I was providing. I could expose the dark side of me.

But even an all-accepting relationship can end. Again and again, we heard women describing friendships that seemed loving and close and then, inexplicably, just withered away. "I can't explain it," forty-five-year-old Wilma, tears sparkling in her eyes, says of her former best friend, Anne. "We were so close, talked every day. I don't know what happened. She is still polite when I call, but she gets off the phone fast and never has time to see me."

Inconstancy in women is hard enough, but for girls new to friendship, the abruptness of change in the emotional climate of friendship can be shattering and incomprehensible. They feel that their own personal value is on the line when a relationship fails. Just as girls agonize over what will attract friends to them, they struggle with trying to understand what makes love in friendship disappear. Rachel, twelve, writes:

> I had this friend, Sandy, who was on all the teams and had the lead roles in all the plays, and I thought that it was kind of neat that she wanted to be my best friend. When we got to middle school, I don't know why, but she totally ignored me. Somebody told me she didn't like me because I wore my socks the wrong way, but I think that is a sort of stupid reason. Somebody else told me that she didn't like me anymore just because I don't have a cute boyfriend. Like Andrew is a real prize! Then she started spreading rumors about me that were really false. And now we are total enemies and we are each spreading rumors about each other. I wish things were like they used to be.

At twelve, Rachel shows that she has internalized the cultural standard of femininity—that a woman's value rests on her capacity to promote harmony in relationships. She describes herself as "loyal" and dissociates herself from other girls she knows "who always put themselves first, and think one-upping everyone is cool." Her mother, a teacher, has taught her to value consideration for others, a lesson she endorses. Yet when her former best friend betrays her by spreading rumors about her, she has no way of understanding what happened and she spreads rumors about her friend in return. Paradoxically, she still wants the relationship to be as it was: In the heat of anger, embroiled in retaliation, she cannot make sense of what happened and why it can't go away. Such tussles are terrible passages in which innocence is lost and the knowledge of one's own duplicity is learned. "I wish things were like they used to be," Rachel says in all sincerity, yet she'll continue to "hate" and act hatefully toward her former friend.

Friendship and Phases

All friendships go through phases, periods of closeness followed by periods of distance. Sometimes, especially during adolescence, friends get too close and need to get away from each other as intimacy collides with the need to remain distinctive and go one's own way. Because people grow at different rates, there is often pain on one side or the other as the bonds of friendship realign themselves.

"Why do I have to tell you everything?" Leila, fourteen, demands of her best friend, Ellen, who mutters, "But you used to." Ellen tells us: "I'm the same. I do the same things, say the same kinds of things, but now Leila just goes, 'Yeah, yeah.' She used to want to know everything, and now it's 'boring.'" As Ellen sees herself change in her friend's eyes, she loses her audience and her sense of her own importance.

Conflict, even when suppressed, often leaves unhealed wounds. Quarrels and violent fallings-out change our feelings, but just as deep a breach can be those minute disenchantments such as "going off," being "narked" or annoyed by someone. Intimacy can cloy and wear us down. The conversation with our friend grows as tedious as it seems to our mother or brother, who is waiting to use the phone. "I'm sick of hearing her go on and on about this huge Bat Mitzvah her father's planning for her," Daniella complains. "She even faxes me pictures of the decorations. I need a break from her. I need a break so bad I can't even think about whether I really like her." And yet then she adds impishly: "I guess I still really like her, but she just talks too much. Sometimes when she calls, I just put the phone down on the bed and go get a soda or turn on the TV for a while, and when I come back she's still talking." In friendship we not only learn about others' fickleness, we also experience our own. As we struggle to know what it means to "have" a real friend, we also struggle with what it means to be one.

As we experience the reality of friendships, we learn about the changeability of human nature: A girl is betrayed by her friend, rebuffed, rejected, ridiculed, or she finds herself betraying her own ideals of friendship—she grows irritated by a friend whose company she once craved, or feels stifled by the closeness. In this dilemma we experience the terrifying frailty of human emotion. An attachment that seems secure can crumble. Our own likes and dislikes can change. How, then, can we make decisions about who to be with? How, then, can we live up to our ideals of friendship? How can we trust others? How can we trust ourselves?

Yet these questions, which can lead us to conclude that relationships are unreliable and unworthy, do not subdue the urgency and need for friendship. Girls create new ideals, new hopes, new friends, and experience new disappointments, but as they experience these, they also discover new pleasures. They realize new depths in their need for friends, and acquire new ways of knowing that increase their friendship skills. So we keep "doing friendship," enjoying it, suffering from it, coming up against the rough edges, stepping back, moving forward.

Each new friendship offers a new chance at love, and many girls wish for a best friend who will offer the unconditional, celebratory love they may have longed for but missed from their mothers. One of six children, Carla felt her mother was usually overburdened and frustrated and seemed frequently to be angry at the children because of their demands. Her first real best friend, Jill, seemed to love her in a way her mother did not. "She spoiled me," Carla said. Jill did special things for her, came to her sports matches and kept track of where she was. As Carla, now thirty-eight, looks back, she says, "Friends were more and more important as a way of getting love. I'd say, 'How is it that my friends love me so much and my mother is always angry at me?' Even now that I understand my mother did love me even when she was angry, I'd say that having my friends' love was just as important."

With its intensity and sense of fragility, girls' friendship has the structure of a romance. With girlfriends, girls have a chance to enact and reenact these dilemmas of choice, trust, loyalty, and responsiveness—which is why it often seems that girls are so far ahead of boys when it comes to knowing how to "be" in a relationship. Some girls, disillusioned by the fickleness of a former best friend, turn to a romantic interest in a boy in hopes that he will prove more constant, be more "there" for her. Women tend to understand their first relationships with men in the vocabulary of their friendships with girls, sometimes trying to reproduce what was special in the closeness, sometimes searching for a lost ideal. But sometimes, too, we can accept the limitations in a partner because we find what we need in a girlfriend. Emma, who is in her thirties, describes a common complaint and a common solution: "He never remembers what I tell him, because it's not really important to him. The details that fascinate me, he doesn't even register. He doesn't remember who Annie is, let alone care about the next episode in her saga. So," Emma concludes, "I need my women friends to talk to. If I didn't have them, I'd go crazy."

Even when we feel that we are no good for anyone, a friend can restore our balance. Kirsten, a magazine editor battling to reach a deadline, called her best friend, Dinah, after a particularly bad day, to relate that she had been growling at everyone and was so upset by her own bad temper she didn't know what to do. "You need a good talk with a girlfriend," Dinah said, and Kirsten found herself smiling for the first time that day. As Kirsten heard Dinah's wicked laugh, a comic image of the witchy woman was conjured between them and dismissed. Sometimes only a girlfriend can break through that surface tension to remind us that we are lovable even when we are not nice.

Chapter Three

"WHOSE FRIEND ARE YOU, ANYWAY?"

Kathe, fourteen, has taken me into her room, where we "can talk without everyone around here interrupting me." As we enter she informs me, "It's an organized mess," and she stares grimly until she sees that I'm appreciative, not judging, and she smiles, embarrassed by her "rudeness." She offers me a seat on the desk chair, while she sinks into a beanbag chair. The floor is bare, the furniture basic, and the walls are plastered with posters—some are of horses, but most are of Jennifer Aniston, Rachel on the TV show *Friends*. When I ask Kathe about her friends, she describes an all-too-common scenario:

> The thing is, Megan—my best, best friend since last year, last fall—just doesn't want to be with me like she used to. I say, "What's wrong?" and she looks blank. "Nothing's wrong!" A real chill. So I think: She's depressed. I'll make her feel better. Talk to her. Do stuff with her. Then I see her with Steffi. Then I know she's not depressed. She's laughing. The conversation's swinging. The thing is, she likes Steffi more than me now—way more, even though I'm supposed to be her best friend. And Steffi is fun to be with, but she's basically shallow, and I think Meg will see that and go back to liking me best.

Friends aren't supposed to be exclusive in the way that lovers are—at least that's what we're taught to accept. But deeply, at the dawn of friendship, we all crave the sense of being the one who is loved best. The love for a friend in early adolescence—passionate, binding, and vulnerable—carries with it the longing for exclusivity and the accompanying deep pain of jealousy. But girls also learn to be ashamed of this yearning: You don't "own" your friends, they are cautioned by "wiser" elders. In their own value system, too, "being possessive" isn't good. They try to adopt a nonchalant attitude when warned by a friend not to be "pushy" or "bossy": "Whatever you say" or "Have it your way," they murmur in response to the inevitable disappointments. But this does not salve the wounds that develop inside. We know them in ourselves: Here are the familiar contours of pain as a woman I thought I'd made friends with races past me with a superficial smile. Yet when we see a daughter's unhappiness and learn the reason—friend trouble—we think, "Oh, is that all?" and are relieved that she is not pregnant, not failing a class, not in what we think of as real trouble.

Rivalries and jealousies among friends may seem mean-spirited, stemming from selfishness or egoism rather than basic humanity, but as we follow Kathe's feelings—from her empathy with her friend's supposed depression, to her startled discovery that her friend is not unhappy, but cooling off to Kathe—we can understand the feeling of loss at the root of her jealousy. Displaced as the best friend, she experiences a new isolation and is angry at the outsider who inter- feres with a valued relationship. What Kathe's thoughts catch on is the tension between a girl's special need for intimate connection and her wish to protect herself from loss, rejection, and pain. Problems then arise: How does she know when a relationship is in danger? What should she do when it is threatened? How can she avoid being hurt yet satisfy her need for something as uncertain and volatile as friendship?

That a friend is freely chosen is what makes us so proud of having friends. If one is chosen, it means one is liked, admired, singled out among others. But this freedom is also what creates the anxiety: One can just as easily become unchosen, and the pride gained from the friendship can be utterly—and irretrievably—lost.

The special love of a best friend also confers a sense of identity. Girls know who is best friends with whom and express an exquisite awareness that "who" a friend is in the larger world also has implications for how others see them. Kathe may not have the smartest clothes, but since Megan always wears the latest styles, Kathe is seen as a sharp dresser, pretty much regardless of what she herself wears. And she stands to lose this if she loses Megan as a best friend. Gail, fourteen, may feel "real awkward and on the way to being nothing," but if she is an acknowledged friend of Pam's, then she borrows that "cool, gutsy manner" and takes it wherever she goes.

We also find ourselves in the selves our friends reflect back to us. Our friends allow us to feel witty or attractive or perceptive or caring. And through them we learn that our views of them matter: A friend's concern about how we see her emphasizes our importance. Being cast out of the friendship, therefore, creates a vast shift in our own identity and our sense of having value. The connection and sense of belonging we achieve with friends, however supportive, leads to vulnerability and exposure. The enormous gains they offer can be brutally withdrawn if the friendship ends. We deal with these shifts on a day-to-day basis, but we also have to work at containing fear and disappointment.

"I can't play tennis Friday," Sara, a thirty-five-year-old full-time mother of four, breathlessly tells her friend Maddy as soon as she answers the phone. Her voice is a mixture of sheepishness and excitement. She wants to apologize, but she can't contain herself. "You'll never guess who invited me to one of her luncheons." Pause. "Go on, guess!" Maddy doesn't want to guess, sensing danger amid the exploding cadences of her friend's enthusiasm. "Brenda!" Sara exclaims triumphantly, knowing that volumes are communicated to Maddy in this one magic word. Brenda—the socialite, revered by all in the country club, Brenda of the "best" parties, arbiter of fashion and taste, darling of their community. Maddy feels pierced by Sara's excitement. She wants to share her friend's pleasure; she wants to enjoy her success. Instead, she feels something very close to envy and resentment as she wonders, "Who am I, and what can I offer a friend? Maybe not so much, if she is so thrilled about being chosen by someone else."

The same scenario is played out every day among women of all ages, from girls in high school to women at the highest levels of business, among secretaries, nurses, university professors, cooks, and doctors—wherever women gather and form friendships. In the role of Sara, we wish to share everything with our best friend, even parts of ourselves that may threaten to hurt her or our relationship. In the role of Maddy, we are torn between pleasure in our friend's joy, envy of her success, and terror about what this other "special" person may mean for the friendship itself.

Our ability—and difficulty—in coping with this everlastingly repeated triangular drama is rooted in our earliest experiences with it. We learn as girls about our drawing power in the friendship market: Who can we attract to us and keep with us? And how do we do that? What happens if we let our feelings show—if Kathe tells Megan she thinks Steffi is shallow, if Maddy confronts Sara and tells her that she thinks it's inexcusable of her to cancel their regular tennis date to go to Brenda's luncheon? What will happen to a friendship if we speak our minds and show our feelings? How can we learn to temper our yearning to be special, to be loved best, to demand exclusivity? How can we come to make room for another's autonomy—room for this other who, unlike those in our family, is bound to us only through feeling? How can we gain security without appearing greedy? These are questions each girl and woman works through, striking her own balance, now overreaching in one direction, later overreacting in the other.[1] If we understand how common and complex these tensions are, we can be more confident in feeling our way through these uncertain passages of friendship.

Possessiveness

We are born into a relationship that often seems exclusive: baby and mother. The power of the interaction in this relationship is overwhelming, as the interaction is the basis for life-sustaining needs. But even a baby, clamoring for her mother, will know that there are other people in her world, and enjoys the father, siblings, friends, and other relatives who respond to her and care for her. At the same time, inevitable interruptions from others can fill a baby or young child with fear and rage. Sharing is not simple. We can accept the need to share those we love with others, but we continue to be driven in our relationships—with lovers, children, and friends—to re-create an ideal of faultless communication, of a perfect one-on-one match. Usually in a family we learn to share those we love with other people we love, or ones who in other ways are deeply significant to us. In a family we can often set aside fears of abandonment, but in friendship we learn about inevitable risks in relationships. We must learn to share the person we love with others who we may not even like. And we must learn to love someone even with the full knowledge that that person can turn away from us without even a backward glance.

Sharing is always threatening, but there are certain points in girls' lives that are marked by a particular possessiveness. In junior high, many girls move into a larger school and lose the protection of familiar networks and norms. At this stage, they feel especially self-conscious. Jabbed at each moment by the critical or mocking eyes they imagine everywhere, they need a friend with whom they can find their way, and in whose presence they feel protected.

Another common period of intense possessiveness is during the first year of college. Away from home and family for the first time, away from her high-school best friend or friends, away perhaps from her high-school boyfriend, the young woman must secure herself with others. She scans the faces of her sister students. Who among you will be my friend?

"I had learned in high school not to trust girls," says Debbie, a college freshman who anchored herself in a group of guys "who adore me" in her first month at Berkeley. "With guys you know where you stand," she continues. "Girlfriends are too fickle—they're always dropping you for someone else."

Enid, however, as a college junior, feels she only "made it through" because of Veronica, her roommate and best friend. "But sometimes I think Veronica needs me too much, expects me always to go to things with her and no one else. But I do because I don't want to lose her."

Enid needs her friend and so tolerates the possessiveness she doesn't like. And her fear of resisting a friend's possessiveness is based on an unspoken awareness of just how dangerous such resistance can be. The potential desperation caused by losing a friend is revealed in a recent tragedy at Harvard. One morning in May 1995, just as the spring semester exams were coming to an end, Sinedu Tadesse, a third-year undergraduate student from Addis Ababa, woke up, as usual, at eight A.M., then took a hunting knife and repeatedly stabbed her roommate, Trang Phuong Ho. Thao Nguyen, an overnight guest who was Trang's true "best friend," tried to stop Sinedu but was also attacked. After she murdered the friend who, in her eyes, was abandoning her, Sinedu hanged herself. Sinedu, who wrote in her high-school yearbook that "friendship is one of life's most precious treasures," thought she had a kindred spirit and exclusive other in

Trang, and so when Trang decided not to room with her the following year, Sinedu felt bereft of the one person who had once liked her
and wanted to be with her. Without the protection of this close
friendship, she saw her world become an impossible place. No
longer whole, no longer a good, acceptable self, she enacted the final
despair by committing murder and then suicide.

This tragedy, however extreme, highlights common conflicts in
girls' friendships, wherein jealous passions are aroused as a girl fears
that she is to be supplanted by another as a friend. The fierce need to
feel connected and to have the reassurance of exclusivity can throw
one into a tailspin. A girl may think she has found the perfect soul
mate in a friend, and then find that the person upon whom she is so
deeply dependent prefers someone else. To mark her specific position in relation to a friend, a girl will pack great meaning into an outing ("I want you to come with me"), a revelation ("This is our
secret"), or a well-defined relationship (such as that of roommates).
For some girls, a Saturday-afternoon expedition is a ritual and can be
changed only by an emergency—or a betrayal. For some, the ritual
marker lies in being told first about a date, an exam, a college application. For Sinedu Tadesse, the relationship of roommates took on a
certain gravity in that she depended upon that relationship to center
her life at Harvard. The question of loyalty—the question "Whose
friend are you?"—splinters into anxious assessments of the significance of certain actions of friends.

Experiencing Disappointments

What do we expect from our friends? How do we know that we
really matter to them? And how do we deal with being loved—but
not exclusively? None of these are easily answered, and a major task
of adolescence is to begin figuring it all out. But there is no ready
language for the intense and often baffling experiences that come

from the vagaries of girlfriends. How can we talk about the gaps between expectation and experience, between hope and what's actually happening? Here is Melinda, an energetic, athletic eighth-grader, trying to make sense out of a hurt in a friendship and reflecting on what she has learned about friends in the last year:

> This year different things have happened to my friends. I had a best friend, Carol, who was almost best friends with another girl. This girl had a lot of other friends, too. Every time she got around her friends, she was making fun and being mean to Carol. But when no one else was around, the girl was really nice to her. Now that girl and Carol talk but are not really as good friends as they used to be. They are kind of still good friends. This has taught me that you can't trust anybody. People who you think are your friends are really not. You have to think about your old friends and not just forget about them. When you make a new friend, the old friend might be the true friend. No one wants to be around someone that changes their ways around different people. They might make you feel that you are too cool for your old friends.

The confusion in Melinda's statement is a beautiful testament to the intricacies of friendship that girls must puzzle through. Here Melinda is wrestling with her hurt from Carol's desertion of her, and her sense of triumph that Carol seems to have returned to her. At the same time, she is a sympathetic participant in Carol's experience; she takes notes on the general condition of friendships found and lost. Whom can you trust, she is asking, and how far can you trust anyone? And woven into this question is the ever-present issue of hierarchy: Who is better than whom? Who is too cool to hang around you?

This peculiar and oppressive intermixture of loyalty and status comes as a tidal wave to the young teenage girl, and persists as a gnawing issue through a woman's life. "She used to be my friend, but now she thinks she's too good for me," says Juanita, age sixty-three, bitterly, of her oldest friend, who had recently become a member of an elite bridge club. "She never calls me anymore—and I'm certainly not going to call her." How can we help our daughters negotiate these conflicts if we remain burdened by them ourselves?

Old dynamics, reflexive responses, are branded on us by past sufferings. We see the mean or false friend through the cloudy impression of betrayal rather than the flux of human connection. Yet Melinda is struggling to know this sense of flux. What makes her comments both charming and inscrutable is her effort to name and come to terms with the complexity she experiences. She struggles to articulate the distinctions between "a best friend," "almost best friends," "not really good friends but kind of still good friends," "old friend," and "new friend." All of these imprecise phrases signify Melinda's dawning awareness of the gradations of feeling and commitment in friendship and the expectations that attend each one.[2]

No one, we learn painfully as we mature, will ever love us absolutely the way we once imagined our mothers loved us when we were infants. People will love us, but imperfectly and never exclusively. We will have to learn to recognize the signals of the kind and extent of love that others offer us—those who will be "best friends" and those who will be "kind of still good friends" and those who will betray us and cause us pain. Seventeen-year-old Nan is described by her mother as "gutsy, often difficult," and by her teacher as "one of the tough ones in a very mixed school," but now there are tears in her voice, and her fingers shred the spread of the bed on which she sits, as she tries to take the sting out of her best friend's decision to go on her first "just girls" vacation with someone else. "I understand why she asked Alicia and not me. Alicia likes to do the same sorts of things. They're both great walkers—you know, the ten-mile-a-day thing. I don't go in for that. So it's not that she likes Alicia more. . . . But I wish she'd talk to me about it. It's the not talking that's hardest to take."

Desertions and betrayals always rankle, no matter at what age, and affect the ways women take up new relationships in their world. Throughout high school, Janet took solace in the comfort of her "best friend," Wendy. Janet was a "brain," a bit awkward and shy, while Wendy was bubbly and outgoing, easily liked. Wendy admired Janet for her intelligence and academic success and relied on her as an always-available ear for the recounting of her exploits with boys. Janet learned vicariously from Wendy's experiences, since Wendy dared to do things Janet was too hesitant to approach. Although they never spoke of it, they had an understanding—they came first with each other, stood by each other, took up for each other. Wendy saw to it that people included Janet and got them to look past her quiet demeanor and try to get to know her. Janet, on her side, ran interference when other girls, out of their envy of Wendy's success with boys, spread rumors about her. "She's not" and "How can you say that?" were phrases she often used to slice through rumors.

Janet and Wendy became friends just before ninth grade. For Janet, being friends with Wendy was a move "up" in the social world, and without a second thought, she gave up her former friends, who were considered "nerds" in the social hierarchy of the high school. For her part, Wendy was glad to have a loyal friend. Her previous friends had been, it seemed to her, opportunistic—they "used" her to get invited to her swimming pool or to meet the many boys who always seemed to surround her—but when she wanted their attention or favors, they were too busy or unresponsive. In Janet, Wendy found a friend who was "always there." But Janet remained the more dependent of the two. It was Janet who was always available to accompany Wendy on her shopping trips or to spend the night when Wendy didn't have a date. Saturday afternoons were nearly holy, though. Every Saturday they would "do something"— usually of Wendy's choosing, but Janet never minded. Wendy was her social life, whatever she offered. One Saturday, though, Wendy told Janet that her mother had something planned for her—they had to go visit an old aunt who was sick, and Wendy's mother didn't think it wise for Janet to come along—so this Saturday Wendy would have to beg off. Janet was sad, and disliked the prospect of a lonely Saturday afternoon, but she understood. She decided to take the bus to the library to get some schoolwork done, but as the bus stopped at a busy intersection, Janet looked out the window and saw Wendy walking with Sandra, a girl whose liking for Wendy had always worried Janet. "It was like someone stuck a knife in me," Janet said, feeling it still, even now, as an adult woman.

Janet is now a forty-year-old social worker, married with children. She has many friends. "Oh, I trust people," she says, "and I've had some good friends since, but I've never fully trusted anyone the way I had trusted Wendy. People always have other fish to fry. You can never be sure you really come first with anyone."

Janet never confronted Wendy. She "played dumb": She didn't speak to Wendy about what she had seen, and listened forbearingly to Wendy's account of her day with her aunt. She chose to go along with the lie, fearful that confronting Wendy would widen the fissure in their friendship yet more. As adult women, Janet and Wendy are still friends although they live a thousand miles apart. And as an adult, working over this incident many times, Janet has come to understand that she had been so possessive of Wendy that Wendy couldn't have told her that she wished to spend the day with Sandra. In some ways, that would have hurt even more. To this day, Janet laughed, they've never spoken of it, but in Janet's life, this small incident was a kind of epiphany. She returns to it again and again for what she learned about relationships. And her lesson was not just a simple "You can't trust people" or "Friends may betray you." Rather, it was a complex lesson about trust, possessiveness, and exclusivity—about what it means to "have" a friend.

When she went to college, Janet no longer sought a "best" friend (as Wendy had been), but learned to manage several close friendships—friendships with limits, friendships with less predictability and loyalty built in. It was only many years later that Janet realized that she'd tried to find Wendy again in a man: She married the first man she met who seemed to offer the loyalty she had felt she had had, if only for a few years, from Wendy. That, of course, did not fare much better in the long run, for the loyalty that she—and other girls—seek in their girlfriends is a fictional perfection.

If we recall the pain of disappointment without learning the realities of human connection, then our past experiences lead to future mistakes. If, instead, we learn from our experiences with girlfriends to tolerate a range of responses, and if we learn that relationships are never solid rocks but currents we must learn to negotiate, whose flow and course vary, then we will not search for what we can never have, and we will develop the skills for dealing with what we can and do have. For Janet, as for most women, hard lessons about love and loyalty come in the arena of girlfriends. Nan is struggling with these lessons, too, but finds it difficult because she has no help in acknowledging her conflict as something more than mere jealousy. When these lessons are learned, we can move forward to more realistic expectations of friendship and connection. We can feel safe even when we share our friends with others.

Fickleness and Change

Girls learn, from their first foray into the friendship world, that friendships have an eerie instability. They must be vigilant about shifts in alliances. A friendship never exists in isolation. It grows and withers within a network of other relationships, all threatening its exclusivity. Silvia, thirteen, who works to preserve her delicate best friendship, reflects that attaining a best friend is the "ultimate achievement for any girl over the age of three." But how long does such an achievement last? It can be lost in a heartbeat as new alliances are formed. There are always other girls around to threaten a special twosome; there is always someone our best friend might prefer to be with or talk to.

What makes this all so difficult is that in their first serious friendships, girls are trying to attach to other girls who are themselves in flux, who are also trying to get a reading on who they are and who they want to be. We had the opportunity to witness the complex drama among a group of three eighth-grade girls as their loves and alliances were shifting. Sally told us:

> Things have been changing with my friend Estelle. She was starting to eat with other people. That's okay. I'm not possessive or anything. Her new group of friends is nice except for one person, Jacey, who seems to want Estelle all as her own. Jacey pulls Estelle over to one side and starts whispering to her. They'll both turn and look at me and start to giggle. That hurts! Estelle is drifting more and more over into the other group—which is fine—but when Estelle is with Jacey, they are very mean to me. But I have to put up with it because I carpool with Estelle, and my mom would hit the roof if I didn't. I like Estelle and her group, but her group hates my group. I am the only one both groups like and I like both groups, but to get to know Estelle's group, I would have to leave my group, of which I seem to be the chosen leader. In my group are some of my best friends. I want to be part of both groups, but I can't, so now it's just my group.

And from Estelle we hear:

> This year I grew apart from my old seventh-grade friends, who seemed childish, immature, and rude. Sally used to be my best friend, but I'm more mature than she is. I made a new best friend named Jacey and we have become very close. As we started to get a little boy-crazy, friendships were a stop-start thing. And then there were other things, like how we looked. We wanted boyfriends and then got kind of jealous of the friends who had them. A new girl in our class wasn't interested in boys, and you know, she just turned into the class joke because she didn't go to things—dances and stuff. I felt sorry for her, but I didn't want to lose friends by being her friend. With my friend Jacey, we can talk about boys, and say how we really feel. I hope we don't grow apart. I think as we grow up, our friendship will grow stronger.

And now from Jacey:

> Last year, there was a new girl in school named Estelle. She was not the kind of person I liked very much. There was a party that year and both of us were invited. That's where the biggest rumor of all time started. It was *not* true. I believed that it was not true. In school the next week, everyone thought that I spread the rumor. Estelle and her friends were all mad at me. This year I came into school with all of that behind me. I guess that Estelle did, too, because now I am her best friend. You've got to realize that a best friend doesn't have to be just like you. You have to get to know a person like Estelle, and once you do, you get to know a really great person!

Girls' friendships become a laboratory for the exploration of human affection and loyalty. Each girl has her own experience of what is occurring, but each also thinks that her experience is shared by others. As girls grow at different rates and have different needs, the connections among them mutate, and the sense they make of these shifts becomes the scaffolding for their understanding of relationships.

Loyalty and Popularity

Who will we ever find who will bond with us, who will protect us from aloneness? We want to be at the top of our friend's list—phoned first when she returns from a vacation, invited first to a party, told news first, and chosen above others. As girls deal with their worries about loss in friendship, they come up with ways and means of making their lives safer. When I was in high school, being popular seemed the greatest good. If only I were popular, I would be safe. In every situation—in gym class, on the lunch line, while looking for a place to sit in the lunch room or walking home a little late, there would be someone who knew me and wanted to be with me. So if I only knew how to dress, put on makeup, and what to say and when, I would be the ideal popular girl, the girl others would always want to be with.

A girl who is popular seems to have greater protection: Someone who is liked by many other girls will have a much better chance of replacing a friend when one lapses. The popular girl has a magic knowledge, and we want to learn from her. Barrie Thorne remembers watching the most popular girl in her fourth- and fifth-grade class.[3] Judging herself to be of "middling social status," she used a "kind of applied sociology" to figure out her place in a charged social network. As an adult, as a "detached" sociologist studying girls and boys at play, she notes that the magnetism of popularity, and the envy of the popular girl, stays with her. Supposedly observing all children, she realizes she is more attuned to the popular girl, from whom she still wants to learn. Status marks a girl's popularity, and nothing is more valuable to her than being popular. Teachers and parents may extol the virtues of egalitarian ideals and instruct their daughters and students to "be nice to everyone," but the notion that girls' friendships are not governed by status is one of those commonly held beliefs that is blatantly false.[4]

Popularity is a signal of high status because it marks a girl as likable, but popularity, in the world of girlfriends, causes conflict and poses a contradiction in the requirements of friendship.[5] A popular girl is one who has many friends, or whom many people want to be friends with, but a friend is someone with whom you share secrets and intimate thoughts, someone you think of first—someone to whom you give priority. With such high standards of friendship, it is impossible to fulfill them with more than a very few people. So the popular girl lets others down, is judged to be "stuck-up" because she declines overtures other girls make to be her friend: She just doesn't have the emotional resources to be the friend of every girl who seeks her out. Or she may be regarded as "shallow" because she accepts friends and then cannot fulfill her commitment as a friend. "Whose friend are you, anyway?" other girls may demand, and then walk away, leaving her with an uncomprehending sense of guilt.

Popular girls whom we interviewed, those who had been clearly and consistently chosen over time, were likely to describe themselves as having many best friends, all of whom they "love to death." They don't have to call others to make plans; others call them. For them, maintaining friendship involves skills of not hurting others' feelings as they juggle multiple expectations and commitments. Because love comes easily to them, though, they seem to learn less about it. But they do learn skills of tact and diplomacy, which enable them to disappoint others while still maintaining their affection. At the same time, even the most popular girls have their own stories of desire and rejection—the friend *they* wanted who somehow turned away.

Group Protection: Cliques

There are many ways in which girls try to protect themselves from being cast out. One surefire means is to group together to define who is acceptable and who is not. My memory of how difficult cliques are was jogged by two terms' stint as parent-supervisor of recess in a middle school. Daily I witnessed scenarios of girls' cruelty and control over one another as they encircled magic and mysterious markings around one another to discriminate those "in" from those "out." "If you play with them, then you can't play with us," Tashi warns Lynn, who has been rehearsing a play with some other children. Her different activity is defined as a betrayal, and her betrayal will be punished if it continues.

Friendships can be fortified by forming groups whose members share and develop norms and standards that mark what is acceptable, admirable, and likable. The knowledge of what looks "right," what sounds right, and who is right becomes the possession of one set of girls, and other girls are then judged according to these standards: "She's always showing off," "She's weird," "She flirts like a slut" are all judgments that make use of the norms girls construct together. These judgments allow others to learn which norms matter, and they show the power that some girls have over others, especially when they stick together in making judgments. As girls feel the threat of shifting alliances, they make a preemptive strike to be the first to exclude someone else. They may want to strengthen their position by getting others on their side as they cast someone out. These cruel experiments of inclusion and exclusion form the basis of the clique. The sufferings they inflict cannot be overestimated: Ask any girl enduring the numerous punishments meted out by a clique.

Cliques form a counterlife to young girls' friendships, with those shared interests and communal conversations that people sometimes idealize as indicative of the harmonious togetherness of girls' friendships. Indeed, girls do care a good deal about "nice," harmonious relationships, preferring to work together as equals and avoid a hierarchical structure. The urge to cooperate, to listen, to support can be seen in girls' conversation and games as early as the age of three.[6] But these harmonious and cooperative dynamics are not the only ones at play. Such dynamics often disguise fierce battles for status and control, battles often hidden under the cover of a demand for fairness and niceness. On the one hand, to ignore the darker side of girls' friendships is to create confusion about ourselves and our own experiences, making what is common and normal seem strange and even shameful: If I think that a good friend is always nice and always on my side, then what can I make of it when she hurts or rejects me, and what sense can I make of my own ambivalence about her? To understand friendships, we have to see—and accept—the downside. On the other hand, to decry this downside as proof of "bitchiness," as evidence of "bad" femininity, is to obscure the double edges of all human relationships. If we acknowledge the difficult aspects of our friendships, we are better able to contain and bear the tensions that arise.

This counterlife of girls' friendships, this other side of harmony and connection, emerges by the age of eight or nine. As girls group up and link together, seeking safety in the company of others, they also learn how to tease, punish, and exclude. Their friendships are governed by complex rules, which may go unnoticed because they are sometimes implicit and subtle, but are nonetheless controlling. Sometimes girls form a close friendship to protect them from being "outsiders" ("When I play with Sue, it's not so bad being teased by the others," declared eight-year-old Denise), but this protection is often ineffective because the friendship can be interfered with by another girl, who may draw one of the friends away. One member of that "safe" pair may be drawn into the group, while the other member of the pair is left behind.

The clique won't let other girls be both outside and safe. And when cliques change, every girl feels threatened by ending up outside, and in danger of all sorts of suffering. The need to belong can make girls fickle: They would rather be secure in a friendship than loyal. Kerry, at fourteen, describes the wrench she felt as the social map shifted and her own loyalty to her friends was battered down:

> The last year in junior high was my best ever year. I had such good friends! Bea and Vera and me—we were *this* close. Everyone knew it, and no one would dare ask one of us to a party and not the others. We just wouldn't go if we didn't all go. But then we get to high school. There are all these other kids. It's such a big place, 'cause all these kids from other schools go here, too. And Vera wants to know all these other smart kids and make new friends, and I'm like "Why? What's wrong with us as we are?" But I can see Vera looking around, so I know I'd better find some new friends, too, but they don't like Bea, so when she keeps coming up to me, I worry that the others are going to say something nasty, and I'm like "Let's talk later." And I feel so bad—real bad. I mean, I'm supposed to be her friend. But I always call when I say that. I don't know—I guess it must hurt, but I just don't want her to be hurt worse by someone saying something when she's right there.

As Kerry enters a large high school, fed by several different junior highs, she is buffeted by the race to get to know the "in" people from other schools. If she fails to keep up in this race, she will lose her safe status within a friendship group. She is left feeling "real bad" about what she does and who she is when she is "supposed to be

Bea's friend" but is only a half-baked friend. The pull of the clique, which offers safety, makes her break faith with herself.

Cooperation and Control

Girls' friendships may seem less competitive than boys', yet competition is rife; it is, however, indirect. This indirectness creates confusion as to what the competition is about, which in itself is distressing. A girl sees something going wrong and then rushes through a maze of questions in an attempt to discover what she has done. Why is her gaffe clear as day to others but unfathomable to her? As nine-year-old Elsa shows two other girls, Julie and Susanna, her watch, displaying its dual function as both timepiece and calculator, Julie and Susanna begin to talk about their sisters' watches and what they can do—store telephone numbers, act as stopwatches, and the like. Suddenly Elsa walks off, complaining that the other two girls are "being mean" to her, and so what initially was a topic of common interest becomes, at least to Elsa, a competition: Julie and Susanna are challenging the status that Elsa is claiming through the possession of her watch. What is upsetting to Julie and Susanna is the sudden and mysterious accusation: It's the quick shift from friendship to animosity that makes interaction so tough. As Elsa rejects them, they conclude, "She's boasting." Elsa's inability to engage in cooperative conversation makes her lose the very status she was trying to obtain.

In her novel *Cat's Eye,* Margaret Atwood explores the controls imposed on girls by other girls as they become friends. Elaine, age eight, having had her brother as her primary childhood companion, begins to go to school with other girls. To her new friends she is a novice who has to be taught what it means to be a girl among other girls. Elaine is surprised at how easy girls' relationships are: All you have to do is sit together, comb one another's hair, look through women's magazines, and be able to name your favorite actress or model. These are the apparent requirements of friendship. There are none of the war games, challenges, competitions, and tests of skills and prowess that occur in the games her brother plays. The girls' group Elaine joins initially offers quiet lessons in feminine grooming—a mark of connection and care—but as the girls mature, these become covert lessons in conformity. Cordelia, whom Elaine idolizes, and her sidekick Beryl expect Elaine to be "just like them." When Elaine later shows that she has her own mind and is critical of their brand of femininity, they punish her, through taunts and criticism, and finally they accost her on a winter walk and corner her, so that she falls into a ravine. In self-defense, Elaine must walk away from them, but walking away from the friend she idolizes is "like stepping off a cliff, believing the air will hold you up."

Friendship becomes a school of correction: To be included or acceptable, you have to meet certain standards and follow the rules of the group. The message is: Conform or you're out. This is a lesson most of us learn well, and how we take this lesson affects us forever in terms of whether we feel safe when our life paths or our values diverge from those of our friends. It affects us when we decide to speak our minds or bite our tongues when we disagree with friends. It affects the ways in which we count the costs of being ourselves and being different. The power of the forces to conform in friendship is what frightens mothers and frustrates teachers who hold out different values for young girls.

Try to persuade a teenage girl to resist the social obsession with how she looks or how much she weighs, and one will run headlong into the brick wall of the norms of her friendship circle. Laurel, sixteen, home on spring break from her boarding school, was brought to a therapist because her mother found her throwing up after meals. Laurel's account of her world at school was of a society of girls ruled by bonds forged at the scale:

Every morning, everyone's there. And this time—well, there was one time I lost two pounds in one day. It was—it was like I was this real star. And everyone told everyone. And they all wanted to sit with me. "I'm going to eat what you eat," they said. I mean—even the really popular girls that hardly ever look my way were staring at me: "Oh, really." I've never felt so warm and tingly inside.

Girls watch what other girls eat, predict who will weigh what the next morning, and all troop to the weigh-in together. They share a sandwich or a sundae, protecting one another from "eating too much," and giving one another the comfort of company in any guilt they feel for eating. Laurel laughed at her therapist when she raised the idea that she pay less attention to her weight. "But then I wouldn't have any friends," she protested.

As we blame the diet and fashion industries, including the model culture, for girls' eating disorders, we should never forget the power friends have to bring us into intimate contact with ideals that can only work against our best interests. The best preventative against eating disorders are friends who resist the social preoccupation with female thinness and beauty.

"It's for Your Own Good"

The "corrective" function of friendship is rooted in a convoluted mix of affection and teasing. Where does one end and the other begin? Teasing can be friendly, and one is not supposed to take offense. The great thing about friends, it is said, is that you can tease them all you want, and no one feels insulted. After all, the jibe may be affectionate. "You have a funny nose" can mean "Your nose is distinctive and lovable," but it can also mean "Your nose is peculiar, odd, wrong." A girl who teases another about the way she speaks or walks may be intentionally cruel but appear to be kind. Cliques increase the power of teasing: Somehow the "inside" girls know that the jibe is genuine, while the targeted girl is being a poor sport if she hears the jibe as something more than "only teasing." Criticism, too, is a double-edged sword. Someone can claim to criticize in order to correct; one corrects because one cares; one is mean to be kind.

Think of the new girl at school in the film *Clueless,* whose "in" friends are drawn to her as a project to "make over." Cher sees Tai as someone who doesn't know anything: She needs to be told how to dress and act and whom to like in her new school. Tai, as a new girl, feels lucky to be befriended by the most popular girl in the school. But her luck is questionable, for at the root of the relationship is dependence: Cher is the one who possesses the significant life knowledge and who, therefore, makes decisions, even decisions about which boy is the appropriate boyfriend. Cher is the one with authority. In the film, Cher is ultimately shown to be the truly "clue-less" girl: So keen is she on controlling other girls' love lives that she nearly misses out on her own. But in real life, the all-too-common relationship of dependence between a girl who "knows" and a girl who doesn't can lead to an awful entrapment. The "clueless" victim may believe that the friend who criticizes her knows what is right, and she must rely upon the friend's greater knowledge and critical appraisal. Because it is so often impossible for the girl to figure out on her own what makes for acceptability or popularity, another girl, one more successful, can easily hold herself forth, and be valued, as an expert. The girl, desperate to be sought out like the others, assumes that if she behaves correctly, or learns to be good, then she will be accepted. This may leave her dependent on her "expert con-sultant" friend, from whom she cannot break away, even if the friendship becomes extremely painful.

A girl who is able to exclude another also holds the key to who is included, and can set the rules. This provides the authority to teach other girls how to dress, how to speak, whom to approach, and whom to avoid. A girl may come to believe that if only she can follow these rules, she, too, can become the ideal girl, the girl whom everyone likes and always wants to be with—the girl who is always safe in friendship. Girls learn early to hide their hostility, fear, and competitiveness under the cloak of niceness; to speak words that can always be retracted or recast as something else; to stick a knife in someone's back while greeting them with a smile. One learns to fight with velvet gloves. These are the lessons of the girls' playground.

Sometimes there is no content at all to girls' teasing of one another beyond the demonstration of superiority. Status among girls is interpersonal power. In a class of eleven- and twelve-year-olds, children gradually come in from the cloakroom. They are assigned tables, but not particular places at the table. Lena is already seated. She leans back in her chair, with her feet touching, massaging each other. Through the canvas tops of her thin "indoor" shoes, you can see her toe jabbing the air. Another girl, Gabby, tall and slim, slinks by, smiling above the seated girl's head. They both face the window, looking onto the playground, which now looks friendly, well washed as the rain ends. Then Pam enters the room and wipes her straight wet hair from her forehead.

"Hi there, Lena," Pam says.

Lena reddens. With the toe of one shoe she picks at the loose plastic sole of the other. "Hi." She seems pleased, anxious, and embarrassed, all at the same time.

"You busy this weekend?" Pam asks her.

"What?" Lena giggles. "I don't know."

"That's too bad. We're all going to the ice rink. We really wanted you to come."

"Oh . . ." Lena lets her book fall flat onto the table and sits up. "Maybe I can. Probably I can. I'll ask. . . ."

Gabby, who has watched this interaction intently, is now laughing—not with Lena, not at her, but quietly, to herself. With her chin pressed against her chest, she starts chewing her sweatshirt, pretending to be trying to suppress the laughter, which does not sound sincere. Without raising her chin, she catches the eyes of two other girls sitting opposite her. She leans toward them and dissolves in laughter.

"She thought Pam meant it," she chokes out in a harsh whisper. She shares with her friends the amazement that such a girl as Lena could believe she would be invited to one of their select outings. The girls shake away their tears of laughter as the teacher's voice calls the class to order.

This awful event, carefully yet spontaneously contrived, serves many functions. First, the group defines—and justifies—its existence by the ability to prove that certain people are excluded from the group. Second, by acting as a group, it can construct a kind of moral authority. The members mark the value of the group itself: This group is so valuable that it is a crime, punishable by ridicule, for a nonmember to suppose that she can join it. This is a female version of a ritualistic lynching, performed in order to demonstrate the power of one's own attractiveness, which, because it is ineffable, can only be felt through such demonstrations. And what of the effects on Lena? Lena is left baffled and hurt. She knows that she has been punched, but is not quite sure just how—there is nothing overt she can ever accuse anyone of—and is certainly perplexed as to why.

The Structure of Teasing

Teasing is so effective that it can hurt and exclude even when we don't know what we are being teased about. Children aged nine or ten develop the knack of teasing simply by implying some criticism, though they themselves barely know what they are teasing someone for. They huddle together, murmur among themselves, or laugh.

This is enough to isolate a girl. It is this isolating focus that is the cruelty, not the specific criticisms. Here is a precursor to a teenage girl's terror of having bad things said about her behind her back, when she is unable directly to defend herself or counter her accuser. It seems as though girls can set up the gossip structure—connecting to one another by criticizing someone else—even before they understand what they should be gossiping about. What matters, first, in gossip is that it can set up markers of who is included (in the conversation and the judgment) on the one hand, and who is judged and excluded on the other. As grown women we may feel such situations reverberate. We walk into a party. A group of other women are laughing, and there is that awful shudder: "Are they laughing at me? Why? What is wrong? How have I been found out?"

Both children and adults often fail to understand why one girl rather than another is picked on or teased. Lena's mother believed that as an early developer (Lena was large and more physically mature than her classmates) she was targeted for her appearance. When children are called names, they often think that what they are teased for is the cause of the teasing. A friend makes a girl feel uncomfortable about wearing glasses, and she believes that the glasses are the problem. A girl is called "Fatty," and she becomes convinced that she is overweight and teased because of that. But a child is targeted as vulnerable, and then the reasons follow. Girls seem to be teased for whatever they feel most self-conscious about: glasses, voice, body shape, clothes. But they cannot escape teasing by changing the way they speak or dress, by getting contact lenses or even by losing weight: teasing marks another child out as globally unacceptable, as simply not belonging. While boys' bullying systems center on the question "Who is stronger?" girls' teasing defines other girls as acceptable or unacceptable, "in" or "out." The question is not "Who's dominant?" but "Who's included?" For girls, power is the authority to exclude.[7]

Girls band together to tease other girls in order to display pride in their inclusion and to demonstrate their power. A girl puts up with being teased in the hope that she'll learn something from it, improve herself, so that the teasing will give way to approval. Lena's mother sees her daughter's tears, learns the reasons, and then despairs: "This happens all the time! Why doesn't Lena learn that Pam is not really her friend? Why doesn't she stay away from her?" Lena protests that Pam sometimes is a friend: "She was being nice to me all day. I thought she was really inviting me out." Lynn's mother, when she hears why her daughter has dropped out of the play, demands to know why Lynn lets herself be ruled by Tashi: "We decided to be friends again." The volatility of friendships cannot yet be controlled, and so it has to be accepted. The goal of having a friend is greater than the desire to avoid pain; the suffering is tolerated because the girl knows it may change, for exclusions, like inclusions, are not permanent. There is always the possibility that being "out" is temporary. And that is why so many girls take their punishment: There may be a rapid reprieve, and they will be "in" once again. But forgiveness invites trouble: Rejection and criticism are likely to erupt again. Friendships always involve risk.

Safe Havens

The cruelty of teasing situations can also define what is best in friendship, by marking positive bounds of loyalty as well. Marilyn, in eighth grade, reveals what for her was an initially painful situation through which she discovered new strengths in friends she had previously taken for granted:

> Lorraine was really bossy, the sort of person you wouldn't want to go against, the kind of person who is your friend but you are afraid of at the same time. Well, one day Lorraine

and I had a disagreement and she started teasing me. Being who she is—you know, *Lorraine*—my other friends were almost afraid to step in. But then Mandy came to my rescue along with Lisa. Both of them had been there before, laughed at by Lorraine. They knew how I felt. It was then that I found out what friendship was.

And so other friends can offer support against someone who is too "bossy," and new alliances are formed as girls protect one another from teasing and coercion. But sometimes girls have to act alone in the struggle to have their feelings and needs respected. Bronwen, fourteen, resists the charismatic force of Pauline, whose friendship she has worked to sustain because "Pauline makes me feel safe," but she sees that this "safety" carries with it risk to her independence and self-respect:

> Every time she has to baby-sit her sister, she asks me to come around, and then she'll get me to play the games her little sister likes and put her to bed while she just watches TV or does her homework. And then she goes on at me, "Bring your homework," and she'll copy it and get real annoyed if I ask her not to: "I'm just looking at it!" Last time she asked I said, "I don't have to do this, you know." She looked at me, like, and my heart was in my stomach. It was so awful, but I just looked back and said, "I want to be your friend, but I don't have to do everything you say." And she said, "Fine." But I don't know whether we are still friends. And if we're not, then things will sure get nasty at school.

Bronwen takes the great risk of losing a friend as she resists her manipulative power. She confirms the rightness of her decision to make a stand as she concludes that "bossy friends aren't any fun," but

so deeply do these confrontations touch her fear of losing a friend
that she feels "sick and dizzy afterward."

Teasing, criticism, and shaming set up clouds of confusion about
who we are and what we are worth. Maeve wears a jacket or skirt or
styles her hair in a certain way. Other girls "know" it's wrong. Their
knowledge is clear. But she doesn't know what they know or how
they know. "Why are running shoes all right to wear with a long skirt
but not a short one? And why is Lucy's hair just fine, but mine,
which is just a little different, somehow completely wrong?" Who we
are and whether we are "right" or "acceptable" seems clear to others:
What's wrong with us that we don't see it?

These dynamics persist into adult life as grown women remain
acutely sensitive to who is sought, who is deemed admirable, and
whose inclusion seems to have special value. Maggie, fifty-two, a
well-established accountant, married with three grown children,
finds great satisfaction in having lunch with a group of women
friends after her aerobics class, and what appeals to her is that these
women accept her, although she is never quite sure just how much
they accept her. These are women who always look wonderful, have
the right clothes, the right husbands, and get invited to the important social events—the women who used to be the girls who never
wanted her around them in high school. Somewhat guiltily, Maggie
takes delight in feeling that she has finally arrived, but is continually
anxious that her "friends" will somehow find her out. An invitation
to dinner from one of them brings more of a sense of triumph than a
new million-dollar account at work. A compliment on her outfit
from another, she tells us, "makes my day." Maggie feels embarrassed
by these feelings, knows at some level that she is being ridiculous,
but as is the case for all who have grown up female, her sense of
worth is embedded in the value of those who choose her as friends.

The "having" of friends and the dynamics of loyalty that accompany friendship form a bedrock of self-esteem or self-hatred. Our

sense of worth is enhanced when we are chosen, included, accepted. We feel a strange division of self-esteem when we are chosen by chance or misunderstanding, as when someone makes of us something we are not, or when we make of ourselves—to others—something we may not be. When we care about inclusion in a group or acceptance, we may judge ourselves to be weak, or shallow. Sometimes we can want to be included in a group we ourselves do not really value. Maggie recognizes the absurdity of her elevating these women, for whom at some level she also feels contempt. But her long-unfulfilled dream of being included in the magic circle of the "in" crowd is too powerful—and brings her too much pleasure—to resist. Like many women, Maggie feared that she could never get herself right if she didn't get her friends right.

Old Enough to Know Better?

In our adult world, as we make friends of colleagues and clients, women are thrown back into the tensions experienced during the intensely possessive adolescent phases of friendships. Eileen, thirty-five, decides to move her departmental newsletter from one printer to another, who has more up-to-date equipment and has given a lower quote. She explains this to her previous printer, but finds old friend issues make things messy:

> I knew she wouldn't like it. No one likes losing business. But she's a pro—she knows the ropes and I figured she would understand that I want a quick result and a low price. Yet when I told her, I got "How can you do this to me? How can you handle this like just another contract?" And then there were warnings: "Well, if you go down this road, don't bother to come back." And then—I can hardly believe this, but she even said, "How can you do this now, when I'm budgeting

for my daughter's wedding?" I know people can be difficult and childish, but this really threw me. She was trying to make me feel bad. Trying to make me feel guilty. She argued that I was wrong because I wasn't caring enough about her and being loyal to her. The issues were not business ones. They were about being a good friend. But she ended with a coup de grâce: "I don't care what you do." This is the stuff of fourteen-year-olds who are hypersensitive to rejection. We're pushing forty. But that doesn't seem to matter.

Getting older helps—but never, we notice, as much as we think it should. Mara, forty-five, tries to explain to a doctor who has delivered her children and seen her through various gynecological problems that the particular procedure Mara now must undergo is not one that she would choose this doctor to perform. She has various explanations. This is a tense, awful time for her as she faces a prophylactic operation that may save her from the cancer that took her mother's life. She recalls the botched operations performed on her mother, and though she does not expect this woman to repeat such clumsiness, she needs the reassurance of having a world-renowned specialist, a doctor highly recommended by a number of other people. She cannot, Mara explains, deal with any more blips in her life than she has to. She is sorry to give this news to her long-term doctor, with whom she has something approaching a friendship, but her doctor is a professional woman, and surely she will take her decision professionally. Instead of hearing a professional doctor's response to her decision, however, she hears a rush of anger: "Of course I can do what I want, she says, but how do I think that makes her feel? How could I suppose someone would do a better job than she would? What future contact can we have, now that she knows my doubts about her work? Why do I prefer someone to her?" What Mara hears, in other words, is not a doctor's professional response, but a fourteen-year-old girl's demand: Whose friend are you, anyway?

Yet as often as we are haunted by this ghostly accusation, "Whose friend are you, anyway?," we can catch a similar response within ourselves. I discover that one of my friends has set up a regular lunch date with another woman, and my mind hums with a hundred thoughts: "She finds Sandy more interesting than me" or "She knows I'm not so generous with my time" or "I'm not as much fun" or "I'm not as nice to look at." Or, I make up a hundred unnecessary excuses: "She and Sandy are working in similar fields" or "They have children the same age" or "They both like the same kind of food." What I, the adult, the realist, want to say is: "This is fine; I'm glad my friends are friends with one another." I want the sharing of friends to be nothing to remark on, nothing to respond to, being simply one good way of the world. But this is not how it will be, until I can learn from experiences with girlfriends to trust the stream of imperfect affection and to bear quietly the deadweight of my wish for an exclusive bond. Our lives remain shaped by past patterns of threats, which we thought were left behind in high school, even as new patterns and a new sense of balance emerges. We learn from our friendships about the inevitable variations in the connections and spaces between us. Distinguishing past from present can help us develop better strategies for observing and relating to others, but we can only distinguish past from present if we acknowledge the past emotions and conflicts.

As girls grow into women, they learn to demand less exclusivity in friendship and to better tolerate its vagaries. "I thought friends would be more like family," said thirty-three-year-old Millie, after recounting a tale of disappointment in her women friends, with whom she had founded a group living arrangement. For a while after the group dissolved, she retreated to her family, then married, suspiciously eyeing women who bade for her friendship. By age forty, though, she had close friends once again, friends who understood the time constraints both she and they were under, friends who welcomed and offered what affection each could bring to the relationship. "I've learned to be more selective of my friends," Millie said, "but also to recognize that there are limits. Someone can be my friend and have other things and people in their life, too."

Over time, our needs in our friendships change. The girlhood fantasy of the perfect twosome of soul mates, the loyal dyad, the discovery of a person who will always make us special, may move into romantic relationships, into our relationships with our children—or it may be transmuted into more complex forms of relating. Yet it is a fantasy that dies hard and never completely vanishes. My best friend from the seventh grade is still my friend—Jenny, who trod with me the earliest steps in loving a friend. I still have a letter she wrote me in the eighth grade, in which she tried to patiently and kindly explain to me that her being friends with Tina did not mean that I wasn't still her best friend or she mine. Throughout middle school and high school, Jenny was the rock on which my life balanced, the friend to whom I always turned for understanding and comfort. But Jenny had demanding family responsibilities and strict, restrictive parents, and she was rarely available on weekends. So I found, a few years later, an additional "best" friend, a friend for companionship and exploration of things our parents would not approve of. As far as I could tell, neither seemed to mind the existence of the other, and when I would sense some unease in Jenny about the things I did with Betty, I was always careful to make some critical remark about Betty to Jenny in order to reassure her that I still loved her best.

Sitting across from each other on an outing to celebrate our fiftieth birthdays—I have flown across the country for the occasion—I tell Jenny unguardedly about my sense of how important she was to me during those years.

"But it wasn't like that at all," she says. "We weren't really friends after ninth grade. You had Betty and I was best friends with Diane. You had ditched me."

I feel a stab of pain, of unreality and confusion. This doesn't matter anymore, I tell myself as I choke back tears. But I feel humiliated and begin to babble: "That's not so," I protest. It feels as if a thirty-five-year-old grievance is unexpectedly whipping me in the face as I recognize that I haven't meant to her what I thought I have, nor can she recognize what she meant to me. And I still want to fight to set the record straight. At a deeper level, though, I am face-to-face with the recognition that I, too, must have been an imperfect friend, capable of betrayals that escaped my notice, hurts that I was unaware of inflicting. Oftentimes it's not so easy to know, in the end, whose friend anyone is.

Chapter Four

"I KNEW YOU'D UNDERSTAND!"

Friends coach others to talk. Without fully being aware of it, we learn how to listen each other into speech. Again and again we discover that we may not really know what we think about something important until a friend makes a space for us to try to express ourselves in language. Then, as we hear the words tumble out of our mouths, we may contact feelings that reveal what we hadn't quite known about ourselves before. Claudia tells us: "I didn't know how angry I was at my husband until I started to tell my friend about this argument we had last night. I was kind of joking about it, but when she listened without laughing, I realized, 'Hey, this is serious,' and I began to cry without really knowing why. Now I see this is something I really have to deal with in my marriage." This capacity to listen empathically, to pick up and shape ideas together, is not simply inbred. Rather, it is a talent constantly honed in the world of girls' and women's friendships.

Beyond having our friends clarify our own voice, friends solidify our sense of self by knowing us. When asked to describe who she is, Audrey, thirty-three, an experienced social worker, married, mother of two, talks about her family, her job, and her goals, but concludes, "When I think of myself, what I really think about, too, are the people I care about and who care about me. It would be hard to feel what I am if my closest friends didn't also know who I am." In this conclusion, she speaks for many women. Who she is, in part, is shaped by friends' understanding of her. As we connect to others, we share private thoughts and ideas in hopes of being acknowledged, understood, and validated. We quickly learn that some of our questions are difficult to articulate, that some of our responses are deemed inappropriate, that many of our thoughts are out of the mainstream. It is in the earliest experiences of friendship that we learn what of ourselves can be understood by another—and when there is a resonant response, we know the joy of feeling understood.

Vicky, fourteen, finds that as she talks to a friend, what emerges is a recognition and reflection of her own feelings:

> I thought, before I got to know Clare—before I got to know her like I know her now—that I was the only one in the whole school, maybe in the whole world, who thought about things and wondered about things like I do. These are things you just can't talk about to other people. I sometimes feel so weird, the way I look at everyone and see them. But with Clare, I can talk about this without feeling I'm such a weirdo. And sometimes we just laugh at ourselves, and that's a relief. But, you know, sometimes we can really talk about it and get somewhere—like get to understand more about what we're thinking.

Vicky catches sight of her own peculiarities, her individual slant, the questions and doubts raised, for her, by the ordinary process of living. Clare offers reassurance that she is not alone in her way of thinking and seeing.

We can only be sure we are what we are when someone else knows with us what and who we are. We become self-aware through our awareness of how our thoughts and feelings are the same, and different, from those of the people around us. This need to share our thoughts, however, rests on a fine balance. We want to feel special, which in part means "different" or "unique," but—one of the constant dilemmas in our sense of self—we also want our feelings and thoughts to be shared. We want someone to know what matters to us deeply, to hold sacred our dreams, to sympathize with our pain and disappointments, to laugh at what delights us, and to share our sense of the ridiculous. From the trivial to the intensely serious, we want a friend to understand.

Early in friendship, we may just want a partner in our experience, someone to breathe the same air we do, to share a climate of understanding. In our first friendships, such basic fingerholds on life are provided even in apparently silly exclamations as, for example, when we invite a friend to mock teachers or boys: "Did you see what he did to his hair?" or "Can you imagine her in bed?" or "Do you think she screws up her eyes and talks in that voice all the time?" The shared giggles that reverberate are crucial to an understanding and acceptance of ourselves—part of the sense of who we are that we try to map in our daily lives. We need this as children and we need this as adolescents, and although the voice and tone may change, we continue to need these self-confirming responses from friends as adults.

"I was amazed," said fifteen-year-old Linda, "that when I got to know Beryl, who always seemed so sure of herself, that she has the same doubts and fears that I do." "I am so relieved to know," said forty-five-year-old Harriet, new to an Al-Anon group, "that other women struggle with the same conflicts and confusions I do. I'm not really alone." We often see others as so much more well-defined than we know ourselves to be. As we tune in to our thoughts and feelings, we note the fragmented nature of our own experience and think that, somehow, for others it is different—much more clearly defined, much less often hedged with blurred borders and questions. We hone ourselves against the surfaces of others as we search for our own reflection in them. Our friends provide the best assurance that we are not mad.

We're Just the Same

The first ways in which we learn to communicate shared understanding of someone else is to say—and hear—"Me, too."[1] Being identical feels like the highest form of knowing and being fully known. As adults, we continue to believe that no one can really understand unless they have been there, too—and certainly, hearing our own experiences in another feels reassuring. Not only are we not strange, but perhaps our way of being has some larger meaning, and not just of our making. The soul-filling pleasures of being understood by someone who feels, in some important ways, like our twin are so intense that for those lucky enough to find such a friend, the illusion of sameness can become highly seductive. In search of someone "like us," we may come to feel that we have found someone "just like us." And while this sense of merger is blissful for a while, it can become devastating, particularly in adolescence, when the realities of difference become inescapable. Tamara, at age twenty, writes of such a relationship:

> For two years, seventh and eighth grade, it was as if we were the same person. We understood each other perfectly. We thought the same thing at the same time, finished each other's sentences, felt the same way always. We were so in sync with one another that I started to get confused about who was who. I would look at her handwriting and think it was mine. I would look at her, and though we looked nothing alike, I would almost think it was me. I lost myself in her, so that after a while I couldn't figure out anymore where she stopped and I began. Together, we were invincible—it was me and her against the world. The only thing that either of us feared was losing the other. She wrote me a letter once, the only one I still have, where she confessed to me that the

thing that most frightened her was when she realized that we were different. I felt the same way. Yet we naively believed that those differences didn't matter. We were one and nothing could change that.

But we were wrong, because no matter how hard we tried to deny it, we were different people. Ninth grade turned out to be the most traumatic year of my life. On the first day of school, she came all dressed in black because she wanted to be part of the punk crowd. I wanted that, too, in a way, but as far as I was concerned, she came first. We were best friends and everyone else was expendable. But I felt that she betrayed me to be cool for punks who were just so hardcore, for some guy with green eyes who could play the guitar. She seemed like such a hypocrite, yet she didn't want to lose me either. Throughout that year, we tried to get back the absolute oneness we'd had. Every night, we talked on the phone for hours, trying to work things out. Neither one of us could understand what had happened, what had gone wrong. Each night, we would resolve things, but then the next day in school it would turn sour as soon as we met in freshman hall.

Feeling helpless, tormented, utterly alone, I turned against everything and everyone but her. I blamed other kids in my class, teachers, myself, but nothing helped. Finally she was the only thing left to turn against. And I knew her so well that I knew just how to hurt her. Every arrow I shot at her hit its mark, but it hit me, too, because I still loved her. Toward the end of the year, I destroyed everything I had that was connected to her. I cut off my hair, stopped eating normally, destroyed my journals, letters, cassettes. I couldn't deal with the loss because when she changed she took everything with her. We had been like the same person; I had given my whole self to her. Then she became the enemy and there seemed like there was nothing left of who I had been. I promised myself over and over never to trust anyone ever again.

At the end of the year I thought would never end, I left the country for the year and she ended up on the maximum dosage of Prozac. When I came back a year later, I had forgiven her. I had realized that it was not her fault, but though I didn't know it, I was still hoping that I could have her back the way we once were. It took another year before I finally accepted that we were two different people, that we had different personalities and desires and had made different choices.

At all ages, girls and women wrestle with the distinction between being liked and being (just) like. The similarities between them can be romanticized: "We're different from other people; we're just like each other; we're special." Many girls experience a wonderfully comforting identification. If they admit differences between them, then an awful question arises: "Who am I?" Tamara knows who she is when she is just like her friend, but feels terror and confusion when she notes differences between them. Viewing this from the outside, perhaps as mothers watching our daughters suffer, we may miss the significance of what seem like minor events: Tamara finds that her friend has come to school wearing different clothes, and she falls apart! Yet there are deep meanings about identity and connection in the minutiae of a girl's social world. "You just don't understand" is a common cry to a mother who forgets the symbolic forces in a daughter's daily life. Tamara, noting her friend's different clothes and attitudes, confronts questions about how her identity is shaped by someone with whom she closely connects. If she likes that person, does she have to be "just like" her? If she depends on a friend's understanding, then does their experience have to be the same? And if it isn't, then what is the nature of their knowledge of each other?[2]

Care and understanding across differences present an ongoing challenge, and the problem of discovering difference where one thought there was sameness in a close friend is a recurring anguish. Most adult women recount similar shattering episodes in their own lives. Wistfully, they tell of old, formerly much-loved friends who drifted away on the waves of difference, ending up too far away for mutual understanding to bridge the gap.

After her first year in college, Merle felt she had made "the best friend ever." Yet at the end of her third year, she feels "like stone" because something in the friendship has "died":

> I've had lots of girlfriends, but before there was always something missing. And then I got to college and someone from an entirely different background, who lived in a totally different city, was like the neighborhood friend I never had. We agreed about everything. We liked the same people. We took the same courses, and then we joined the same sorority. The sense of closeness was special, like we were really twins, separated at birth. Can you imagine what kind of a bond that's like? And for a while it seemed that we were getting more and more alike. I noticed she'd be looking at my handwriting and hers would get more like mine, and once a teacher wasn't sure whose paper was whose, because there weren't names on them. And we were thrilled. And then I'd choose clothes that were clothes I knew she'd choose. We had this great repartee going. We were always on the same wavelength, and we knew what was coming next because we just understood each other's mind.
>
> And then I started to realize how much pressure I felt to say, "Yeah, I know exactly what you mean." And sometimes

I knew she felt the same. We stuck together, but we really started to hate each other. This summer, for the first time since we met, we spent the whole vacation apart. There was not even a phone call. I dread going back. It's so hard to know where we stand. It's not like she's done anything unforgivable, and I know I still like her, but that sense that we're really one and always understanding each other—well, that's just gone, and I'm not going to fake it anymore, and I just don't see how we're going to stay friends, but it will really get nasty if we don't.

Merle is dealing with an insecurity that strikes many college women as they step away from their homes and try to establish, with a girlfriend, a familiar base. At a time when college women expect to feel mature and independent, they experience a crisis of confidence and identity that may be far worse than anything they experienced during adolescence.

For most young women, college friendships are exhilarating. Nancy, now thirty-two, reflects on the freedom she felt in college, where for the first time she could make friends with girls who understood her goals and drive. Among the girls in her suburban high school she was "brainy, but with hairy legs, so brainy didn't matter." In her college setting she found girls offering confirmation of her values, whose conversation was "like a sharp intake of Alpine air." For Nancy, there was a new surprising pleasure in having "friends who dreamed along with me." But many young women, like Merle, are overwhelmed by the new "freedom," which they experience as an overwhelming lack of self-definition. For Merle, the problem is "solved" by an identification with another young woman. Connected, she feels supported. She depends on this support, and hence denies any differences that may threaten the connection.

Though this kind of merger and need to be "just the same" may seem like a phase, and something we will "grow out of," it can strike at any time, for at any time in our lives we may have an intense need for the support only a girlfriend—with her capacity to be just like us—is likely to provide. And when we have that need, the old dilemmas confront us—the need to be close, the association between closeness and similarity, and the subsequent fear of what impact our differences will have on the friendship.

Stephanie, thirty-nine, has for many years enjoyed support from a friend she first met in the maternity ward during the birth of her first child. The bond that was forged as they underwent labor together, had similar experiences in delivery, and both had sons, continued while her children were growing up, and then intensified during the process of her divorce. She describes how the discovery of sameness supported her in a crisis, and how the discovery of difference felt like a betrayal of the friendship:

> This woman was so supportive. I needed all that support to leave a very uncomfortable marriage. There's no way I could have made this decision by myself. My thoughts kept circling: "He's not nice to you, but what else can you do, and what else is going to be better?" I'd swing from "I just have to put up with it" to "I can't put up with it." Oh, it was awful. Randi just wrenched me out of that loop. She told me how she'd been through the same thing, and how it was really worth the fight to break free, and that my kids would be fine, just fine. And we talked about men and life, and everything was so clear because she felt exactly the same way about marriage and men and mothers as I did. But as soon as I got divorced, she fell in love! And instead of hearing that she felt just like I did, she was telling me that happiness lay in the right man. I felt betrayed. I was like a wounded bird. It was like I only believed I should separate because that's

how she saw things. I know that's not how it was, but I half thought that then. How could she change on me? Looking back, I guess her life changed, but she was still ready to spend time with me. She'd call, and she'd try to be as supportive as ever, but things just weren't the same, and I didn't feel any better after talking to her, so I'd put off phoning her back, and we gradually drifted apart. Divorce was terrible, but when I think about how terrible it was, the end of that friendship—because that's what I have to say happened—is one of the still-awful things about it. It was just so confusing to see how different we were after all.

There is no "natural" or inevitable resolution of this dilemma, no release from the battery of disappointment at discovering and rediscovering how different we are from someone we're close to. The adolescent within each of us keeps open questions about how we can connect with someone who is different from us. And, constantly in touch with that adolescent identity that hasn't quite formed, we can still shudder with doubt as we wonder, "Can this be what I feel—if it's different from what my close friend feels?"

Shared Feeling

For girls, friendship without talk about feelings, and without reciprocal understanding of what each feels, seems little more than a shell. Friends seek each other's help in understanding and managing their feelings: "Jana ignored me today and I just feel so awful," one friend says to another. "Nothing I do seems to go right" or "I can't deal with my new stepfather." They work together, carefully assembling the pieces of a story, in an attempt to understand their world and how they might handle it. They sift through their reactions to their families and to their other friends. As friends explore the world of emotions, one girl is careful to help to make the other's emotions bearable and to describe her behavior in an acceptable light: "You did the best you could." "It's not your fault." "He's the one who's strange." One friend gets the message across to the other: "You're okay." And that acceptance is the gift of understanding.

Here Ginny and Francine, both fourteen, work to sort out Ginny's problem with a third friend:

G I N N Y: When she says things like that—"What've you been up to?"—right in front of everyone, it's like—how can you answer?

F R A N C I N E: She's slipped the criticism in, hasn't she?

G I N N Y: Yeah! So everyone thinks "What's up?" and something's wrong, and it makes me feel so strange.

F R A N C I N E: You looked upset.

G I N N Y: You could tell? Was it obvious?

F R A N C I N E: I knew—'cause I know you. It wasn't obvious. I mean, they were just thinking about what she said, and 'cause you didn't say much, I don't think—

G I N N Y: You know, I was just about to cry. It's silly, isn't it. I mean, there was nothing to it. I was just embarrassed.

F R A N C I N E: My eyes sometimes fill with tears when I'm embarrassed.

G I N N Y: Yeah—it's not really crying. Your eyes just sting.

F R A N C I N E: And you hurt inside.

G I N N Y: It's just so confusing to see everyone looking at you and wondering about you. 'Cause it makes me feel so strange. It was like she wanted to push me away before I got there.

F R A N C I N E: 'Cause she feels bad about spending so much time with those guys. You know how she used to always wait for you after lunch.

G I N N Y: So she was covering up—making me out to be the odd one for walking up to her.

FRANCINE: Maybe . . . you could just shrug and walk away.
GINNY: Like she's the one who's strange.
FRANCINE: Well, isn't she?

Here two girlfriends engage in a remarkable emotional-education course. They shift from sympathy to analysis to advice to comfort: Francine acknowledges Ginny's feelings ("You looked upset") and the gravity of the situation. She then sympathizes with her, as though to say "I know how you feel," because she, too, feels pain, and her eyes also water when she is embarrassed. But the conversation does not stop with a simple "I know how you feel." This girl talk is a beautiful example of emotional coaching—a process in which we learn to identify emotions and to understand how emotions arise. As they understand why the third friend behaved as she did, Francine convinces Ginny that the fault or problem is not hers but the other girl's—a comforting, positive spin. Together they read another's feelings from how she acts, then, as they go through possible ways of managing an uncomfortable social situation, consider how other people might be handled. Only another girl who inhabits the same social world can understand the nuances of this interaction.[3]

In talk, girls create and learn the contours of their interpersonal worlds. Friends frequently engage in plotting sessions whereby they ask one another, "What should I do?" They discuss how to get a boy to notice them, how to deal with a difficult mother, how to get out of trouble with a teacher. Should I confront this girl, they may ask, or ignore her? Should I give her a dose of her own medicine? How can I ask this guy out or start a conversation with him? How do I tell my mother? These coaching sessions also offer help with a girl's attempt to handle her feelings—especially that terrible adolescent self-consciousness and the anxiety that accompanies it: "Do you think he noticed?" "What did they think?" "How did I look?"

A friend provides an outsider's view—but is an outsider who

understands. Francine, as a good friend, understands that Ginny was upset, but she can also assure her, as an "outsider," that no one else noticed. They discuss others' reactions to them ("Why did she react like that? I didn't mean to upset her"). They form an alliance against those who do not understand, and their mutual understanding of each other allows them to form an elite. The need for being understood is primitive and deep, arising in infancy from our need for others to respond to us in ways that, first, simply keep us alive (as we communicate hunger, pain, and fear) and then, later, shape our basic humanity. Throughout our lives, talk with friends continues to offer emotional feedback and helps us make sense of our experience.[4] In Marge Piercy's novel *Braided Lives,* which describes a life-molding friendship, Jill feels the urge we have all known to tell a friend something in order to make our experience real:

> I begin to walk fast and then trot, wishing I was already in my dormitory room, transported instantly to Donna so I can spill out to her verbatim, gestures illustrated and pauses marked, the afternoon. Then it will be real for me, secured, understood.

Friends can support and confirm our feelings. Though the danger remains that as they crave understanding, girls—and women— may change what they are to fit what a friend understands, they often help us to see more than we can with our single vision. And so we continue to search for the boundaries of ourselves in the reflections of our friends.

Mirroring

Friends become mirrors. Part of the awful pain of adolescence arises from a fix or focus on what others see. How one appears in others' eyes is both magnified (teenagers always assume they are seen) and distorted: They may not know whether they are fat or thin, cool or nerdy, pretty or plain, ridiculous or savvy. Acutely aware of others' views, yet unable to gauge them, they work with a friend to focus a perspective: I am sixteen, shopping with a friend, and I try on a suit. "Oh, yes," Mary tells me, "it's very you." And I look in the mirror and think, "What does she see as very me? Can I see it, too?"

Speaking of her best friend, Shelley, sixteen-year-old Gabrielle explained:

> Shelley and I talk about me a lot. Because I'm so hung up about how I look. And she says to me, "You really look great" or "Your skin's not so bad!" Or she might say, "Try your hair this way" or "Why don't you wear a certain color?" and I feel like she's putting me together, giving me a spare skin of confidence. I need someone to tell me how I look, otherwise I feel myself falling to bits. I know it's silly, and we laugh about it, but I'll remember her help all my life.

Much attention has recently been given to girls' loss of confidence during adolescence: As their bodies change and develop, they grow increasingly dissatisfied with their weight, shape, skin.[5] To understand each girl, we have to understand that how she internalizes and resists the cultural pressure to be both concerned about and critical of her looks—and how she resists these pressures, or succumbs to them—will in large part be shaped by the reflections her girlfriends give back to her.

Sometimes a friend can see things about us that we cannot see ourselves, or understand things about us before we do. A good friend knows how to use this knowledge, to wait with it until the right moment when we, too, are ready to allow our own awareness. Gilda, age eighteen, recalls how a close friend would "tease me about how

little I was eating. I guess she knew before I did that I was becoming
anorexic. Finally, one day, I asked her if she thought I was and she
said, 'I was wondering when you were going to figure it out.' She
didn't hate me for it. She helped me get the courage to ask my
mother to get me some help."

And this theme reverberates among women of all ages. Tracy, age
forty-two, tells of a conversation she had with her friend Mindy following her, Tracy's, divorce.

> Mindy always knew I shouldn't have married him. I remem-
> ber in college when she would ask me gently if I knew what I
> was doing. But she always supported me; she figured I must
> have had my reasons. But now she tells me what she had
> been thinking all along, and I know that she was tuned into
> that other part of myself, the part I kept trying to push away
> because I was so scared of it.

Often, our friends can see the whole of us when we feel lost
among the parts. Telling a friend what we really feel, no matter what
our age, commits us to being who we are. Once out in the open,
what we feel is real—there is no taking it back or turning away from
it. When what we are or what we feel is nourished by the acceptance
and understanding of a friend, we can make it part of ourselves and
we feel more whole. "Dale and I are so close I can tell her
everything," says Kay, age fifteen, "even my darkest secrets." "What
is the darkest secret you've told?" I ask her. "Once I even told her
about how sometimes I think bad thoughts—like wanting bad
things to happen to people—people I like, but still want—oh, you
know—dead, or maimed. Maybe even my mom, or some girl that
just gets at me. I feel terrible about these thoughts, and I normally
don't tell anyone about them, 'cause they make me into such a shit.
But I told Dale. And she said, 'Yeah, sometimes I feel like that, too.'"

Kay sounds relieved: Even the terrible parts of her can be accepted—and shared—by her friend.

Over and over again we hear of the importance of being understood in girls' and women's lives. But early experiences in friendship teach us that being understood doesn't just happen. Girls have to make themselves understood, and so they do lots of practicing. Kelly, age sixteen, tries to analyze the process:

> We spend hours talking. Just talking. Sometimes it's about just one thing, like what happened last night, or yesterday at school. I tell her what happened, and then she'll ask a hundred questions. "What did she do then?" or "How did she say it?" and "Who else was there?" And it goes on and on, but the best part is when she says things like "That's because you're the kind of person you are," and she goes on to say these things about me, like "It's all so interesting" and "It's going to lead to something." And that's why she's my best friend. Because she wants to know who I am and what'll become of me.

Kelly sees a best friend as someone who wants to understand, and who works, through talking, at seeing how things really are, then creates a story about what kind of person she is.

Our great concern with how people describe us starts in our earliest relationships. "You're a clever/pretty/good girl" is one of the most basic descriptions we may take to heart. Other aspects of our sense of self develop as our family tells us we are "helpful" or "clumsy" or "lazy" or "hard-working" or even "lucky." "I'm not a naughty girl!" a child protests when being scolded. But even as she protests to save face, to save something deep within her self-esteem, she fears it is so, because someone has said it. Sticks and stones don't hurt as deeply as names do.

Names construct stories about who we are, and we continue to care about these stories.[6] Even as we grow stronger in our sense of who we are, this self-awareness is always fluid, under constant revision. "Am I fair? Am I honest? Am I stingy? Am I sympathetic?" we ask, several times each day, as we go about living our lives. These questions are usually microthoughts that pass unnoticed once we are adults, but teenagers work on them daily—and work on them by asking one another.

As women, we continue to use friends to talk about the meaning of a situation, defining our role and someone else's.[7] We also know how broken we can feel when someone doesn't understand us. Several years ago, I failed to give my father the gift his wife had suggested. Instead, I gave him something that, in my stepmother's view, was far too casual, utterly failing to mark the event that was, for her, so special. She wrote to me describing my thoughtlessness, my coldness, my fundamentally deficient character. Though over forty, I felt beaten down, stung by the criticism from someone whose goodness I trust. My husband could comfort me and tell me the accusations were "absurd." A male friend comforts me by describing the letter as "abusive." But only my girlfriend Janet could look at me with that special friend look, that "I know who you are and you are not that" look. Only a close friend could combine objectivity and understanding to say, "That isn't you, girl!" So my fault is packed into a very small space, and I am once again someone who, at worst, may have lacked a little judgment, or could be a little careless, but not someone worthy of such criticism. As I feel the weight of that punishing description of myself ease away, I think how many times this has happened: A story about who I am and what I am worth is put right again by a counterdescription, which only the friend who understands me can convincingly give. Having a girlfriend tell us we're okay is the closest thing to telling this to ourselves—and believing it.

Understanding as Comfort

Not all the explorations of oneself are purely verbal, though, nor does growth in understanding who we are always come from verbal exchanges. That strange concept of "women's intuition"—the way a woman knows certain things without apparent evidence—is actually a source of knowledge that is meticulously built up during the long years of important work within girls' friendships. Some girls say they "hardly know what they talk about," and that what matters is "we're just together," but a close look at what girls do when they're just together reveals the interplay of comfort and understanding. Here Gemma, at fifteen, articulates her awareness that understanding can be implicit:

> Sometimes I can feel so down. I don't think most people can know just how low I get, how sometimes life seems so awful. And when I'm with most of my friends—especially Sam and Dee—I can joke and stuff, but I don't feel better. With Cari, who's really my best friend, I can just mope, and we'll listen to music or eat or watch a video. I don't have to be bouncy or happy. I don't even have to smile. She'll look at me, and I'll nod: "Yeah, I feel better than I did." Or sometimes I have to shake my head, and she nods, like "Okay. I understand." And sometimes there will be this phrase in the music, or something will happen in the movie, and we're suddenly laughing.

We don't have to talk about our depression to know whether, if we did, it would meet with avoidance or sympathy. As girls feel the power of a friend's comfort, they experience the subtleties of communication: Gemma notes that Tess can ask a question simply by looking at her, and her emotions can be acknowledged without speech. Together they acknowledge the precariousness of their moods. Somehow, without speech, they share secrets and jokes. It is often said that girls and women are more tuned in to feelings than men. When we listen to girls talk about their friendships with other girls, we can see that "women's intuition" is not brought about by magic but by a meticulous learning process. Gemma and Tess stay in their rooms, looking at magazines and listening to music, and "keep the busy, roaring strange-tongued world at bay."[8] Instead of cracking the code of the strange-tongued language of that outside world, these girls, in the dense privacy of friendships, crack interpersonal codes and experience a resonant togetherness.

The Mysteries of Sex

Although girls may learn the "facts" from adult women (often their mothers), they need one another to explore and work out the tangled set of emotions that litter the road toward integration of their sexuality. Girls develop a private but shared idiom for talking about body parts and the desires, anxieties, and guilt that riddle them. Vicky, now fourteen, describes how important Clare was to her when her mother first explained to her some of the basic facts of human sexuality. Her mother insisted that sexual intercourse was not "disgusting," as Vicky first proclaimed it was, but a beautiful human experience. Her mother could not have done a better job of conveying positive and responsible messages about sex, but girls also need something else. Vicky needed to explore with her friend Clare—as she couldn't with her mother—how odd and disturbing it was to her that people she knew actually engaged in such activities. Laura's mother, too, does a good mother's job, telling her fourteen-year-old that her body shape is normal, not "fat" or "repulsive," as Laura sometimes fears, but it is not until her friend Diane tells her that she's "really gorgeous" that Laura can walk down the school hall at ease with herself.

Parents and teachers emphasize the need to speak openly about sexuality, without demeaning it through embarrassment or anxiety. But until maturity and experience bring a certain level of comfort, sexuality—both one's own and that of others—is embarrassing. Girls need someone to giggle with.

Flannery O'Connor, one of the few writers to attempt to enter this world in descriptive prose, observes the dawn of sexuality through the eyes of a child watching two older, early-adolescent girls. She begins her short story "A Temple of the Holy Ghost" with the sentence "All weekend the two girls were calling each other Temple One and Temple Two, shaking with laughter and getting so red and hot that they were positively ugly." The child's mother finally asks them why they are calling each other such silly names,

> and this sent them into gales of giggles. Finally they man-
> aged to explain. Sister Perpetua . . . had given them a lecture
> on what to do if a young man should—here they laughed so
> hard they were not able to go on without going back to the
> beginning—on what to do if a young man should—they
> put their heads in their laps—on what to do if—they finally
> managed to shout it out—if he should "behave in an
> ungentlemanly manner with them in the back of an auto-
> mobile." Sister Perpetua said they were to say, "Stop, sir! I
> am a Temple of the Holy Ghost!" and that would put an end
> to it. . . . "I think you are pretty silly," [the mother] said.
> "After all, that's what you are—Temples of the Ghost." The
> two of them looked up at her, politely concealing their gig-
> gles, but with astonished faces, as if they were beginning to
> realize that she was made of the same stuff as Sister Perpetua.[9]

What Flannery O'Connor captures in this story is the need for girls to work out these feelings in their own way, with one another. Girls squealing behind the closed bedroom door are probably exchanging some erotically tinged tidbits and thereby helping each other grow in a way that no amount of conversation with adults ever could.

As Judy Blume records in *Are You There, God? It's Me, Margaret,* parents can do a good job at giving some information, but adults who pretend such matters are totally serious become ridiculous. In this novel, loved by so many girls and women, the twelve-year-old narrator, Margaret, and her friends share their concerns about their sexual maturity. Forming a secret club, the girls scrutinize the physical development of their classmates: Whose breasts are growing? they ask one another. Who's started to menstruate? The girls we spoke to, like Margaret and her friends, are curious and anxious about their own physical development. Like Margaret, some girls admitted (and women remembered) giggling about adults' attempts to convey information about "the facts of life" while evading questions that girls really want answered: They know what menstruation is; they know it doesn't hurt; what they don't know—and what the sex-education teacher can't tell them—is what it feels like to be a menstruating person. It takes another girl—of the same developmental level—to do the kind of talking that mitigates shame, tempers anxiety, expresses the excitement, and creates shared fantasy.[10] To fully understand, a girl, of any age, needs to find a close friend at the same emotional level as her with regard to eroticism.

The emergence of sexual feeling and sexual anxiety is one of the powerful forces that bond girls with one another. Beyond "Did he kiss you?" is "But how did you feel when he kissed you?" This world of girls' exploration of sexual feeling is one closed to adults and one we can remember, but one that was entered only sporadically with the girls we interviewed. With adults, girls talk in adult language. With one another, they speak the emotionally laden vernacular that captures the uncertainty, the excitement, and the forbiddenness of their experience. We could only know they were thinking about it if they blushed and said that with their best friends they talked of "you know—other things."

Sharing a World

Friends can understand in a way no one else can because only someone sharing similar pressures and goals can be available as an alter ego, and this is why friendship with a girl (or woman) has unique qualities that cannot be duplicated in a friendship with a boy (or man). Friends share a sense of the "lay of the social land" and the social meanings of moves and gestures. When Eva tells Lana that Cassie saw her in the hall but just looked straight ahead, Lana knows at once why that matters. She knows how friends are supposed to greet one another in the hall, and how they snub one another. She can easily guess who else would have seen the incident and what they would have thought about it. But when Eva tells her mother, her mother asks whether she is sure Cassie looked away, whether she actually saw her, and whether Cassie's behavior really had anything to do with her feelings for Eva. "I can't get her to see. It takes an hour just to set the scene."

As I reread the "notes" Jenny and I wrote to each other in the eighth grade, collected and saved over all these years, they make no sense to me. All that passion and turmoil about what seems to my adult mind utterly inconsequential things—who sat where in chorus, who put what note in whose notebook, who tried to get who in trouble with another group of people. I can no longer empathize with my adolescent self because I don't live in that social world anymore, yet I wonder ruefully if my E-mail correspondence with my current close friends is really any different—who is getting invited where or moving to a different job, what my daughter wants to do

("Should I let her? How do I handle this?"), what films I've seen, what other people say about a recent book. I know my daughter finds these interchanges as "boring" and inconsequential as I find my old personal notes. But don't they amount to the same thing? I want to know from my women friends who's "in" and who's "out." I want to test my sense of "doing the right thing." I want to share some experiences—like seeing the same films or reading the same books— even if we are thousands of miles away, and then I feel a pleasure, whose intensity I'd be hard-pressed to explain, when we have the same response.

In Search of Understanding

In looking back to earlier friendships, adolescent girls often claim that they did not really like some of their friends. They only played with a girl because she wanted to play with them. They played with someone because they were used to her—or liked the food at her house, or the basketball hoop she had in her driveway. Many girls, in early adolescence, shift from seeing friendship in terms of familiarity or comfort, to searching for a friend who is interesting: As a child, Lynda accepted friends who were "okay," and she made use of their "warm bodies," which provided the support that "just someone" can give in a difficult situation. Now, as a college student, she is critical of these early relationships: Her previous friends accepted her by recognizing her idiosyncrasies ("Oh, there she goes again"), but her current friends want to explore the feelings behind her behavior. This shift involves an altogether higher order of relationship: No longer is a friend needed primarily as a partner who provides space within a group, or as a playmate ("someone to do things with"); what's sought is someone who engages her mind and enables her to see herself through their eyes as someone who is interesting. No longer bound by a parent's choices or by convenience, teenage girls act upon their own preferences for friends.

A girl confronts a two-way challenge in trying to find a friend who will register who she is. First, she needs to find someone who is receptive, and so she engages in a search-and-selection process. Intellectual Violet, growing up in a small farm community, chronically estranged from the girls in her class whom she regarded as silly and immature, began to blossom after Meg moved into the next town and began going to her school. Meg seemed to bring distant places with her, to have breadth in her hopes for a future that, in Violet's view, the friends she had known since first grade lacked. In Meg, she found someone who could understand her, someone who was like her. Violet felt she needed no more than that to hold on to her own view of the world.

But in order to have a friend who registers who she is, a girl has to learn how to say who she is: In order to be heard, she has to speak. She must learn how to present herself so that she is not only understood but also appreciated. Before girls can sit down and talk about "everything," and get from one another the responses they need, before they receive confirmation or understanding, they have to be able to make themselves understood. The verbal barrages of female friendship provide girls with the opportunity for developing practical skills in self-explanation that will get other girls' support and hold their interest. Girls learn to tell about themselves by testing the waters, alluding to feelings, wading slowly into the depths of self-disclosure, gauging all the time their friends' reactions. But friendships are reciprocal, and so a girl must also learn how to offer effective support and understanding in return.

Karen, fifteen, describes how this reciprocity gives her a thrilling sense of a maturing, new self: "At home it's 'Well, you think you know everything' from my sister, and 'Look, honey, I know a lot more about life than you do' from my mother. So with Emma it's 'Wow! Do you really think that? I never thought about it that way, but you're right!' She really thinks I have something to say."

Girls worry over their developing responsiveness and may consult other friends for advice about how to respond effectively to another friend. "Talia tells me her mom gets so mad sometimes and really hits her and stuff. She called me late one night and was crying and crying and she asks me, 'What can I do?' What do I tell her?" Marianne asks another friend. "I try to just listen, but I'm afraid that isn't enough. Sometimes Talia seems so down. I wonder if she might try to run away or something. But I promised not to tell anyone else. It's really her problem. But I feel so bad for her. I wish there were more I could do."

Often it takes many years for girls to learn that "just" listening and empathizing is enough. Especially when our friends share with us what pains them, it takes time to learn to bear that pain with them, not minimizing it, not trying to reassure it away, not allowing it to overwhelm us, too—just to contain it and to understand.

A wonderful document of a girl's need to explain herself, to explore herself through telling and to believe that she has something to say, is *The Diary of Anne Frank*. Deprived of friends as she is in hiding during the Nazi occupation of the Netherlands, Anne constructs her diary into the perfect friend. Naming this friend "Kitty," apologizing, as she would to a real friend, for "neglecting" her for several days, asking "her" not to be shocked by what Anne tells her, pleading for patience and understanding, Anne pours her intellectual energy into explaining herself and her mix of feelings: Her mother annoys her, preferring her sister, her coldness makes her mother cry, she is in a state of high irritation with all around her— and yet her diary, her friend, will understand. This understanding means that her friend will see that her bad feelings do not make her a bad person, that she struggles to sustain both a sense of who she is and a sense of her own goodness. (Would it please Anne to know how many people in the world have, as readers, taken the role of her friend—understanding, sympathizing, and admiring her struggle for a sense of a good self? Or would the exposure be too harsh, given that Anne saw herself as writing to her one and only friend who could really understand?)

Perhaps this is the quintessential struggle of us all: to have someone acknowledge and accept all our feelings, even the socially taboo ones like ingratitude or hard-heartedness, and to endorse the enduring struggle for authenticity. During the past few years, much has been written on the ways in which girls are at great risk during adolescence because their environment—at home, at school, and in the culture at large—works to undermine their self-confidence. They receive messages about the importance of their appearance; they feel the pressure to be the perfect girl, whom everyone likes and whose feelings are as sweetly arranged as her clothes and face. They put energy into their appearance and lose out on authenticity. Because they lose out on authenticity, their confidence and sense of self-worth plummets. One safety net is a good friendship—and women who can help girls understand and negotiate the intricacies of all friendships.

But Do You Really Understand?

Even with our best friends, we cannot always count on being understood. We make friends, and the quality of our friendships changes. There is always the danger that when we tell a story about ourselves, our friend won't understand; instead she'll say, "How could you?" or "What a terrible thing to do" or "I don't believe you said that!" And so while we grow through a friend's understanding, we may also live in fear that one time—maybe this time, maybe next time—she will judge us, not understand us. Luisa, fifteen, describes her own careful moves to discover whether her situation will be understood:

> I did this real dumb thing. But when I do something like that, I don't know how bad it really is. I said I'd go on this school thing with Katie. I said yes because she really didn't want to go alone. But now I've made this other promise, because I couldn't say no to Trudy either, and I feel so bad. I want to tell Katie, but it might be "Oh, my God, you didn't!" I couldn't take that! I want to say, "Look, I've done this dumb thing. How do I handle it? How do I feel okay again?" Because sometimes when I feel like this, it's "I'm never going to feel okay again." And then she'll just say, "Don't worry." But she'll say that because she sees how bad I'm feeling, and I want to know, "What do you really think?"

As Luisa tiptoes around her friend's responses, she shows awareness that her friend, to "be nice," might utter soothing words just to comfort her—and silence her real feelings. But Luisa knows that "being nice" is very different from *really* being nice. We implicitly give a friend the power to hurt us with their judgment of us, spoken or unspoken.

Both girls and women learn, often through painful mistakes, to gauge who will understand what—and when. Kia, forty-five, distinguishes her innermost circle of friends from all others by who knows about her affair. "I need to talk about it," she says, "but only a couple of my very closest friends would understand. Marge used to be my best friend, I guess, but I know she wouldn't approve of something like this, and because I can't tell her, I feel myself pulling away from her. I feel fake or something, but I know she couldn't handle it."

Somewhere in our lives we need to speak forthrightly, unguardedly, and from our hearts. Not to do so risks crippling our very being. We keep talking in the hope of being understood, yet when we talk, we know we may be condemned. If we want to understand girls' and women's emotional worlds, and the ways in which connections are important to us, we must also understand the divided ground on which we stand when we connect to others. The ease with which some women silence their own thoughts and needs; the hesitation or indecisiveness that characterizes many women, and that many of us have to push aside with effort; the terror of not pleasing—all of these have been located in our relationships with our mothers, in our dependence on men, in the subordinate position of women. But we can also see that they have a primary location in the pleasures and perils of our friendships, as we need the connection and know that it can go wrong.

Our messages can be misunderstood both in small and large communications, and in both cases, the misunderstanding hurts. Jody tells Trish she likes her hair, and Trish says, "Stop being sarcastic." Jody feels outrage: "She just can't understand what I say." When Beth tells Leslie that she is going to New York during the school vacation and Leslie is heard saying to another girl, "Beth is always boasting," Beth is shocked: "I wasn't boasting. Leslie doesn't understand!" In everyday exchanges, we count on being understood. We are hurt and offended when someone takes something we have said "the wrong way," or when someone takes offense at what we've said when we meant none. Or perhaps someone refuses to respond to our need for sympathy, as Josie reported when she was telling Gwen how uncomfortable she felt about her weight and Gwen said, "You're not still going on about that!" Josie needed reassurance and got criticism instead. So Josie concluded, "Gwen just doesn't listen." Or perhaps someone finds our remarks insignificant, a disappointment Roxana suffered when she ran to Eva with the news that a couple they knew had split up. "Big deal," Eva said and turned back to a conversation she was having with someone else. For Roxana, her friend's lack of interest in the news was proof that she "didn't try to understand." When we seek a friend's understanding, we seek far more than *just* an understanding of what we say. We also seek a reverberation of sympathy and interest, a dancing probe into what we think and feel.

The craving to describe our feelings and thoughts and problems so that someone—a friend—will understand puts girls and women at serious risk. We are never more vulnerable than when we open ourselves to another. The most painful clashes of misunderstanding come when we work hard to make ourselves understood, when we expose ourselves in order to be understood, and something goes wrong. Once past middle childhood, when the volatility of friendships and feelings is accepted as part of the rough social structure on which they climb and swing and from which they fall, girls brood over the meaning of what was said and why it was said. They look back over previous conversations and interactions, especially those involving disharmonies: Why did she say that? What did she mean when she said that? Why did she take what I said in that way? Girls brood over glitches in their friendships, nursing the wounds of the failures of understanding. And where empathy is fruitlessly sought, lasting scars can result. Faith, who just received her master's degree in art history, was reflecting at age twenty-four on her own growth:

> For me, adolescence was not a stage to "pass through" or "get over." It totally shaped my sense of myself as an adult. When I was so confused as an adolescent, I drew closer to my girlfriends, hoping that their "wisdom" could straighten out the confusion. I had feelings of intense despair and sadness and did not know where they came from. When I leaned toward my friends for support and understanding, they moved out of the way. They were confused by my feelings and words

and so left me because, I guess, they were scared. When my best friend turned away from me, I felt loss, rejection, and abandonment. It seemed absolutely no one could understand or help me. I felt alone, worthless, isolated, and helpless. I had no self-esteem or sense of strength. Being rejected by those I trusted, confided in, and needed was the most devastating experience of my life. The confusion grew within me to the point where I felt enveloped by a big black emptiness. It was then, at the age of fifteen, when I first had thoughts of taking my own life.

I've carried pieces of the fear and pain of those years into my adult life. I am still afraid of abandonment. Though I know I can handle rejection logically, it still shakes me to the core emotionally. As an adult, I'm very independent and in control. To be dependent or to feel out of control is too much of a risk. If this side of me emerges, I feel defenseless and fear that the person who saw this would be disgusted and leave—just as my most trusted girlfriends did. My girlfriends rejected me for my weaknesses, and the pain I felt then was so strong that I fear feeling it again with all my soul. As a result of my failed teenage friendships, I developed a bad habit of keeping my feelings and "unacceptable" thoughts to myself. I don't wish to be a burden on anyone, so I keep my fears, insecurities, and weaknesses and confusions to myself.

This isn't something that I do on purpose—it just happens. Since high school, I have come to recognize that this practice of "keeping things to myself" can be damaging. It leaves me with an overwhelming feeling of loneliness that "no one could ever understand." I begin to wonder if there is anyone out there who will accept me—my bad sides as well as my good ones—unconditionally. Sometimes I think of trying to really talk to my fiancé about these deeper feelings, but then I remember how my girlfriends were and I back off.

Friendships between girls and friendships between women come to rest on the dilemmas that arise from the need for understanding. Like Faith, friends seek the support of shared emotions, and they want to assert their individuality. They want to express themselves to their friends so that their friends will understand them, and yet they know that as they expose themselves, and as they hope for a good response, they may be leveled by a poor one. The problem is that our individuality and our exposure make us so vulnerable that a friend seldom responds perfectly, admires with sufficient intensity, or sustains the necessary quality of attention. At any stage in girls' and women's lives, friendship can be threatened by the contradiction between friendship as a relationship of understanding and friendship in which real thoughts must be withheld. And so parts of the self—crucial parts—may be locked away.

In his novel *The Manticore,* Robertson Davies defines a therapist as someone who "listens to people say things they very badly want to tell but are afraid nobody else will understand." It is in this sense that therapy takes over where friendship ends, a process for excavating and putting into words all that got buried for fear that no one would ever understand it. When we come to fear that we have no friend who can understand the muddled or unsightly aspects of our character, we imprison ourselves with psychological symptoms or lapse into depression.

With enough experience of being misunderstood or having our feelings deemed unacceptable, we learn to include in our relationships with others only those aspects of ourselves that are likely to be valued. This is perhaps the most powerful, pernicious force that ultimately silences girls—and women. Many girls learn, early on, that they must tailor the feelings they disclose to the prevailing atmosphere of acceptability. What cannot survive being told goes underground to fester in shame and fear. Many adult women we interviewed, tracing their own histories through friendship, stress moments of understanding or failures to be understood as critical junctures in their own development. Over time, as we pass from girlhood into womanhood, some of us maintain relationships with "best friends" who have been there, understanding all along. Others get better at judging who might understand, who might be recruited into friendship as an empathic ear. Yet there remain some women who, like Faith, feel they have never found the understanding one and must stand guard at the gates of their deepest selves, hiding out even from their closest friends.

In early adolescence, we can still scream angrily at a friend, "You don't understand!" and storm away. As we grow, we learn how complicated the processes of sharing and understanding can be, and we learn to negotiate the pitfalls. As women move into adult life, more firmly shaping their own individuality and unique lives, they come to treasure those moments of deep sharing with a friend, moments when they feel the treasured resonance of "Yeah, I know just how that is for you." The true loss of innocence is the knowledge that others will not always "understand" in the sense of seeing things from our point of view, telling us we are "okay," and confirming that thread of reality in our dreams. But women also learn, with time and maturity, to accept—without despair—that no one will ever completely understand.

Chapter Five

"I'M NOT WHO YOU THINK I AM"

A s girls reach out to friends in hopes of finding a soul mate, one who will listen and understand, the fear of losing face is an ever-present shadow that haunts each act, each revelation. An eternal dilemma of all relationships is exposed: How can I say what I think and do what I want, and still be accepted by others? How can I preserve my authenticity when I would do anything for my friends' acceptance?

Leslie, having just turned fourteen, describes the care with which she tends her conversations:

> We say we tell each other everything, and that's just about true, but everything's a tall order. There are things that I just don't want her to know, even if I trust her. And you have to trust a best friend, don't you? But just her knowing could make a real difference to how she felt about me, and I can't take the risk. Sometimes I want to. Like there's a crossing, and I'm there and I'm really just about to tell her. I think it's obvious, but it's so hard, I'm sweating. And then I just chicken out. I mean, what if I see that look? There's that awful look on someone's face when their feelings suddenly change, and you can't go back to where you were.

Even girls who foster a "tough" image and exult in their ability to shock the grown-ups tread carefully with a girlfriend. Dina, Leslie's classmate, tells me, "There's nothing funnier than my mother's face when I speak my mind. It can look as white as yours, I tell you." But her "wicked" laughter ceases when I ask about speaking her mind to her close friend:

> Sure, I tell Char most things. But you gotta take care. These girls—the best of them have some high horse stored away, and start thinking about you in a certain way, once you've told them something. I say, "We're taking my little brother with us because we have to take him and that's that." See, I'll tell her I have to do it 'cause my mom's in a mood, you know? But I'm taking him 'cause I know he wants to go. It's just—it's just a little maneuver to save some face.

For girls in early adolescence, new to these intense friendships, the joy of acceptance is so great that the qualities that ensure acceptance get amplified in what the girl presents to the world. Girls learn quickly what they may not talk about to other girls, and all the things they can't show about themselves may go underground. Leslie and Dina exemplify the process by which girls' friendships pose a series of interlocking questions, one giving rise to another, each presenting a potential (and usually lasting) conflict. If I earn a friendship by being what another girl wants me to be, or if I present myself to her in a way she will like and admire, then what happens to who I really am? But if I show who I am and, as a result, my friend no longer likes or approves of me, how can I cope with that loss? It can seem to a girl that she has the choice of keeping herself or keeping her friend.

What we label "peer pressure" is often not pressure at all, but the subtleties of friendship in action. We build up a sense of who we are by experiencing our friends' understanding of us. A girl's knowledge of her thoughts and feelings is not simply "there," fully formed and ready to be expressed. We find our authentic self by trying to speak it, giving it shape, tentatively, with words. We "try out" emerging or inchoate aspects of ourselves, and as we hear ourselves speak, we discover whether we "mean" what we say. Exposing these murky parts of ourselves to our friend's gaze puts this part of ourselves on the line. A friend's enthusiasm may lead us to take this thought, feeling, or plan more seriously than we may have intended. On the other hand, a quizzical look can smother it for good.

"I was maybe thinking about learning to play the harp, " Lorraine, age thirteen, confides to Sally. "That's dorky," replies Sally, and the harp is forever lost to Lorraine. But we might imagine another response from Sally: "Gosh, that would be so cool. Have you asked your mom about it yet?" And Lorraine's hazily formed fantasy might result in a new direction for her life. "Did you see Jed play Clarence Darrow in the school play?" Sandy, fifteen, breathlessly asks her friend. "Oh, yeah. He sure can act—but what a creep," Ruth answers, and Sandy's attraction goes stone cold. When Jed asks her out, she declines brusquely. Not only can her sense of who is attractive be undermined by a friend's disapproval, but also that rejection gives her the right to be rude. Jed becomes a "nonperson" in her eyes.

These meandering conversations with friends have enormous power to challenge our thoughts, our feelings, our very selves.

We cannot understand ourselves without building up a vocabulary in which to think about the complex and constantly changing thoughts and emotions that make us who we are. As we talk with a friend about others, we are in part building a lexicon of traits and dispositions, words with which to fashion a portrait of ourselves. "That Kara is such a drip," Sally exclaims to Lorraine. Not exactly sure what makes someone a drip, but not wanting to be one herself,

Lorraine agrees, but later asks Sally if she thinks she, Lorraine, is sometimes a drip as well. "No, except sometimes like when you want to do your homework on weekends instead of go to the mall." So now "drip" is added to Lorraine's vocabulary of things she doesn't want to be and must be vigilant against in herself.

Friends are also the center of our emotional education. Girls learn together about what it means to be in love or how to calibrate and express vengeful feelings. A girl also registers her friend's values, what she counts as "normal," and what she "just can't stand." As Lorraine criticizes Carole for being "a slut," Sally learns that she had better not describe to Lorraine the fun she had flirting with Joe. In this way, girls learn the knack of selective exposure necessary to retain a friend's good opinion. If certain thoughts and feelings will render me unlikable, I gradually learn to barely acknowledge them myself—or change myself so that they seem to disappear.

Intimacy becomes dangerous because disapproval is possible. That the tenterhooks on which girls live as friends become as necessary as air is an uncharted story in their lives. Here we see a dangerous dilemma: To preserve this friendship, a girl may hide from her friend who she really is. On the other hand, a true friendship involves authenticity and self-revelation; paradoxically, girls learn to preserve the "friendship" by curtailing its honesty. Booker Prize–winning novelist Pat Barker expresses this dilemma perfectly when she writes, "You know you're walking around with a mask on, and you desperately want to take it off and you can't because everybody else thinks it's your face."[1]

Designing Images

We learn, over time, that there are ways in which we can count on our friends for understanding and support. But girls learn that they can also use conversation to deliberately shape—and sometimes disguise—who they really are. Self-distortion becomes a way of trying to ensure friendship. Beside the pleasure of shared understandings lurk problems. Do we really want to be understood—fully and completely? Aren't there some things about us we would rather have remain hidden, or at least not be in such direct focus of a friend's gaze—especially if we want to retain a friend's affection, or admiration, or approval? But then what is this self that is revealed? Built into the need for closeness through self-revelation is a need to manage information about the self, or even to create illusions about the self. At the very same time that girls are learning the value of sincerity and developing skills of self-expression, they are also learning new ways of presenting themselves as their friends wish them to be, often with disregard for who they know themselves to really be.

Girls tell their friends about themselves, but this information is not made available in a straightforward way. Instead, it may be carefully packaged, with increasing designer skill. Fay stares at herself in the mirror, trying to see every angle all at once. She runs from one mirror to another as she searches for the whole, the true image. But her careful makeup, her endless search for a new look—a better, more original look—are only part of her work at self-presentation. Just as important as clothes, hair, and makeup is the way she designs information about herself. There's the picking and choosing of what to tell, whom to tell it to—or even where to tell it. At thirteen, Fay likes to regale her friends with stories of how bad she was in English class because it seems "cool" and rebellious. But if she finds someone who seems interested in literature, she is more likely to highlight her love for *Catcher in the Rye*. Nadia, also thirteen, professes a great love for the band Fugazi because she thinks they are deliciously punk, even though she has never heard their music.[2] Mothers smile at a daughter's antics, performed in the anxiety of pleasing a friend. But when do we leave this anxiety behind? Nadia's mother, Roxanne, at forty-three, carefully reads the *New Yorker* before going to a party in an effort to appear sophisticated and intellectual. Even as we distance ourselves from this need to "impress," even as we laugh at ourselves, we don't lose the thrill of seeing a good reflection of ourselves in a friend's eyes.

Small wonder, then, that so many adolescent girls complain of a parent's hypocrisy, and reject that parent's wise or forbearing advice. As Nadia's mother acknowledges her own participation in these friend dynamics, Nadia says, "I always knew she liked to impress her friends. She dresses up for them, and gets excited about going out with 'the gals.' It bugs me when she's patronizing about me and my friends. But when she said, 'Yeah, I do that, too,' I felt so much better. It's sometimes strange to think of your mother as having a life, too. But it's good to feel she understands." It seems that girls can deal more easily with their own friend conflicts when their mothers acknowledge theirs.

How Self-Presentation Is Managed Can Make or Break a Friendship

As girls work their way through the dilemma between wanting to speak about who they really are on the one hand and being the sort of person who will be thoroughly liked on the other, they develop a sensitivity to meta-messages—those messages in conversation that go beyond the meaning of the words spoken, the implicit meanings that denote a girl's value, her status, her goodness, her luck. Girls begin to use these meta-messages, along with information management, to help design themselves. Since "boasting" remains a culpable offense (after all, we've heard other girls condemned for "showing off" or being "too full of herself"), certain information—about grades, vacations, academic awards, raises in allowance, successes of parents—has to arise "naturally" within the normal flow of conversation, rather than be delivered deliberately, with the obvious intention to impress. When Fay rushes up to Julie and asks, "Are you going to the party?" Fay is creating an appropriate opening to tell Julie that she has been invited. When Gloria tells Corinne, "I feel so bad about Mary," she may be expressing a sentiment that shows she is caring and loyal—or she may be expressing concern, but in truth highlighting the fact that *she* is now the focus of Mary's former boyfriend's attentions.

But girls learn to anticipate another's intention, and a meta-message can be preempted. When Elizabeth asks Hillary how she did on a history essay, and Hillary says, "A C-something or other. I can't be bothered to remember. It was such a dumb assignment and she's such a dumb teacher," then Hillary is denying Elizabeth the appropriate opportunity to announce her high grade. Hillary catches Elizabeth's intention to "boast," and so she trips her up, undermining the assignment's importance even before she can speak. The successful dissemination of positive information about oneself must be developed into a fine art if it is to be tolerated.

A girl who fails to learn this art will be punished, said to "think too much" of herself, be "too full of herself," and therefore deserving of group disdain. And she may even alienate her best friend. Corinne complains that Gloria "is always dragging the conversation back to her problems, like they're so important—real grand dramas. But everyone else just has these little problems. I feel she's just turning me into an audience, and doesn't care about my little life anymore."

Teenage girls, with their myriad insecurities, are easily threatened by a friend's presumption of importance or status, but even as adults, with—supposedly—a more robust sense of self, we can rankle when a friend manipulates the conversation to slip in positive information about herself. "Hali just has to yawn, and I know she's then going to explain how much traveling she's been doing and how many clients she has to see, and then, oh well, there are compensations in the money she's making." At twenty-eight, Andrea wants to enjoy her friend's success, but finds the clumsy style of information management hard to tolerate. "I'm back in high school with this. I've only known Hali for three years, but the relationship is just like one I had when I was a sophomore. I want to stick out my tongue at her. Well, I couldn't even do that then, could I? But that's what I wasn't ashamed of wanting to do then, and that's what I want to do now, even though I think of myself as pretty tolerant." Hali, in Andrea's eyes, breaks the rule of reciprocal admiration. So caught up is she in designing herself that Andrea feels there is no room for her.

And so girls tread the daily routes of making themselves up, showing themselves in a good light, asking to be seen for who they are, and feeling the pinch of various disguises. Each girl suffers from a sense of being off-balance, as Penny, seventeen, explains:

> When I got the news about this really great part-time job, I just wanted to run to Lee and tell her. Yes! Yes! I wanted to grab her and we'd jump up and everything. . . . And it's sometimes like that, but you can't just go up and say, "This really great thing happened." So I waited until she had some good news, and then I gave her mine. She goes, "Yeah?" But I then had to play it down because I was sort of taking the focus from her. So here I was, pretending it was no big deal, that I didn't really care about it, but I was thinking, "You just don't know how much this means to me. You just don't see how determined I am." The thing is, when she looks at me with that mild smile, I get to wondering, "Maybe it's no big deal, maybe I'm not on such a fast track after all."

For Penny, the problem of how to tell Lee how pleased she is about a new job means that she has to hide her feelings. To avoid bragging, or being too full of herself, she omits showing a friend who she is and what she is determined to do. For Devia, fifteen, the problem of concealment strikes even deeper:

> Other girls will talk about all kinds of stuff—like the fight they had with a brother or some really mean thing they said to their mom—and they'll just laugh at it, like they're so pleased. So I do the same thing. I tell them what I said to my mom, and I make it funny, even though I've been feeling so down about it. And I tell them things she does, and I pretend that I think she's wild—kind of fun. I sure don't tell them about her crying. So while I'm drawing this picture of what a cool and cruel daughter I can be, I'm slicing my insides up. My image of the whole thing—my mom, you know—goes way out of focus.

Devia registers the violence her pretense does to her own feelings: While she shows her friends a false picture, she feels cut up inside. She wants to fit in—as most girls do—so she presents feelings she does not have, disguises those she does, and carefully selects what she tells her friends about her mother. But both Penny and Devia realize that by not revealing who they are, their loneliness increases. They try to hold on to a sense of who they really are, but when they disguise themselves from friends, they become confused. As they present an image for a friend and ignore what comes from inside, everything "goes way out of focus."

Ironically, the impulse to show a friend only the feelings and attitudes that make one "cool" or gain approval is strongest in early and middle adolescence, just when girls value honest expression and become hypersensitive to adults' hypocrisy. Many girls see clearly what they are doing but cannot resolve the conflict. Devia has no trouble catching her mom out as a "phony": "She switches on this voice like a warm water faucet. 'Oh, *hello,* how *are* you? I'm *so* glad you called.' She starts to sweat if someone asks her what she really thinks about something. I sometimes think she doesn't know the difference between what she thinks she should feel and what she does feel." But Devia finds herself cornered into similar insincerity by her need for friends. In that corner girls learn their own rules for hypocrisy—for being "two-faced," saying one thing and feeling another. They are trapped by the worry that if they spoke the whole truth, they just wouldn't be any fun.

For some, the temptation to create illusions, to create a fictitious self, is great; fabrications feel easier and safer than authenticity. For Lynn, thirteen, self-presentation is sheer disguise. She feels she can be liked only if she blows a smoke screen over everything she is. As she starts a new boarding school, she snatches the opportunity of a "clean slate" on which to draw a new self:

> No one here knew anything about me, and I could become whoever I wanted to be. Day one, and I told everyone I lived on a farm. I wasn't really from Denver, but from outside Denver. I told everyone this, even though I live on the most ordinary city street in the world. And I kept on drawing pictures of it—all the cows we had, and the horses. And everyone thought it was so cool, and they thought I was nice. They thought I was lucky. And I felt so good, because I could—well, I could reach out and touch that much nicer image of me.

By seeking approval through this false self, she leaves much of herself untested, unknown, festering in a needless sense of shame. Being "ordinary," she thinks no one will want to talk to her or be with her.

Hiding Emptiness

Just at the time when girls need friends to help them describe and recognize who they really are, they may feel a panicky emptiness, leading them to feel they are nothing and ignore who they really are in a desperate attempt simply to be interesting. Connie, fifteen, is performing way below par at school. She takes comfort in food and controls her weight with self-induced vomiting. She is, she thinks, anything but what she should be, if others are to like her. She describes her humiliating sense of inner emptiness, and her compulsion to create illusions for her friends: "I can't helping making up things. Other girls always have something interesting to say, and seem to have so much going for them, and going on around them, so I get ideas from them, and once I start making something up, I keep going and going. Nothing can stop me."

When Connie sees that someone is impressed by her, she feels immense pleasure. "There's a kind of glow. 'They like me now,' I think, and it makes me happy, even if I know it won't last." If, later, someone discovers she was lying, she still savors this scrap of time in which she has a moment's glory. Yet she is often plagued by the anxiety of being "found out": "When my mom comes in and starts talking, my heart just goes *bang, bang,* because any little thing she says could just blow the whole picture." She forgoes peace of mind and risks embarrassment all for one glowing moment of a friend's acceptance.

Even in this exceptional case, we can see the rule of friendship—be what a friend will find interesting and likable. A compulsion as extreme as Connie's—to pay any price for momentary acceptance in a friend's eyes—arises within several contexts. Connie explains that she is "not brainy" like her mom wants her to be, that she is "too fat" for her father's liking, and that her brother, to whom she was once close, is now "this stranger, tall and handsome and getting these amazing grades in law school." She avoids her mother because "Mom keeps nagging me about my grades." She avoids her father because she sees "this awful disappointment in his eyes." She is used to disappointing people, who are likely, she says, "to be interested at first, but then get bored." As a child, she escaped an ever-increasing self-dissatisfaction through reading:

> Mysteries, science fiction, fantasy—I could devour books and feel so much better. I could read, and feel just like the best girl in the book. But you can't . . . I don't know . . . Once you're older, and you look a certain way, it's just not plausible to think you can be Nancy Drew. Instead of feeling all cozy when I read this stuff, I now feel like someone's criticizing me. I read about someone who's pretty or smart, and it's like I'm being told, "You're not like her."

Connie's last-ditch attempts with her friends, then, are efforts to get the support she needs so badly—too badly to believe she deserves it. There is nothing she would like more than "a bunch of friends who really liked me, and we could all have fun together. But the best thing would be a really good friend who's just kind of special and thinks I'm special and we could have this really special thing." Paradoxically, she feels she has to make herself into something she is not if she is to get the validation she needs to feel good about herself. Tragically, Connie's creations of a fantasy self led to enormous interpersonal problems. Connie's friends felt betrayed by false "confidences," and betrayal turned girls into harsh judges. "Why did she say that?" Janine demanded when she discovered some senseless lie about an injury Connie claimed to have suffered on a family outing:

> We were all so worried when she described the accident and how many stitches she had to have. My mom was worried.

My little sister was upset. She kept asking for details and getting more and more anxious. But Connie must have known
we would know she didn't have twenty stitches in her leg,
even with the plastic surgeon she was going on about.

The liar's friends feel duped: They have been taken in, their sympathy and attention acquired under false pretenses. When the shock
and anger subside, they often take steps toward forgiving—but not
forgetting—the friend's transgressions:

> I wish she hadn't done it. It floors me—why did she do it?
> What can I believe now? Did she want attention? My mom
> says she wanted attention, but what a stupid way to go about
> it. And my attention! She has that anyway. She only has to
> pick up the phone. She can talk to me. I'm listening. I'm
> right here. I guess she has problems I don't understand. I still
> like her, but this changes everything. I don't know where I
> am with her. And what's real odd is that she's really a very
> sincere person. She's not sneaky or anything like that. I
> always feel she's up front—showing me what she really feels.
> So it's confusing. And I feel bad because I got her into trouble
> by telling my mom about her "accident," and then my mom
> called hers, and it turns out she made the whole thing up.

The girl who lies to her friends, who "makes up things," is not,
as Janine notes, insincere in the usual sense. In girlfriends' language,
"insincere" means showing affection when there is none, or soliciting
information for some ulterior motive (usually gossip), or claiming to
be one girl's best friend one moment and another girl's best friend
another. Connie sincerely likes her friends and does not betray their
secrets. She is still liked, but everything is changed: The understanding she asks for cannot be given.

Many girls battle against the impulse to create illusions. Rhonda, fourteen, explains:

> I make up silly things—like having problems with my dad, problems I really don't have—but it seems to make me more interesting. And [my best friend] has so much to talk about, so when she's finished, and there's—you know—that lull, like "I've had my say, now you say something," I just rush to fill it with all sorts of things. I worry that she'll think I'm dull. I'm like, "Oh, I gotta say something interesting." It's like I'm writing a script, and I just keep elaborating.

Feeling empty inside, terrified of being thought "uninteresting," she spins tales about problems at home, or possible illnesses—even financial problems seem to add glamour to her in a friend's eyes. While mothers expect a daughter will simply "outgrow such childish nonsense," this compulsion can persist throughout adolescence. Molly, seventeen, felt she was being left behind by her girlfriends, who all had boyfriends. When they gathered, they would giggle and compare notes about who had done what sexually, and who had received what romantic gestures and presents. But Molly had not yet succeeded in attracting a boy, which in and of itself didn't really bother her. What rankled was feeling left out with her girlfriends and worrying that they would move beyond her or think her immature or feel sorry for her, all reactions she felt she could not bear. Back from a family vacation, Molly constructed a tale of a passionate brief encounter to share with her girlfriends and kept this fantasized liaison alive for five months by artfully mailing herself letters and sending herself flowers. "I didn't hurt anyone by doing this," she said. "I just wanted to be part of things." Yet her burning face and embarrassed tears show who is hurt: the girl who seeks acceptance by disguising herself.

As adults, most of us have left most of this behind, and have integrated the need for acceptance with the need for authenticity, but the process can easily go awry. Madelyn, thirty-five, is one of those women who seem to charm people without even trying. She has an easy, comfortable manner, ready humor, and is attractive without being flashy. Somehow, she instantly puts others at ease and people enjoy being with her. She has a small business selling promotional products, which is increasingly successful. But after finally acknowledging that she had been bulimic for years, she required a lengthy psychotherapy to discover what in herself felt real and what felt like a mask she was wearing to please other people. Always a very popular girl, she felt she had lost herself for a long period during her twenties by being what others wanted her to be.

> My twin sister was the smart one and my older sister was the pretty one and I was just good at making friends. People have always been drawn to me, but I wasn't sure who "me" was. I learned how to make people think I cared more than I did, that I was closer than I was. And I always worried about being found out as an impostor. But now I know that there are "safe" people that I can tell who I really am. And last night I went to this party, and I was watching myself work the room. You never can tell who will refer you a client. And I realized that being charming is surprisingly easy. All you have to do is get people to talk about themselves and smile and laugh. When I got home, I felt disgusted with myself, like there I was, not really being myself, but doing my charm thing, and I was really getting down on myself when I realized that this, too, is a kind of skill. As long as I know when I'm doing it. And, after all, it is good for business. So maybe it's not such a bad thing after all?

In the end, the tension is tentatively resolved by making the best of our need to put on masks to gain friends—as long as we know when we are doing it and don't confuse our pretense with our real selves.

Being Different

Pulling strong against the impulse to be liked is an adolescent girl's impulse to speak her mind. Yet many psychologists have noted a chronic difficulty girls and women have in stating differences, in saying "No, this is what I think" or "No, that is not how I feel." Girls and women feel more comfortable when they emphasize sameness and connection. There is a distinctive flow of girl talk and woman talk that brings us together. Agreement and assent oil communication: "I know," "That's just how I feel," "I know exactly what you mean" are waves that keep girlfriend talk going.[3] This conversational style has its strong, positive aspect, as it marks a form of listening whereby we track the meaning of what's said and relate to it closely, matching it to our own thoughts and feelings. (In comparison, a more masculine style of challenge and correction can seem tedious and uncreative.) Caught in this stylistic current, however, girls often get stuck in a consensus they do not really share. Sometimes, confused about who they are, girls may not even know if they truly agree or resonate with the other. Galerai, at fifteen, explains the changing tides of feeling:

> I hear myself saying, "Yeah, I know," and then later on I feel bad. Once, one of my friends was talking about someone I know and like. And this friend was saying how this guy went to her house and in one hour had gotten her clothes off. In a group that sort of thing is funny, and you just laugh because everyone else does, but there are a hundred questions

hammering at you: Is it true? Why did it happen? What happened then? How did she feel? But if I start asking questions, they go, "Gali, you're so dim" or "You just don't get it, do you?" So I laugh with them, but afterward I'm not sure what I really think.

Galerai notices how easy it is to fall into agreement when she doesn't really agree, or laugh at something she doesn't think is funny but others do. As a girl becomes more aware of the ways in which politeness blends into insincerity, or solidarity with a close friend shades into dishonesty to oneself, she may feel trapped by the need to think and feel like her friends. She develops a series of strategies, becomes a mistress of tact, until tact bends and twists real meaning and she hears herself described as someone she is not. Yet if she doesn't laugh with her friends, if she sees things in a different way, they will call her "dim." Laughing with the others makes her feel she herself, inside, is unreal. Hazel, fourteen, reflects, "It's easy to catch myself changing with the people I'm with. I hate it when I see that happen to someone else. What's the word? . . . Yeah, like a chameleon. That's not the kind of person I want to be. But it's sometimes hard not to switch your ideas when you're with different people."

A feminine niceness, an urge to accommodate and please, has often been attributed to the way girls are raised to be obedient and conforming. The power of men, and the urge women therefore have to please or placate them, is often seen as the underlying cause for girls being accommodating to others. We need also to consider, however, how girls' experiences of the inevitable tyrannies of friendship teach them that conformity can bring approval and nonconformity can lead to rejection. Groups of friends, with their demand for cohesion and shared norms, determine what can and cannot be expressed. And in close friendships, too, girls come to fear that honesty may sever a life-sustaining bond, and the contours of the self are refashioned to ensure that the friendship will survive. At the first sight of any real difference between us, even as grown women, we can catch ourselves engaging in some conciliatory babble: "But of course you're right," "I didn't mean it the way it sounded," "Yeah, that's just what I think."

The joys of huddling together in a glow of sameness and affection are so great that it may begin to seem that being different is synonymous with being cast out and unloved. The social world of the girl in early adolescence is particularly constructed around the tight bonds of liking and sameness. "I'm like that, too," not only indicates understanding at this age—it indicates love. When girls stick by their own—different—voices and views at this age, they may be condemned for being "stuck-up" or "cruel" or "dim" or "weird." Later in adolescence, toward the latter years of high school, when differentiation is more tolerated and more valued, girls will discover opportunities to be loved and understood for their differences as well. Yet they may still fear to disagree, may shrink from fully articulating their own opinions.

Much is written within psychology about the late adolescent's struggle to declare herself to her parents, to claim her own characteristics, to say, "This is me." But equally important are the moments when the girl, on the threshold of womanhood, holds up her chin among her friends and announces, in effect, "I'm not who you think I am."

The Fear of Success

Tragic consequences can follow a failure to stand firmly on one's own identity ground. Many girls act recklessly—with drugs, with sex, with cars—because they are subdued by someone else's judgment, afraid to say, "This isn't me. I'm not who you think I am." Less clearly highlighted is the way a girl may squelch her talents in order to maintain her friendships, sacrificing her abilities in the service of being like a less gifted friend. Casey, age seventeen, told us regretfully:

> When I was in eighth grade, my best friend, Tara, and I were angry about everything. We would criticize everything, from the "cool people" to capitalism to our sheltered neighborhoods. We thought we were ready for life, but we were stuck. We thought we were ready for anything. I was terrified of only one thing: losing her. Finding differences between us scared the shit out of me, because I felt that if I lost her, all my fears would come back. All my anger and enthusiasm would deflate into insecurity. So I tried to be like her, stay like her. One time I said, "I really like that song by Tori Amos," and she said, "You do?" in this really mocking tone. So I didn't buy the album. Another time, I wanted to learn to skateboard, but she bought Rollerblades, so I did, too. Those are just little things, but it was more than that. I took school pretty seriously and did well, but she was a badass, so I had to hide my interest in learning. I even misbehaved, goofed off, and acted sullen in class because I didn't want her to be more of a delinquent than me. It sounds silly, but I think it turned me off from learning. Although I continued to do well despite everything, I developed a "see what I can get away with" attitude. Some part of me echoes Tara's voice saying, "Learning is dumb . . . so do as little as possible." I was afraid to assert myself because I wanted to stay close to her. I didn't know how to really disagree.

The fear that difference may lead to isolation or loss of a valued friendship is one of the most pernicious threats to a girl's capacity to express herself. It is therefore unsurprising that so many high-achieving women were girls who felt rejected and cast out as adolescents.[4] Barred from friendship by some already-apparent difference, these women, as girls, turned in on themselves and their inner worlds, developing themselves apart from the tyranny of other girls. Anger at other girls' rejection can be productive. Some highly successful women report having a best friend with whom they felt allied against the rest of the world, one girl who seemed to understand them and share their values. "It was the two of us," Muriel, age forty, said, looking back. "We were the top students. We were going to Harvard. We were going to take over the world. We had absolute contempt for the cheerleaders and social bunnies and couldn't have cared less about not being invited to their parties." Muriel went to Princeton, her friend to Duke. Her supportive friend remains supportive: The women are now both successful lawyers—in practice together. "I needed only that one friendship to see those other girls as of no consequence."

Speaking Her Mind

There is a tremendous relief many girls experience when they realize they can disagree with a friend, but this recognition and the skills of disagreement emerge in increments over time. Conflict pervades young girls' friendships. We can see it splinter and fuse the cliques of middle childhood. Among very young girls—between eight and eleven—quarrels are frequent, and frequently nasty; sometimes they destroy a friendship, but often they do not. Some girls seem to practice quarreling, as they engage in play fights with the same enthusiasm with which their much younger brothers will be engaging in war games. Girls of eight and nine gleefully shout abuse at one another: "You're such a smart-ass," "You're one yourself," "Don't you think you're smart." Word games, volleys of taunts, are clearly enjoyable. They engage in devious, mock fighting for an audience, pretending to have a quarrel with a friend, not sitting near a friend as they pretend to others that the friendship is in danger. "It's so much fun, pretending to fight," nine-year-old Ari tells me, her face flushed, her voice hoarse from name-calling. The pretense airs tensions and makes her feel strong.

But entering into real disagreement involves difficult skills and cannot be learned merely by these practice sessions. When a girl can say, "Hang on a minute" or "No, I don't agree" or "No, I don't want to do that" or "I don't have time to do you that favor" or "I don't feel like seeing you tonight," she can have a better handle on retaining authenticity within the friendship. Disagreement is an important way of opening up the debate about norms, such as who should be criticized, who is in the wrong, what a girl should do or say, what her appearance indicates.

More than the views of parents, it is the judgment of a girl's close friends—the type of judgment seen to be most astute and most fair—that she truly feels she has to answer. Here girls may experience a control far stronger than they, or grown women, do in any desire to please men. Modern girls and women are often aware of (and hence equipped to resist) their own efforts to please or accommodate a man, but find it harder to recognize the social control exercised by their girlfriends. How easy it is to recognize Nena's terror in ourselves when we see a fight brewing with a close friend:

> I'd rather have a fight with my boyfriend or my mom, any day, than with my girlfriend. I'm not sure just why. There's just this awful panic: "Oh no, this can't be happening" sort of thing, I guess. Even though I can stand up for myself most times, I just hate fighting with a friend. It's like something coming at you, real fast, and you don't know whether to freeze or run. I'm basically honest, up-front, but I'll say anything to get out of an argument with a friend.

At eighteen, Nena stands on the fissure that marks these relationships: She wants to stand up for herself, she sees herself as someone who can speak her mind, yet that ability is sacrificed to the need to be liked, to be accepted, to avoid conflict. She sees herself as "basically honest," yet she also sees herself sacrificing this for being liked. This sacrifice of self is far deeper than the social pressure to "be nice": We can be nice in the living room and swear in the kitchen; we can smile sweetly at Grandma but still know how to be feisty with our mother. "That awful panic" that leads Nena to "say anything to get out of an argument with a friend" compromises integrity. We learn through this panic that we have to hotfoot from one side of the dilemma to another to avoid falling in. That authenticity we seek has to be created each day, just as each day, in each interchange, we look to what we can say, and weigh what we'll risk and what we won't. In the lives of most women, the battle for authenticity is never won fully and finally, nor is it fully and finally compromised. Instead, we work on this in each exchange we have with our friends. When we look at girls' friendships, we see what we knew all along, but maybe hoped was not true, or would not always be true: that attachments are forever complicated, and constantly in need of negotiation.

Changing Friends

Sometimes the dilemma can be too difficult to bridge—not because a girl is weak-voiced but because the friendship is wrong. Particularly later in adolescence, a girl may opt for herself over friendship by seeking out new friends whose values and outlook promise that they will be more tolerant of her own. When a girl finds that a friend no longer accepts her, or her version of herself, she may have to change friends.

But as Kay tells me she has "outgrown" Maureen, who used to be her best friend, I wonder whether the fifteen-year-old is moving away from an inadequate friend or from a true friend's uncomfortable knowledge of her past self. In adolescence, a girl may discard a friend whose only fault is seeing her as she used to be. She may believe that new friends allow her to start again on her journey of self-discovery and self-creation. As she changes, the previous friendship becomes wooden, empty, and she needs new relationships to match her emerging self. As Kay puts it:

> This is a pretty shitty thing to say, but you can outgrow someone. I've been friends with Maureen for years. I can't remember a time we didn't play together, and then our parents became friends. It used to be so much fun, staying the night at her house, preparing midnight feasts, and talking. But I feel strange with her now. I say something, and she'll be looking at me like I'm this real strange person. You can't be friends with someone when you never know what they're thinking. It's like I'm always putting my foot in it, when I'm simply being me. She says, "That's not really you, Kay," and I want to say, "I'm not who you think I am." She's all disapproving of me when she sees me in the hall at school. It might be okay if we were just friends outside of school, but that's hard. I can tell she takes it personally when I choose to be with other kids.

We want to be known, yet we may come to feel trapped by our friend's hold on the image of what we really are. Kay, like Angela in the television series *My So-Called Life,* has to change friends and "betray" a friendship when she herself wants to change. Angela wants to be different, and so she does two things: She dyes her hair and switches from one best friend to another. The false-colored hair goes with the new friend who is less conventional and represents the kind of person she would like to be, the kind of person who has a "life." Like Angela, Kay feels the bonds of an old friendship, and also the weight of parental expectations that this is a friendship that should last. Like Angela, Kay wants to change herself by changing her friends. Staying best friends with Maureen feels to her like being chained to one stagnant identity. Within this friendship, she is not allowed to change or grow. She has discovered that change of friends is a fast track—though often an experimental one—to changing oneself.

The Adolescent Within

Much has been written recently about the "child within"—the still-whole, clear-sighted, outspoken innocence within us. Adolescence, by contrast, is regarded as a painful, awkward phase that we pass through and leave behind. It is seen as a "not really me" phase, a time when we play at being who we really are, discarding our true identities. But the adolescent within us is also alive and well—the insecure, confused self, recurrently pinned on the horns of relational dilemmas. The adolescent in us is not a foreigner, nor has she been left behind. We meet her daily in ourselves, and a daughter's struggles affect us not only because we love her and want to help her, but also because we know we cannot protect her, cannot make these adolescent tribulations go away.

Jane watches her adolescent daughter struggle through trying to be like her friends even though Jane is certain that is not who her daughter really "is." But Jane, despite having many friends, feels intensely alone. She goes to a therapist to share her fears—fears that her husband may be embezzling from his company. She does not dare to tell her friends. "What would they think of me? Of us? I couldn't even tell my best friend. Things would never be the same." Having made this choice, she deprives herself of the potential comfort; the risks are too great. Similarly, Marjorie becomes more and more emotionally isolated from her friends, who regard her as sophisticated, well-organized, leading a perfect life. How could she shatter that image by letting them know that her husband has been alcoholic for years—a secret she has never told anyone?

When we ache with the realization of not being the person we have convinced our friends we are, our problem reaches back to those of adolescent friendships: I'm not who you think I am because I don't let you know who I am. Girls struggle bravely to overcome impediments to true speech. Each time we stand on that edge between pride in ourselves for speaking our minds and fear of reprisals for speaking our minds, we meet the adolescent within us.

Time and again we heard teenage girls focus on the same challenges that women face on a day-to-day basis, winning one point, only to look back and find it lost after all. Fifteen-year-old Laurie explained:

> I thought we'd really made it. I'd gone over with Jessica how I really liked her but didn't want to go to this party she was having. I just didn't want to be with some of her other friends. And I was so careful. I explained that I liked Pete and Sue, and I could see that she liked them, but that something different happened when they were all together, and I just wasn't going to have a good time. And it was "Yes, I understand, and of course you can tell me this," and then she's at her locker with those guys and they're whispering and laughing, and when I walk by they all turn away, and this one guy goes, "Ooh, ooh," and swivels his hips, and Sue is biting her lip to keep from laughing.

The "ordinary courage," which psychologist Annie Rogers defines as the ability "to speak one's mind by telling all one's heart,"[5] is sought each day, even as girls (and women) see themselves failing to summon it up. In repeated small interactions, Laurie learns how to find a balance:

> I told her how I really felt about her piece for the yearbook, and she goes, "You're always setting yourself up over people. You just have your own ideas and won't listen to anyone else," and I kept saying, "I didn't mean it the way you took it. I want your piece in here and it's fine." But she had this . . . momentum. It was "You ask me to do something and then all I get is criticism, and I feel set up." That version of what I was doing just slapped me in the face and I crumbled. I told her the piece was fine.

And today, even as a grown woman who should know better, I can catch myself doing what Laurie does—feeling my way across the tiny but treacherous bridge between speaking my mind and keeping a friend, the tiny but treacherous difference between showing what I feel and causing trouble between a friend and me. I begin to explain to a friend that I don't want to join her for dinner. I'm simply not in the mood. It is an evening I would like to spend at home, "doing nothing." And so I begin to reel off a list of reasons why tonight just isn't good, but I see, or think I see, some contraction—pain, judgment, withdrawal—in her eyes. And while I see this, I remember an uneasy conversation we had the week before about how we had different ideas about organizing a seminar, and I wonder what these differences will mean for us. So I silence what cannot be accepted, and I say, "I'll see if I can make it." She sees right through me and laughs. Her laugh frees me both from subterfuge and from doing something I don't want. "I don't feel like going out," I admit, laughing with her at my own cowardice, and our relationship is momentarily clear and open-faced.

The "Perfect Girl"

The desire to be seen in the "right" light by our friends can be compelling. But how does a girl feel when her friends admire her, look up to her, think that she is "just right" in what she does, what she says, and how she looks? Does this girl feel more secure, more satisfied with herself, more confident?

We all live, or have lived, in the shadow of the perfect girl, the one whom we befriend because she has everything, is everything we would like to be or think we should be. Every girl and woman we spoke to described a time during her adolescence or early adulthood when her own sense of worth was shadowed by an ideal other girl, a girlfriend who, by contrast, diminished her. For me, there was JoAnne Baldwin, an academic highflier and a cheerleader, who had a flawless complexion, whose pleated skirts hung perfectly on her hips, who would choose just the right college, just the right job, just the right husband. Her best asset, however, was others' admiration of her. No one had a bad word to say about her. "She's too nice to envy," other girls said, but I managed nonetheless. She collected admirers—both female and male—as easily as I collected slights and embarrassments.

Such girls and women seem to others to be unencumbered by the self-doubts and dilemmas that cling to everyone else. But what is the subjective reality of these friends whom we look up to? Instead of the inner perfection and ease that seems to go all the way through them, such "perfect girls" experience a special dread.

Constant and total admiration by one's girlfriends is stifling. Girls who are widely admired and liked have the most to risk by seeking understanding and comfort for a sense of failure, or of misfit. Sylvia Plath once described herself as strangely disguised by the way other people knew her as "the girl who wins prizes." She was seen by her classmates as a star but was isolated because no one knew her anger and her hatred. Therefore she suffered a depression too awful to voice, a depression that occurs in the context of relating to others through a false self.

Lois is also a girl other people think is perfect. Already working as an occasional professional model, she is thin, tall, doesn't wear glasses. She has a smooth olive complexion, beautifully cut hair, and a smile that radiates calmness. She looks older than her sixteen years—more graceful, apparently more confident than her peers—yet when she speaks we can recognize the sixteen-year-old's fragile self:

> Everything's been going so well for me, and I was so pleased to get these modeling jobs, but I just can't keep together inside—and now I'm not eating. I was in the hospital before—last year—because I was anorexic, and I can feel it coming back, though my mom hasn't noticed yet. She was so worried last year, and when I got better, I thought I would never worry her again. . . . My friends all say they envy me. . . . I must be really bad inside, because all these things are going so well for me, and I still can't eat. I don't think anyone else can see what it's like. I smile at people and they gush at me, but I'm just feeling like shit inside. Because I hear someone say how good I look, and how wonderful it was I got into *Seventeen,* and I get this dread—like I'm going to be found out, like no one knows who I really am. I've tried to talk to some of my friends, and they just don't get it. Can you . . . ? Do you see? How it's like being on a roller coaster that's out of control, and there's going to be more and more people disappointed in me?

Lois talks about how she is seen versus how she feels, and because she cannot be what she seems to be, and feels she will do nothing but accumulate disappointments, she feels "like shit" inside—unable to eat, on a roller coaster to hell. It isn't her mother's view she cannot stand up to honestly and openly, as she would like, but the view of her friends—a flattering looking glass she cannot, or will not, break.

"I'm not who you think I am" is the cry of a walking mask, and the dilemma is between removing that mask and being known, really connecting, and keeping a friend's approval safe. There is often punishment meted out to those girls who try to remove the mask, punishment in the form of ridicule ("You're not such hot stuff"), gossip ("Do you know what she's really like?"), or rejection ("I don't know you. We have nothing to say to each other"). Few of us, in our relationships with parents or siblings, feel that awful judge lurking in the shadows as we do in many of our adolescent friendships. Ariadne is a sixteen-year-old national swimming champion, idolized by the girls in her class, but Ariadne feels the tenuousness of their admiration: She senses their hidden wish to see her fall. She tells us:

> They are all so excited about my swimming. "How did you do in Michigan? Did they offer you a scholarship? Isn't it great? Things are going so well for you!" They sound like their mothers when they talk to me! But I sometimes think they think I'm weird. If I started to lose—and that's easy to do—they'd be pleased. I can just hear them saying, "She always thought so much of herself."

As proud as Ariadne may be of her achievements, she feels they form a block between her and her friends, who cannot see that she has ordinary problems. But as she notes this commonplace fact (a version of "They don't see I'm simply a person like everyone else underneath"), she gropes for something else, something even more problematic, for the problem lies not simply with the girls who idealize her, but also with her desire to retain their idealization. She feels that the loss of her star status would leave her unprotected. She also feels, hidden behind her prizes, unable to interpret her friends' enthusiasm and kindness. They do not seem genuine to her, and if they are nice to her when she loses, it may be because they feel good about her disappointment.

Lois and Ariadne hide behind their perfect images because they are afraid of what it would feel like to be outside that wrapping. They haven't had the opportunity to feel a friend's support when they fail, when they disappoint a parent, when they are embarrassed and humiliated. Being seen as perfect by their friends, they feel both unknown and afraid to be known. What will happen if their friends no longer find them interesting, if they discover a fault or failing?

Therapists know this to be an enduring dilemma in women's lives. Marisa, at age forty-five, comes into therapy because she realizes that she has never forged that link between who she feels she is and who she is to others. This gap leaves her with a sense of not knowing who she "really" is. Increasingly, she avoids going out because she can't decide what to wear; doesn't invite friends over because she is unable to decide how to decorate her new apartment. She has the best designer in town, but she has her own ideas. Which should she honor? Which is "really" her? At a party the week before, Marisa's best friend, Nadine, whispered to her, "I think you are having a hard time being good to yourself." "What do you mean?" Marisa asked. "Your dress," replied Nadine.

On the surface, of course, this conversation makes no sense at all. But friendship has its own delicately encoded language, so that Marisa and Nadine were quite clear what they were talking about. And in this brief exchange lay a complex history that contained the key to Marisa's troubles. Marisa understood immediately that Nadine was criticizing her dress as deliberately unbecoming and was implying that Marisa was being aggressively careless of her appearance. Marisa was also aware that Nadine, knowing her as well as she did, was fully aware of her sensitivity to how others thought she looked.

Unlike many of the women we have interviewed, who feel they had been the marginal ones as teenagers, shut out from the magic circle of popularity, Marisa had been one of the most popular girls in her large high school. Beautiful from childhood, she set the standards in adolescence. She often thought of herself as a Barbie doll and loved dressing herself in special ways, which everyone else then copied. Her teenage years, she recounts, were "perfect." Everyone always liked her, she had more friends than she had time for, and it was an easy matter to date the "best" boys and eventually find the "Ken doll" who seemed made for her. After they married, she became a professional model until they had children, and then she devoted herself to raising suitably "perfect" children. But what Marisa hadn't seen in all this ease was the degree to which she had become addicted to others' admiration of her. She found that she had become who others expected her to be—and lost herself in the process. From time to time over the years, she had tried to say to a friend, "I'm not really who you think I am," but the friend would always regard this as false humility and respond reassuringly, "Of course you are."

Nadine was a particular problem for Marisa because Nadine seemed almost a caricature of all that Marisa felt others expected her to be. Nadine was very, very rich and always looked spectacular. The two of them together were reigning queens of the political crowd, and Nadine expected Marisa to keep up with her, to engage in the kind of friendly competition that would keep both women striving to outdo themselves. Marisa recognized that Nadine's comment about her dress was double-edged. On the one hand, it put Marisa down ("You're really a disappointment tonight"), and on the other, it demanded that she resume her role as trendsetter. But the trouble was that Marisa wasn't sure she wanted to be in this game anymore.

She wasn't sure she even wanted to be on this ladder, let alone at the top of it. But she could imagine no other way to live her life.

Shortly after this conversation, Marisa developed severe psychosomatic symptoms and took to her bed, refusing to see anyone but her therapist, her husband, and her children. "How can I see anyone looking like this?" she asked—she had lost about twenty pounds and looked skeletal. She had withdrawn from the world, experiencing what her worst fear had always been—that to be other than what others took her to be would mean being all alone.

Eventually, Marisa was able to recover. She shifted into a new career, entering a program to get a Realtor's license. She could eat. She could go out. But she could only maintain a grip on herself by avoiding anything but the most superficial interactions with other women. Even after several years of therapy, girlfriends continued to feel toxic to her.

Marisa shows us how deep the fissure can go between who we think we can be and who we think other people think we are, and how this conflict can remain localized in the world of friendships. Many psychologists believe that such powerful feelings must echo early problems within family relationships, but what I have become convinced of, from twenty-five years' experience as a therapist and researcher, is that women can function in many areas very well—as Marisa does with her husband and children and with her work—yet feel unsteady and afraid because of abiding problems with their sense of self, problems that have arisen within the realm of friendships. So important is our sense of self in relation to our friends that the threat of their rejection, their incomprehension, or their demand for us to be other than we are can make us ill, even if we have strong and healthy relationships with a partner, parents, and children.

A potential malignancy in friendship is the growth of a false self, the mask we are afraid to be without. This covering keeps us from connecting with the healing and nurturing aspects of friendship.

Much of psychotherapy is the excavation of the true self beneath the false one, allowing it voice and providing a safe relationship in which the true self is welcomed and validated.[6] With time, a woman may feel secure enough that she dares to reveal herself to her friends as well—and to find out that they are not who she thought they were, either.

For Connie, who tried to keep rejection at bay by lying to her friends, the path to a new acceptance was found as she discovered a friend's ability to integrate her faults and virtues into an acceptable person. The route is terrifying: She has to face up to someone who knows she lies and who won't be taken in again by stories of high drama or fantastic prize-winnings. She has to remove the cloak of shame that kept her stony and silent after one lie had been discovered: "I didn't talk to any of my friends for two weeks after Janine's mom talked to mine. I kept waiting for someone to be real nasty." But her friends registered her vulnerability, even though they suffered from their own confusion. Their tacit willingness to forgive allowed her to "come out of hiding." Six months after first speaking to us, Connie, now sixteen, explains how she is fighting her way from disguise to authenticity:

> Janine and I don't talk about it much, but it's there, out in the open. She knows I've lied—lied to her a lot. The worst thing she said to me was, "I don't know you anymore." Before that, I was too ashamed to say anything. But when she said that, "I don't know you," I fought back. Maybe she got some facts wrong, but we still spent time together. We had fun together. Like I'd go to visit my dad, and the first thing I'd do when I came home was call her. Maybe some of the stuff I made up, but the important thing was for me to talk to her. I wasn't properly back until I talked to her. And anyway, I know her—not everything, but I have a feel for what she'll

say and do. And then she said that best thing, ever. She said she was only pretending to be shocked, because she knew just what it was like to want to tell loads of lies. So we're still friends—maybe now better than ever, because we have this secret. She understands me at my worst.

Connie finds that a friend can help free her from the constraints of her disguise. There is, of course, always the danger that her closeness with Janine will inaugurate yet another disguise, a new mode of being that accommodates to this new intimacy. But when we can tell the truth about ourselves—at least to one special friend—we are that much closer to living without our masks.

Chapter Six

"PROMISE YOU WON'T TELL"

I usually feel so good talking to Grazi. I can say, "You won't believe what I did. It was the stupidest thing, and if you tell anyone else, I'll die." Or maybe I've been real mean to Mom. I know it's not my fault, 'cause she's made me real mad, but I'll still feel like a shit, because you're not supposed to feel like that about a *mother*. So we talk—and she'll tell me stuff about her, so I know she isn't judging me, and what was so awful before just isn't awful anymore. There's this relief, a huge relief to tell someone else your problems so you don't seem the awfulest person in the world. When your friend knows about stuff, you feel good. But anyone else knowing would be worse than the awful feeling of no one knowing. These things have to be private. You shouldn't even have to say, "Don't tell anyone else." What you tell a friend isn't for anyone else.

At fifteen, Maria expresses a common dilemma. She needs, urgently, to talk to a friend. Talking about herself and her problems offers relief from being "the awfulest person in the world." But to get this relief, she has to expose herself, revealing unattractive motives and behavior that shames or embarrasses her. That vulnerable self is safe with a friend—at least, that is what we hope. Sharing ourselves is the route to "I knew you'd understand."

Things happen to us, and we do things we need to talk about—and yet we don't want everyone to know. We share our feelings of danger and insecurity, or we confess to behavior that we feel is bad or humiliating. We can tell a friend because she'll be on our side: We count on her to see things from our point of view, to support us, even if she may disagree with what we've done. I don't know precisely what Michelle will say when I tell her I failed to get the job I was interviewed for, but I know she will "understand" things from my point of view and see me in my best light, despite what may have happened to make me "unsuitable" in a prospective employer's eyes. I can tell her how I fumbled for answers, how pathetic I was, without being afraid of losing her regard. The bruised, imperfect self I reveal to her is one proof of our friendship, and is safely revealed in the context of friendship. "Telling" this news outside such a safe area turns what was said into something else. "She didn't get the job," becomes information about failure, stark and simple.

Pieces of news told in private become distorted when they're made public. Lara, fourteen, is outraged when she hears the version of events Kathy reported on the basis of what Fay said. "Everyone thinks I did something unforgivable," she fumes. "They made it sound as though I hate her, but I just meant there were certain things I didn't like about her." In "telling," that safe space is invaded by others, and the tentative steps we have taken toward self-revelation are turned against us. We reveal our secrets and then we set up structures to protect ourselves after we make ourselves vulnerable: "Promise you won't tell," we plead, and confidentiality becomes part and parcel of what we mean by friendship. Over and over, as we interviewed women and girls, we heard that the worst betrayal of friendship is to "tell."

In this arena of friendship, our close friends become interwoven with how we manage our sense of ourselves and our shame about those parts of ourselves that feel unacceptable to us. Shame is a social emotion. It arises from the sense of finding out, in the presence of others, that we are not what we supposed ourselves to be. Intense shame can feel like annihilation—a person may simply wish to disappear in order to avoid the stares of others, which feel like knife blades cutting into the core of the self. And yet, paradoxically, the only vaccine against and remedy for shame is the reassurance of others that what we feel (and are) is not nearly as unacceptable as we imagine.

Maddy, age thirty, is ashamed of "not having a life." Attractive, intelligent, and witty, Maddy was, up until now, caught in a guilt-ridden relationship between her controlling mother and slowly dying father. Angry and depressed, she kept people at bay, was polite and affable at her work as a dental hygienist, but never allowed herself friendship or dates. Coming out of this depression, lonely and longing for friends, she feared what would happen if she got close to someone, who would quickly learn of her isolation. Surely, she reasoned, they would run from her. Who, after all, would want to befriend someone with no other friends? And if they did, she figured, it would just be because they felt sorry for her.

Maddy remembers, when she was thirteen, having a friend, Jane, and going to her house after school. But what was most fun about this was seeing Jane's older brother, about whom Maddy was having "delicious" fantasies, fed by the briefest encounters with him at Jane's house. It didn't take too long for Jane to notice Maddy's blushes and giggles when Jerry was around, and as Maddy later put it, "She got it out of me." Uncertain of and confused by these intense, powerful, and exciting feelings, Maddy tried, in the language of the thirteen-year-old she was, to tell Jane about the "butterflies" she felt when she saw Jerry. This felt like the deepest and most secret part of her soul, but this revelation seemed rather strange and amusing to Jane, to whom, after all, Jerry was just her irritating, intrusive older brother, who "got on her nerves."

Shortly thereafter, another girl at their Catholic school, someone whom Maddy hardly knew, approached her and asked mockingly, "So, how are your butterflies these days?" As Maddy later described it, "Something in me sort of died. I wanted to run away forever. I was now sure everyone *knew*." All her secret, deepest, most confusing longings felt open to everyone's gaze. "It was much worse than being stripped naked. It was more like being skinned alive." For weeks, Maddy didn't go back to school. She developed an illness the doctors could not diagnose. When her parents forced her to return, she avoided looking at anyone, just did her work and went home. And she never went back to Jane's house.

For other girls, this scenario plays out differently, toward a positive resolution. Imagine here that Jerry is not Jane's older brother and that Jane is developmentally in the same place as Maddy. When Maddy reveals her secret, Jane responds by saying, "I know just what you mean. Roger makes me feel that way, too. When he's around, I feel all hot and strange, and I'm afraid that anyone can see it. And I can barely talk to him." Maddy is now not only understood and reassured, but Jane also offers her a reciprocal secret, establishing a bond of trust between them.

Friendship as a Context for Secrets

We tell our friends things about ourselves that we would not risk telling other people who are close to us. We do not tell a parent, because the foibles and poor behavior we reveal to a friend would, if told to a mother or father, arouse anxiety, and possibly set off a parental maneuver to control us. We may not tell a partner, because we don't want to expose ourselves to criticism, or be "told what to do next time." The friendship talk between girls and women has all sorts of structures preventing someone from acting the "expert," as a parent or partner might.

For this reason, what we say is for a friend's ears only. Girls repeatedly describe how betrayed they feel when a friend tells someone else what they said. "It doesn't even have to be mean, but when a friend tells someone else your problems, they somehow get a different perspective." The protected arena of friend talk allows girls to use friendship to understand their world and look at things in new ways.

In talking we try out different versions of our histories, our futures, and our present feelings—we work on possible selves. We rehearse our thoughts and feelings and plans—plans of how to deal with a parent or a boyfriend or a teacher or another friend. And this rehearsal space needs to be private. When we have an audience whose feelings and views we cannot trust, we no longer have this safe space in which to grow.

It is with girlfriends that we learn to live at the boundaries of the "personal." Young girls are often taught to respond to intrusive questions of their friends with "It's none of your business!" Mothers, remembering their own histories of betrayal and shame, counsel daughters not to tell too much to their friends. Lines of privacy are drawn around such issues as family finances, parental discord or other problems, special body characteristics, and sexual behavior— all areas with the greatest risk of shame from exposure. But a girl wonders how she can reap the rewards of intimacy without letting her best friend in on her sense of financial stress, her worries about her parents fighting, her fears about her body, or her growing interest in sex. The first telling of a vulnerable secret often marks the girl's first real step out of childhood and into the world of adolescence. For the first time, the girl realizes that to love outside her family—to love a friend—she must reveal herself.

We open sensitive, vulnerable parts of ourselves in this form of friend love, and expose ourselves to the possibility of ridicule or scorn. "I trust you," we say to our friend. But who is this friend whom we trust to guard what is so sensitive in us?

Betrayals

Lurlene, fourteen, one day found her best friend, Nicole, crying in the school bathroom. At first Nicole was reluctant to tell Lurlene why, but eventually she gave in to Lurlene's persuasion ("She made me tell her"). Nicole was crying because her parents had had a violent fight the previous night and her mother had ordered her father out of the house. Nicole feared the dissolution of her family. Lurlene was compassionate, hugged Nicole, listened to her, and told her not to worry. Nicole felt comforted and relieved that she had been able to share her awful experience and fear with her best friend. But this dramatic incident haunted Lurlene, who, living alone with her mother, had no experience of parental fighting, and over the next days, she found it harder and harder to keep this secret to herself. Taking a walk with Isabella later in the week, Lurlene swore her to secrecy and then recounted the story Nicole had told her. For Isabella, who was not bound by ties of love and loyalty to Nicole, this episode had the quality of an intriguing soap opera, and she had little hesitation about amusing her friend Jill with its details, now somewhat embellished. It, of course, did not take long before nearly everyone in the class "knew" about Nicole's family and before someone, in a moment of temper, made a nasty comment to Nicole, which indicated that she knew about it.

Nicole felt crushed by Lurlene's betrayal. "How could you tell?" she demanded. But Lurlene could not explain her anxiety, her inability to contain this secret on her own. Nicole never spoke to Lurlene again and retreated into a lonely world of mistrust, relating to others only superficially. By the end of the year, Nicole's shame and anger had grown to such proportions that she demanded that she be allowed to change schools.

Friends don't always betray secrets out of venal motives. More likely, the secret is too emotionally explosive for them to hold on to for long. Keeping a secret is difficult—at any age. Our capacity to keep a secret depends on many factors, of which our capacity for loyalty is just one. Sometimes a friend's secrets make us anxious or fill us with other strong feelings that are difficult to contain.

Everyone, though, thinks of herself as someone who can keep secrets. Who has ever responded to the question "Can you keep a secret?" with "No"? "Of course I'd never tell" is a pledge we make sincerely and wholeheartedly. What we don't factor in is our own anxiety about the content of a secret. Again and again, in training psychotherapists, I am amazed at how even experienced therapists, who otherwise fully understand their vows of confidentiality, betray secrets because they are unable to contain them, passing the responsibility of stopping the leakage on to the next person. The name of a client may be withheld, but the problems, circumstances, and even status of the client are often openly discussed.[1] It comes as no surprise, then, that adolescent girls find it hard to keep upsetting knowledge about their closest friends to themselves.

The more feeling and fantasy our friend's secret arouses in us, the harder it is to keep the secret to ourselves. As a therapist for twenty-five years, I have heard thousands of secrets—and I have learned to store them in a special safe in my mind from which leaks are impossible. After so many years of listening to the pain and struggles of many people, I feel that there is not much I have not yet heard or could not contain. Recently, though, a friend, not a very close friend—someone I know distantly and admire enormously, someone who rarely talks personally—chose to confide in me. Her husband had discovered a brief affair she'd had, she whispered, and now she was under constant surveillance. He had even hit her several times since this revelation, and she felt she had to endure anything in order to preserve her marriage. Recently, he'd humiliated her by insisting that she leave a professional meeting when he saw her talking to another man. It was on her way out, by way of explaining her behavior, that she told me all this. I was full of pity and anguish and outrage for her. I knew that this revelation was an impulse of the moment, and I knew that she was not going to discuss this with me further. I gave her the name of a good therapist in her city. For some reason, this story filled me with some special kind of pain I could not keep to myself, and, days later, I found myself recounting it (without her name) to another friend of mine. My wish was not to betray, but to share my distress and helplessness in this situation—to seek comfort for myself.

But adolescent girls do not have an adult woman's years of experience in containing anxiety over others' human complexity or shock at the realities behind people's masks. It is hard for a girl to emotionally bind and manage the potent revelations of her friends. It was just too much for Jane to think of anyone having a crush on her brother. It may be too much for Lurlene to know about her friend Nicole's family problems. These girls may intend to keep the secret when they solemnly swear not to tell, but their own precarious emotional balance, with its contradictory forces, impels them to seek support in their reactions, and so they tell—and make the next person "promise not to tell."

Secret Status

Knowing another's secrets is a mark of closeness and may raise our status. "Cindy always gets whatever guy she wants," Elsa declares admiringly to her group of friends. But Alice, who is very close to Cindy, knows that the guy Cindy really likes rejected her—Cindy told her in strictest confidence. Alice can easily gain status points by announcing this fact to the group. By advertising this marker of her closeness to the much-admired Cindy, she can raise her own value in the others' eyes. Whether Alice yields to this temptation depends on the complex psychological and emotional forces that operate within her.

These dilemmas persist in adult women. Joan's daughter is getting married, but her friend Dawn has a business trip scheduled for that weekend and has told Joan that she will be unable to change it. Miffed, Joan is on the telephone with Mary, a friend of both women. "I'm really angry at Dawn," Joan says. "You'd think we were good enough friends that my daughter's wedding would be more important than this meeting." Mary is torn. She wants to support Joan but also defend Dawn, who, she knows, has a marriage in the process of coming apart and who feels she could not bear being at a wedding under the circumstances. But Dawn has asked Mary not to tell anyone about this, and so Mary tries a compromise solution: "Well, maybe there are some other reasons you don't know about that keep Dawn from being able to come," she offers. But this doesn't work, because Joan immediately comes back with "Like what?" Mary thinks quickly. "Don't push me on this, Joan. I just want to say that I don't think Dawn is a bad friend. I think there may be other things going on. Just don't be too hard on her now." This is better, perhaps, but leaves Joan perplexed and irritated now with Mary as well.

Ask any woman if she can keep a secret told by a close friend and she will unhesitatingly answer, "Of course!" But if she declares she has never betrayed a friend's secret, you can be pretty certain she is either deluding herself or lying—or, perhaps, she means she never got found out, never faced the reality of her betrayal by seeing it in a friend's face.

In the "Promise not to tell" interactions that are so central to girls' friendships, we learn about enlightened trust. We learn we can trust others—but never completely. We learn that others are loyal to us, but within limits circumscribed by their own needs and inner struggles.

Protection Games

Betrayals occur continuously, but nonetheless their probability is denied as loyalties are idealized and controlled by rules of information management: of who is "allowed" to tell what to whom. Risks are not only regulated by promises of secrecy, they are also regulated by assertions of hierarchies of connection and commitment ("I'm only telling you this because you're my best friend") and by *exchanges* of confidences.[2] A girl talks about what she thinks and feels, about the people close to her, about her experiences, and then expects similar revelations from her friend. When Helen talks about her awkward silence with a teacher, Yoko implies that she has had similar social embarrassments ("I hate it when that happens"). When René talks about crying at the dinner table, Helen and Yoko show they've experienced the same sort of thing and are well aware of the sensations accompanying crying and trying not to cry. This exchange of information acts as a safety mechanism: "You know as much about me as I know about you."

Mutual revelations (which ensure mutual vulnerability) are attempts to make relationships safe—even though girls already know they are dangerous. If a friend can spill the beans on me, then I will be more careful what I say about her. So a girl tends to be uncomfortable if her friend doesn't confide in her. If this happens, the friendship is downgraded on the intimacy scale: "We're friends, but not close friends." Even if such a reserved friend does not in fact betray her, Clare, seventeen, feels herself at a disadvantage if she is the only one who imparts confidences:

> I used to tell Harriet everything. I knew she was reserved. This was one of the things I liked about her. It made her special—different from so many of the girls I know who just want you to know everything about them. But when I realized

how little she was ever going to let on about herself, I got—
well, I got a little uneasy. Then I heard she had broken up
with her boyfriend and started dating someone else. I'd seen
her the day before. I'd been talking to her the day before,
and she hadn't even whispered a thing about it. I asked her
why she hadn't said anything. "Well, I wasn't sure how it
would all work out," she told me. All right. Fine. She can
play her cards close to her chest. That's her right. But this
reserve gives me the creeps. There I was, talking about me,
and she didn't say a word about her, just because she wasn't
sure how things would turn out. I never know how anything's going to turn out! I'm not comfortable talking to a
friend like that.

If friends aren't mutually exposed, then where is our safety net?

Gossip

What is often called gossip is a way of slaking girls' enormous curiosity about others—a curiosity about the human world, and in particular about their world. Through the process of gossip, girls learn
how to pool their responses and focus on one another's stories. As
girls move toward adolescence, their talk is increasingly formed by
implicit questions: What are other people's lives really like? What
problems do they have? Who are they, as opposed to who they seem
to be? How does a friend see the other people in her world?

   The need to know what other people are really like may drive
some of the most painful instances of betrayal. One girl may try to
get close to another in order to prod her to reveal information, only
to then offer it to others. The exchanges of vulnerable information
may be a sham, as Heather discovers: "Jody just told me about her
and Sam because she wanted me to tell her about my boyfriend.

What she said about herself wasn't even true, and she posted everything I'd told her to the class blabbermouth."

Talking about the people who make up their world is so important that, once again, girls find themselves talking about another friend without meaning to betray her. They find they are led by the tone of others' conversations. That stylistic consensus can flow against their own thoughts and against their desire to be loyal. Many girls described "feeling bad after a bitch session" or "talking to someone and ending up saying things I didn't believe—like I'm sort of programmed to agree, even against a friend." In seeking out others' ways of seeing, girls sometimes find themselves caught up in another's perspective, agreeing too readily and failing to keep faith with their own individual ideas: "She said Franny was being horrible, so I sort of just agreed, but it was only because Nora kept saying it," Katia, twelve, explains. But some girls, however ruefully they reflect on criticizing a friend behind her back, are sometimes glad to express reservations about "even a best friend," to "get away from this lovey-dovey stuff" and to criticize "someone you like but who still does things that annoy you." No close relationship is perfectly comfortable, and we seek other friends' views of the person who sometimes annoys or hurt us, in order to justify our dissatisfaction. We need to talk and gather friends' views even about our good friends.

Gossip is so cruel because it involves the sharing of information out of its private context. Girls talk about their problems because they seek comfort. They expect a friend to listen and appreciate the tentative searching for self-expression. Girls talk about their reactions to one another to gain clarity about their own values. When we talk to our friends, we need a special space where we can work out what we're feeling, searching sometimes for the right words to describe it. Jayne works toward telling Dee how she feels about Noel: "I don't think I fancy him like I used to. I still like him, but he holds my hand, it's—yech! And I start not to like him at all, even though I

know I do." Jayne trusts that Dee will understand that she is exploring her feelings. But if Dee were to say to others, "Jayne doesn't like
Noel anymore," then Jayne's hedging and groping for clarity about
her feelings for Noel would be lost, the perspective changed, and all
comfort removed. Jayne would be left with the feeling that what has
been passed on to others is indeed what she *said* but not at all what
she *meant*. Gossip distorts information because it takes away the
frame that we trusted.

Gossip, that malicious form of torment, is a central form of
exchange in which girls learn to map the social world. It's the forum
in which they learn what is unacceptable—and how unacceptable
it is. "Did you hear what Lynn did?" expressed in a tone of outrage
or shock is the most powerful vehicle of social control in a girl's or
woman's world.

Though gossip has a bad name, and all girls fear it, it serves the
purposes of creating a group with defined norms. As girls gossip
about others and confess their own secrets, they learn how other girls
might react to their own potential selves. "Oh, my God, she didn't!"
Emma exclaims, and Jean learns, rapidly, that what Lynn did was
"bad"—or delightfully outrageous. Gossip has its own moral vocabulary. It is impossible to gossip with someone whose moral vocabulary you don't know: What can be said? What can be criticized and
condemned?

Gossip is also an important organizer of girls' social lives. Different networks are established by assessing the behavior of absent parties. Jody thinks Trish is Leslie's best friend, but when Leslie talks to
her about Trish, she feels she and Leslie are moving closer together. It
is a source of information—sometimes information about status
(who's in for praise, who's up for criticism), which helps draw the
ever-changing social map that is important to prevent a girl from
making a faux pas, such as befriending a girl who is shunned by others or flirting with a "nerd." It marks the boundaries of acceptable

behaviors and the framework for adolescents unsure of how to manage such things as sex or mind-altering substances.

What is sometimes called gossip, too, is really a pool of common stories that bond us with a sense of a shared history—whether what we are talking about happened last night, last year, or twenty years before. "Did you hear the latest with Pam and Saul?" or "Do you know what happened at the party last night?" or "Have you heard what happened to that girl who always used to sit next to you in junior high?" forge common interests and create a sense of common knowledge.

And this continues on into adulthood as women thrash out among themselves what is expected of them, what makes them admirable or contemptible in others' eyes. "Did you hear that Norma won the regional tennis tournament?" forty-five-year-old Nancy says to a group of her women friends, referring to Myrna's daughter. "It's not a surprise," Gail responds. "Myrna is so pushy with that child—doesn't let her do anything but practice. You should see her at the lacrosse games. Same thing. Cheering and yelling like life depended on whether or not Norma makes a goal. I think it's terrible. She's really making a mess of that kid." The women go on to discuss Myrna and her parenting and seem to conclude that she has gone too far. Secretly, then, each woman in the group wonders if she is too pushy with her own child. No one wants to be talked of in the way Myrna just has been.

"Juicy" gossip, with its overtones of secrecy, is tinged with excitement, marking it as information out of the ordinary. Women and girls know the delicious anticipation that attends a friend coming to them with a gleam in her eye and the words "Have I got something to tell you!" The very secrecy of information makes it sparkle. As Jody tells Leslie that she has something to tell her, something she can only tell her "in private," she sets her information in a context that highlights its importance. As Trish refuses to tell Jody what Heather said, she makes the "my lips are sealed sign," which signals that much could be said. Trish will goad Jody's interest, making her beg for information. The display of "secrecy" spreads signals around, and opens the private aspect of the friendship to the public gaze. Privacy proves importance, and what was once private and confidential soon becomes "private" gossip.

Gossip is something we depend on a friend to have. It's part of what makes her fun. We thrill to our own status when we have a rich piece of gossip, something that is a source of pleasure or excitement or entertainment to others ("Wait till you hear this!"). Our insider knowledge raises our social standing, especially when the information comes from high-status sources: If you are close to a popular girl, then you, too, are popular. You can prove that you are close to her by knowing her secrets, but you can only prove you know her secrets by betraying them, so friend talk and betrayal—those seemingly utter opposites—often fit together like hand in glove.

So basic is this urge to gossip that keeping secrets is pretty nigh impossible. It would seem reasonable, then, to withhold information about oneself to prevent it from being spread around. Few are naturally reticent about their thoughts and feelings, but some girls work hard on themselves to become reserved—forming themselves into inaccessible women forever wary of what others will say about them. Most girls, however, continue to open their hearts to their friends, and act upon trust, even though they know betrayal—through gossip—might be a breath away.

Restitution

The safety net promised by friendship talk is constantly broken. By the time girls are fourteen, most say they have already been betrayed by a friend—betrayed by having a "secret" or a "problem" or "something private" revealed behind their backs. Having one's secrets exposed feels awful, and we would normally run to our friend to talk about how we feel, how angry and vengeful, but if it's our "best friend" who has betrayed us, we are bereft: "Who can I go to now?" Jayne demands of us as she describes her best friend's betrayal. Some girls may then seek another friend for comfort, and so alliances shift. At the same time that "telling" is extracted and encouraged, it is also condemned, and the canny girl can turn a betrayal into an occasion to scorn the betrayer.

The indirect, or secondhand, way girls discover a friend's betrayal adds insult to injury. We seldom catch a friend in the act of betrayal, but find out later, through conversations with others. Surinder (now thirteen, whom we first observed with her friends at age eleven) describes how she heard what Sita was saying behind her back:

> Lydia told me, "You better watch out what you tell Sita." This really got to me. I kept wondering, "What's she saying?" "I'm just warning you," she said, and she wouldn't say anything more, until I said, "Look, you can't just keep dropping hints." So finally Lydia told me that Sita was saying how I took her to my new house and kept boasting and was saying it was nicer than anyone else's house, and that I was really a snob. And I go, "I'm not gonna worry about what I tell her. I'm gonna make sure she stops that talk." Because it's not right—is it?—to take what someone says the wrong way and tell everyone else what I'm "really" like when I'm not. And Lydia said that was the best thing, and Sita shouldn't get away with it, and if Sita denied she said anything, Lydia would say she did.

After the discovery comes the fight to clear one's name, to confront the betrayer, to have her say what she wants to say, face-to-face.[3] Few occasions in a girl's life require more courage: She must place herself in clear opposition to another girl, and she must risk the shame of a counterattack. Surinder needs support before she finally decides on this course, and she seeks Lydia's help in making sure she has a right to confront Sita, and that Sita is in the wrong. Lydia demonstrates her loyalty to Surinder even as she betrays Sita. Surinder, before she can confront Sita, wants to hear from Lydia that "Sita shouldn't get away with it." The two girls bond through criticism of another, and plan to confront her.

Surinder has some comfort in condemning Sita with Lydia, but the process doesn't end there. Surinder goes on to discuss with Lydia what she should do:

> SURINDER: I'm going to talk to her. I'm going to ask her why she keeps saying things like that.
> LYDIA: I don't know. She might just say, "I'm not." She might just not want to talk.
> SURINDER: But if it comes when we're talking about something—
> LYDIA: Like you could just bring it up.
> SURINDER: Yeah, just say it—
> LYDIA: Because it really depends how much you still want to be friends.
> SURINDER: I really want to know why she's saying these things, why she's being so two-faced.
> LYDIA: So you could ask.
> SURINDER: I can say, "I'd like to ask you something."
> LYDIA: And don't let her deny it.
> SURINDER: No, if she denies—
> LYDIA: If she denies she said those things, you say I told you.

Lydia and Surinder work to clear the air, to correct the harm done from "what people think" or "what people are saying." But sometimes we barely know what's been said about us. A girl hears whispers or sniggers, or simply senses that others "know something bad about her," that others are pooling their negative thoughts and drowning her in their disapproval. Rowena, thirteen, has felt her status plummet in recent weeks.

> I don't know what happened. Everyone who mattered used to like me—I mean, really like me. Now it's like there's a dirty film all around me and I don't know why. I say something, or make a joke, and it just goes wrong. The more I try, the worse it gets. I ask, "What's wrong? What do you think I've done?" And Cynthia shrugs. "What?" I ask. "Nothing?" But I know it's not nothing. I just don't know what it is. There's a whole conversation I'm just not allowed to hear.

Desperate to discover what Cynthia really thinks of her, Rowena persuades Toni to phone Cynthia and, while Rowena is listening on an extension, to "say something bad" about her, to see whether her friend Cynthia will agree, or whether she will start to "talk about her" and "tell things she promised not to." An urgent need "to know" pushes her into the masochistic process of hearing for herself what her friend will say "behind her back." Rowena then hears Cynthia say, "The thing about Rowena is she's just so picky. You know what she told me? She said, 'I don't like Julie anymore because I can't stand the way she keeps flicking her hair back.' And she told me you kept boasting about your sister's wedding. She's just picky."

Rowena feels the dark power a friend has to twist her words. Like many girls before her, like many girls after her, she tries to work her way out of misery by putting together the pieces of puzzles—pieces made from glances, whispers, taunts. "I can't believe she told anyone!" we cry, when that in fact is what we have to believe to make sense of what's happening to our social world.

The gravest betrayal, the one most difficult to forgive, involves ridicule. The worst thing a friend can do, we were repeatedly told, is to "use something I said to laugh at me behind my back," to "turn my problem into a joke," to "twist things, so what hurts me turns into everyone else's joke." Teenage girls are exquisitely vulnerable to their social image, to the way others talk about them, and the threat of shame is an ever-present specter. Some girls may be concerned about the fragility of their reputations, but the worry about what others will think and say about them goes far deeper. Because they are uncertain of their own identities, the descriptions others give of them threaten them with a reality that can seem stronger than their own minds. They then confront a conflict: They want to be known, they want to be understood and accepted for who they are, yet they want control over what is known and how they are known. To gain the benefits of the first, they risk losing control over the second.

Betrayals are as common as dust, yet each one comes as a shock, since each girl believes her system of control will be effective. "But she *promised*," "But she *swore*," "But I was sure she'd *never* tell," girls protest, even as they see the promise broken. Some girls are traumatized by these betrayals, which can lead to depression and the conviction that they will "never trust anyone again," and "life isn't worth living." Jules Henry reports, in *Culture Against Man,* one thirteen-year-old girl saying, "I don't have many friends because people who call themselves your friends are really your enemies, sweet in front of your face and gossips behind your back. If you call those kind of people your friends, then I guess I have as many as anybody else, if not more. But it would be nice to have a real friend, someone to tell your problems to." Those girls and women who do have friends note the conflict and danger but insist, "I can't give up my friends."[4]

The Women's Room

We like to think, as we mature, that our identity takes a firmer shape, and we are therefore not so badly bruised by others' views of us, so someone else's version of what we've said or done won't hurt as it did when we were thirteen, or sixteen. But even when we're "grown-ups," there is still something awful in the pain we feel when something we said to a friend has been told to someone else, and is exaggerated, and loses the tentative nature of our telling it, or the safe context in which we told it. At thirty-seven, Micki, a college professor, finds familiar wounds inflicted on her as her friends report what she's said—or not said—about another friend:

> Brenda marched up to me and said, "I was really sorry to hear you didn't stick up for me at that meeting." There was this familiar, sinking feeling. In a way, I knew exactly what she meant, but at the same time I could hardly believe she would attack me like this. Brenda's grant was up for renewal. I'm on the committee to assess these grants, and I was for her all the way. But you have to negotiate in these situations. You just can't have everything, and so Brenda didn't get the full amount renewed.
>
> *Someone*—and I think I know who—must have told her something about what I said after the meeting, because afterward I was upset that I hadn't done more, but it's the kind of regret that's not really logical, because when I think of it, I know that I didn't do more because I just couldn't— not if I was still being fair-minded or professional or whatever. And you'd think a friend would catch on that I'd done my best, and when I said I wanted to do more, I was being too hard on myself, not laying myself open to being criticized by Brenda herself. I really feel screwed.
>
> But the most upsetting thing about this is not that this happened today and it's making me feel lousy, but that this has happened before. I mean, this kind of relaying of distorted events has been thrown at me before. And that's

what's always going to happen in friendships, and that can really get me down.

Though we leave behind the halls of our junior high and high school, where what other girls say seems of paramount importance, we take with us an awareness of friendship's dangers. While on the one hand, this close and complex relationship makes us feel safe—it persuades us to talk about ourselves and expose the doubts, insecurities, and failings that we do not want publicly known, but for which we crave acknowledgment, sympathy, and acceptance—on the other hand, the information we give in private can work against us in public. However positive and strong we feel ourselves growing, we never forget friendship's precarious structure. As we now work beside other women, our knowledge of these relationships makes us cautious.

When as young adults in the early seventies, women, their consciousness newly raised, made the first giant step into the male bastions of the workplace, they were disconcerted by a silent network—a network supplying information and support, a network to which they had no access. Somewhere behind the scenes, somewhere outside both the formal and informal meetings, was a center of activity that aided and abetted men's progress. As women felt their exclusion, they labeled this network "the men's room": There, in the men's restroom, from which women were reasonably barred, information casually exchanged decisively shaped men's careers. The term came to refer not only to the limited number of events that actually took place in the men's room, but to the entire system of knowledge to which men had access and from which women were excluded.

Preparing to enter a difficult world in which they would have to compete to succeed, many women were disconcerted to see how men often did not have to compete with one another. Instead, men befriended one another, mentored one another, supported one another. What many women experienced was not the cutthroat environment they had expected, but a cozy club. When they tried to join it, they were ostracized, by both the men and the women. Trying to be one of the boys was a loser's game. Either she failed and the men ridiculed her, or she succeeded and women saw her as "sleeping her way to the top." There could, at that time, be no comparable women's network. In the workplace women were too scarce, or too divided, or too defensive, to band together and empower one another.

Once women did try to form a corresponding "women's room," they found that, far from its being the place of comfort they had envisioned, the rivalry and backbiting in some groups often seemed to threaten the fabric of women's progress. Women found themselves unwittingly re-creating the "clubs" of junior high, with punishments for those who didn't conform, competition for closeness to the women who seemed most popular (and therefore powerful), and a grapevine of rumors about who said what about whom behind her back. Several women described the sense of doom they experienced as members of a women's group engaged in conflict. As one recalled:

> It would start with just one person saying how the conversation was really getting her all upset and all sorts of nasty notions were buzzing around the room, and then the different armies would group. Over and over, there would be people who were "in" and people who were "out," and people talking about each other and swearing each other to secrecy, and someone who was way beyond criticism one week would be in for it the next.

As Olga reflects on past divisions on the board of a women's center, she describes the format of girls' cliques: They are volatile and mean. But unlike a young girl who keeps going back to the same friends, explaining to her dismayed parents that she has made up with them because "they are not mean all the time," women in their twenties and thirties may avoid contact in order to avoid the pain of divisiveness. "I gave up my position on the board," Olga explained. "It was a battle station, not a group."

In more personal circumstances, too, conflict with friends during early adulthood is avoided. The "mommy wars," or the defensive stances between traditional mothers who forgo work outside the home and look after children full-time, and those mothers who pay for child care and commit themselves to a job during the day, have become a feature of women's relationships. So, too, is the division between women who have children and women who don't. Each woman, facing another, senses some implied criticism of her life choices. The pressing questions that we all ask ourselves from time to time—"Have I followed the right path?" and "Have I given up too much?"—color our friendships, especially in the context of a society in which the balance between family and work is inevitably precarious.[5] Monica, thirty-nine, felt her former classmates looked down on her. Mai, forty-seven, felt that her roles were "belittled by people at college who had struggled so much to make the grade." She understood how their struggles separated them from her: "They see my life as cushy—which in some ways it is, but then they don't see how I have real problems, too." Audrey, thirty-four, was haunted by the memory of how "smug I felt when my friends' marriages broke up. I wouldn't have said it at the time, but I did . . . I felt smug, like 'Poor her, and lucky me.' I needed some proof that I'd made the right decision—not to work—and they'd made the wrong one. The kind of support I got from my friends when *my* marriage broke up was a surprise—and made me regret my old feelings."

Audrey is contrite when she discovers there is no contempt or *schadenfreude* (pleasure at another's pain) in her friends' responses to her divorce. But her initial wariness shows she has learned—as most women do—that animosity can lurk in many friendships. Time and again, women experience other women's support, but time and again, too, something not quite nameable rears its head. Audrey also recalls the political minefield she discovered as she began working in a health-service corporation. The senior partner, a woman in her forties, was eager to integrate her into the firm, and things moved smoothly. As Audrey tells it:

> I was being given more and more referrals. Then I was asked to do some seminars. Suddenly, the therapist working alongside me at some of the seminars declared that "they" could not offer me so much office space at the rate I'd been told. I knew I had to behave as though this were simply a technical matter, but I know there's some other agenda. This has happened to me before. It's like someone in your set turning against you because you're getting too matey with another girl.

These "wars" are so disturbing because the battle lines keep changing, because we feel we should have outgrown them, and because they can always take us by surprise, however much experience we've had in the realm of girlfriends. What we can learn, however, is that one blow, falling upon us with an awful recognition ("This has happened to me before"), is something we can withstand, and we can go on to trust again.

Without a doubt, women's networks have been enormously important in what advancement there has been for women in the workplace. Natalie, now nearly fifty, notes that a woman is more likely to see the value in another woman:

> I don't count her reflectiveness as a weakness. The men describe her as "indecisive," but she listens, and may feed what she hears into her decisions. That's not weakness. Sometimes men just don't see other women as potential candidates. There are all these women around, and they'll look

around the room and say, "Who can we appoint? There aren't any women." They're right there—the men just don't see them.

Natalie treasures the opportunity to befriend other women at work, to "put friendship into action," and is glad to escape from "merely commiserating with girlfriends." But alongside the pride many women now have in their power to aid and abet other women in their careers is an awareness that true friendship in the workplace carries with it the same dangers that it did in high school, that our new public faces in adulthood often need protection similar to that we desired for our fragile teenage "reputations." Many women working with women feel the return of that same doubt: Who is really my friend, and how much can I safely reveal, and what promises of silence will be kept?

The urge toward friendship often overcomes these fears, though, and in their careers, women often make friends and find friendships an important perk of the job. Kimberly, twenty-five, even evaluates a job in terms of whether the workplace atmosphere fosters friendship between women. "You can't be friends and cut throats at the same time. But if I can't trust my colleagues, if I can't make at least some of them my friends, I don't want to work with them."

As women make friends at work, they practice the cautions they used in high school, weighing how much intimacy the friendship can contain. But many women nevertheless have been "burned" by believing it safe to speak unguardedly to a work friend, only to find their private information revealed in a work assessment or in an executive decision. Audrey decides that it is "unwise" or "unpolitic" to make friends at work. She knows where she is with the men at work:

It is easier to be friends with the men, even though they're often more difficult. The thing is—you see the competitiveness. It's up front, and you know that if they have something to use against you, when the time comes, they'll use it. With women, there are mixed messages. I can't afford to be what I call friends with a woman I work with, even though many of the women here are great, and I miss like hell that closeness that I could have with them. But if I tell a woman that I have all sorts of doubts about giving a presentation, or if I tell a woman how easily I might goof up on something— And you see, that's the sort of thing I would tell a woman friend. I'd laugh at myself. I'd despair of myself. Well, you know the sorts of things women friends do! And what if it's a woman who day in and day out has to do what I ask her? Or what if it's someone who's in charge of my next promotion? If I expose my weaknesses, they may think I can't stand up to the pressure of a certain client. You make lots of judgment calls on the basis of personality, and I have to look competent through and through. I have to watch myself with these women. It's not that I don't trust them, but I know what happens with that kind of private information.

At thirty-four, Audrey is learning again that women friends tempt us to reveal what can then be used to hurt us. She knows the "promise you won't tell" contract that goes with disclosures between women friends is unreliable. But this knowledge then gives rise to questions about how to be a woman, how to be herself and still be successful in her job:

I have to be more like a man when it comes to relationships at work. I have to keep a watch on myself. But the best thing is to be so totally honest that you can switch from being a friend to someone and then being an employer who assesses her work. There's one woman I know who can do that. She

has this real special quality. But she has to take a lot of accusation: "How can you be my friend and say that!" And it
would wear me down. I just don't know . . . this is a tricky
area. I knew working with men was going to be hard. I didn't
realize the emotional exhaustion of working with women. But
my need for women friends runs deep, right into my bones.

The "emotional exhaustion" arises from the conflict between the
need to have women friends and the decision to restrict this need.
Like many women in high-pressure jobs, with sparse time to develop
a social life completely apart from work, Audrey grows wise to continuing problems between women, and yet dreads the loneliness of
giving them up.

At fifty, having been a homemaker for most of her life, Gillian is
now catching on to the emotional entanglements of work and
friendship as she becomes a professional detective story writer:

My editor is a real doll. I just love her. She flies over to see
me and says, "We can discuss things at the mall!" She loves
shopping in Minneapolis—it's much better than New York,
she says. So we go around the mall, and I'll be as open as
the sun with her. Then my agent screams down the phone,
"Why did you tell her that!" and when I say, "Why not? It's
true," she'll say, "This is business, kiddo. Behave like it's
business." I get the point. You can't tell an editor that you'll
stick with her even if she doesn't offer a bigger advance, and
you can't tell your editor that you really don't know what
came over you when you got this really good idea and it
probably won't happen again. You just gotta have a strong
front. So I try to keep the lid on. But that keeps the lid on a
lot of other things, too.

I'm just so curious about these go-getting young women

I'm meeting now. And it doesn't seem right to ask them all sorts of questions and then not offer one bean about myself. And I'm used to talking round the clock with my women friends. It's real strange to be biting my tongue when I'm out with a real nice gal. But I know what can happen. I've been there before, goodness knows. You tell someone something, and she nods and puts her hand on yours, and then the next thing you know, she's gone and told the last person in the world you ever wanted to hear of it. So I try to keep up a little reserve all around.

As women enter the professional arena, they reencounter the dilemmas they faced in the world of girlfriends. As always, these struggles lead to a string of questions about who we are in relation to others and who we want to be. Audrey and Gillian accept the imperfections of friendly confidences. They long for women friends but resist the longing as they remember the possibility of betrayal. Yet, noticing their resistance, they wonder whether it is necessary, whether their work culture could be changed to accommodate more human feeling and frailty. Audrey reaches a temporary resolution through new ways of appreciating being with women. "There's a different kind of closeness as we tackle jobs together. I'm not sure how distinctively female it is, and I still wouldn't say I feel close to the women in my section, but I'm glad they're there. It's the worst feeling, that feeling that you'd rather not have women around. When I get to that stage, I'll have to find another place to work." And so she asks whether she wants to be what she has to be if she is to walk among women and not make friends with them.

Women are discovering, along with Audrey, that this is a far more important question about women at work than anyone had previously thought. As Audrey discovers, the emotional exhaustion of schooling her responses to other women takes a toll, and she is not sure how far she is willing to go along that road. Gillian discovers that she must become the person she never thought she would be: the reserved girl who listens to other people's problems without revealing her own, and who must even curb her curiosity about others because she won't prod them or persuade them to talk by offering self-revelations. We frequently note these conflicts but treat them as peripheral—far less important than men's attitudes toward women in the workplace, far less important than the conflicts between work and family that tend to be etched into women's, rather than men's, lives. Yet so deep is the need for good friendships with women that this difficulty in negotiating friendships with women at work can make women feel bad about themselves or the jobs they do.

Belinda, fifty-eight, felt "devastated" as she realized how her professional distance had impaired a friendship. Carla, a longtime coworker in an advertising agency, didn't tell her about having cancer until she was through treatment and well into remission. "She was afraid for me to know, afraid I'd let others at work know, and that she'd lose her chance for the promotion she eventually did get. I found out kind of by accident and I said, 'I am your best friend. How could you go through all this and not even let me know?' I still can't believe she didn't trust me enough."

Even as mature women, the dilemma we experienced with our girlfriends during adolescence recurs: To be absolutely safe from betrayal, we must be alone, but being alone is lonely, and so we seek friends. Our paradigm of friendship involves exchanges of confidence and self-exposure—and hence vulnerability. What we learn to live with is the acceptance that we must take risks because we need friends. And the benefits of friendship with women seem to multiply as we mature. Our growth depends on sharing patterns of doubt, conflict, and desire with other women. With their power to support and confirm our identity, women friends play an enormous role in clarifying women's sense of themselves. The relationships that women worked on as girls remain an important resource in gathering strength to manage their increasingly complex world. Yet we are never completely safe within a friendship: The "promise not to tell" is never fully secured, but being without the pleasures of exchanged confidences—being without girlfriends—is intolerable.

Chapter Seven

"FORGET IT—I DON'T WANT TO TALK ABOUT IT"

One of the hardest things in any relationship is learning how to disagree—how to fight as freely as we did as children, and make up as readily. At times, however, walls spring up and chasms open that may feel—or be—untraversable. Girls may sometimes confront one another outright, but more likely they will tiptoe around one another, burying their negative feelings in order to avoid open clashes and preserve the illusion of harmony.

Girls are simultaneously terrified and fascinated by the dynamics of confrontation. They discuss among themselves scenarios and procedures: "Should I say anything?" "Do you think she's really sorry?" "Can you believe what she said?" "What I should've said is . . ." They enact, reenact, brood, assess other girls' "crimes," and try to hone their own tactics. They address issues about what a good close relationship is, how people should be treated, and what's right, what's fair, what's loyal. Their arguments reveal tensions about possessiveness and independence, questions about how each should be treated and how a girl should behave if the rules for fair treatment are broken.

Girls' intense disputes with their girlfriends are not primarily about hierarchy but about identity and closeness.[1] Boys' disputes about who can give orders or who's the best player may involve tempers, but rarely involve the sense that if one fights back, one is guilty of not being a nice guy. And without guilt, the conflicts can be more easily forgotten. For girls, it's the self-justifications ("I was mean to her because she was so awful") or the nagging self-doubts ("Was I justified in saying that?") that give conflicts their psychological power. Girls are often bound by impossibly angelic ideals of who they should be and how they should treat others. Paradoxically, the ideals of femininity may prevent girls from getting close again. Because girls feel pressure to "be nice" to each other's face, harsh feelings fester. But few girls will risk being openly angry for fear of being called a bitch and losing others' regard in consequence. Worse, they may offend the friend so much that reconciliation becomes impossible. So how can girlfriend conflict be resolved?

Open Conflict

Quinisha, fifteen, a tall girl with bright eyes and carefully braided hair, told us about how she resolved an explosive conflict with her close friend Carmine. After hearing from Rhia that Carmine had been spreading the word about Quinisha's attraction to Darren and that Carmine had said "only whores went for him," Quinisha was furious:

> I told Carmine, "You meet me outside those school gates and I'll rub your face in dirt, you big-mouthed bitch." [She shouts out this threat and then sits back and laughs heartily.] You know, a girl can be my best friend, but she can't go saying that only whores go for the guy I like, because that means I'm a whore, and no one, not even my best friend, can say that about me. I really would have rubbed her mouth on the ground, 'cause I'm bigger and Carmine's no fighter, and was she scared. And I didn't want to hear her lily-livered excuses, and I tell her she's talked enough, so she should just shut up and take her punishment. But she's pleading with

me to listen, and I go, "Well, she's my friend, I'll listen for a minute," and she says she only told Rhia that I liked him and she was worried he'd treat me like a whore, and that's different. And she said Rhia shouldn't have opened her mouth because she told Rhia as a friend, because she was worried about me. I told her that she can just talk to me if she's worried and not go to someone else, and she said she'd learned her lesson, that no friend's problems are safe with someone else, so we're still best friends.

Quinisha describes her heated anger, and it is easy to imagine, too, the frisson within the school as others anticipate the fight, which could goad her further. But she sticks to the issue: that a friend has a right to answer the charges against her, that a friend has a right to make a mistake and be forgiven, and that mending the relationship is better than winning a fight. She makes good use of the "masculine" model of confrontation. Resentments don't simmer away: The accusation and proposed punishment are immediately declared. Then Quinisha steps into the listening and responding modes of friendship, and the relationship is mended.

But this kind of open conflict is rare among girls. More likely, girls will find it difficult to announce their anger and will search for indirect means to seek reparation—or will bury their feelings altogether.

There is a social myth that, in contrast to boys, girls are permitted greater freedom in expression of their feelings. While girls may indeed be allowed greater latitude in the expression of love, affection, and tender feelings, the outright expression of anger is almost completely taboo. While boys can take out their anger and aggression in fights, sports, and other forms of competition, girls are often filled with repressed rage, which leaks into subtle and harmful manipulations that may damage the friend, the friendship—or themselves. This buried rage is often one of the causes behind depression, eating disorders, self-mutilation, or other self-crippling behaviors.

A girl is caught between her need to express what she feels and her fears of being thought a crybaby or a bitch. How far a girl may go in expressing her anger before she is labeled a bitch depends, of course, on the norms of the subculture in her school or neighborhood. In some schools, like Quinisha's, girls engage in fights while their friends cheer them on, but in others, even raising their voices may be construed as excessive meanness, which other girls will, in one way or another, punish.

Smoothing Over Conflict

"I still feel dreadful," Holly, now seventeen, explains, "when something goes wrong—just a disagreement, like you're talking and—*wham!*—there you are with no way forward." While Holly describes herself as "pretty confident and straightforward," she knows she has earned this self-image by honing her courage with friends: "It's an awful feeling, but what do you do? Say 'Oh, I agree' when you damn well don't? But my mouth gets me into trouble. I say what I think, and then things go wrong. So I usually wait awhile. Then I'll phone. We'll meet. But sometimes the damage is terrible."

The confusion and pain girls feel when a friendship goes wrong measures the depth of real feeling engaged by these relationships. Such disappointment stirs primitive emotional responses, ranging from the terror of losing a friend to the fear of being engulfed by one's own anger. Thirteen-year-old Miriam's eyes fill with tears and her voice cracks with anger as she talks about "being let down in the worst way" by a friend who "just turned on me, for no reason, and said there was no point in talking."

In early childhood, before the age of seven, friendships are made and broken and remade constantly. Accusations and counter-accusations pitch back and forth, then friends "make up," the anger forgotten. As girls move through middle childhood and toward adolescence, however, their fallings-out become more problematic as the attachments grow in complexity and depth. A friend is "too possessive," or prone "to use" people. A friend "says bad things" about another, or "stops going around with her," and a girl feels betrayed, let down, edged out. "I don't trust her. She's not a good friend," Ellie declares during a rift with a friend. She confronts the clash that we are all likely to feel in important relationships—the clash between wanting to lash out and hurt someone who has hurt us, and wanting to protect the relationship, no matter what. In short, a quarrel with a friend is like a quarrel between lovers who continue to care about each other even when they are outraged by each other's behavior, and who want a valued relationship to work even when they are so angry they want to smash something.

Most friendship conflicts are maneuvers that draw boundaries ("Don't be so bossy!" or "Why do you think you're the leader?" or "You don't own me!") or establish rules ("I thought you'd tell me first" or "You weren't supposed to tell her that"). Open quarrels keep the friendship up to date and thereby sustain it. The worst, most lasting fights between girlfriends involve evasion—refusing to talk, refusing to engage with the other person. This refusal can be terrifying. Nurit, at fourteen, discovers how she can now suffer a "panic attack" as a close friend suddenly becomes curt and cold: "I don't know why Sara's not talking to me. I don't know what she thinks I've done, so I can't defend myself. She's still *speaking* to me, but she won't *talk*, so I don't know what she's thinking, and I don't know what she's going to do." As the friendship dissolves into animosity, Nurit worries that now "everything we once talked about will get spread around," and because she does not know her friend's feelings, she does not know "who else will side with her." The halt of communication puts her privacy at risk and her social world into turmoil. She wants to understand the failure, as urgently as she would seek understanding of a parent's depression, or their divorce.

Some girls who remain silent, who "bite their tongues," who avoid rather than confront, are trying to keep from harming the relationship further. Speaking out, putting things on the table, does not always end in a good repair. Sara won't talk to Nurit because she feels she would do more harm by explaining how she feels than she does by keeping quiet:

> You can't say, "No, I don't want to talk to you now, I'd rather talk to someone else." Maybe you say, "I just don't feel like talking about this now." But that's as much as you can get away with. Sometimes I just spout off: "I don't like that kind of remark" or "I don't feel like going out with those guys" or "It really annoys me when you nudge me like that." But I can be real sorry for it later. Weeks later, there will still be some remark hanging between us. Often it's just not worth it. I wish it could be like me and my brother or my mom. We can spit words, and then it's over. It can even be funny. But between me and a friend—it's damage. I'd rather just keep my mouth shut till I'm not so fed up with Nuri.

So the call for sincerity is caught by the trap of good manners. Once again, a basic dilemma of communication and connection is confronted in friendship: How far can we say what we think, and keep a friend? How can we handle our annoyance or anger? Can we speak up, to change what we don't like in a friend? What answers we come up with will have enormous repercussions on how honestly we can be ourselves, and be friends.

Bringing conflict into the open may involve a process with much pain on both sides until each understands the other's needs. Samantha, a college junior majoring in psychology, described the wrenching reworking of her friendship with Ariel:

> She was always there, but I needed space for myself. I really liked her, but I started to say nasty things about her to other friends; I hid from her, ran away from her. When she talked to me, I was unresponsive—not because I didn't like her. I just felt she was encroaching—I needed other parts of my life. I didn't like it when she watched out for me to come back to my room. I didn't like it when she knew my other friends. I felt like she was oozing into my skin. But I was afraid of telling her.

"Why?" I asked. "Because I wouldn't want someone to say something like this to me. You don't want to do something that will hurt another person." So what happened? I wondered.

> Finally she wrote me a note saying, "I feel like you've been avoiding me. I feel I'm making all the effort in this relationship. Tell me if I'm a pain in the ass—just tell me." The note shocked me into realizing I had to make a decision about what our relationship would be. So finally I said to her, "Look, I really like you, but I need to see you a little bit less." I realized I just needed to be clear with her about the limitations and what they need to be. I said, "I'm sorry. I was just feeling a need for space."

"What were you sorry about?" I asked.

> Sorry to have to hurt her feelings. We had different needs, and when there's not a perfect match, you have to work

around it. And usually someone feels hurt. I think our friendship was stronger once we had other friends and could still be friends but have separate lives. At the same time, I don't want her to get too close to someone else. When I see her close to another girl, I have to say to myself, "This is fine. This is good." But still I have to fight being jealous. Even though I want space, I don't want loss. There's a difference.

Negotiating Arguments

When things go wrong, girls search for some explanation. "What happened?" and "Whose fault is it?" girls ask themselves and one another, trying, in retrospect, to put the pieces together again. Their conversations fill with discussions of past conflicts, how they arose and how they were resolved. Vivienne Griffiths, observing adolescent girls and their friends, was amazed at the amount of detail the girls remembered—who said what, how long the argument lasted, which girl played what role in the process.[2] Girls remember such events in minute detail because these interchanges matter so much. Were they able to save the friendship, or has it been permanently broken? When they spoke out, did it have the effect they wanted, or did things spiral out of control? Did they make up without losing face? Did they give in, did they grovel—or did they succeed in having their say, gaining recognition for their grievance, and striking a better balance?

Ellie, fourteen, tells me about her rift with Kerry. She gives me a blow-by-blow account of an argument they had that took place two months before. Whether or not Ellie's account is thoroughly accurate really doesn't matter. What she shows is how important all these steps in the argument are to her, and how they have stayed with her—a significant story in her life:

I told Kerry I couldn't go around with her because I didn't
trust her. And she said that wasn't fair, and I'd just decided to
go against her without even talking about it. So I said we
could talk, but when we started to talk, she just walked
away: "I'm not going to listen to this shit." So I ran after her
and really gave it to her: "You say you want to talk and then
you push off!" And she said she walked away because I was
shouting and I wasn't listening to her. And I said I was
shouting because *she* wasn't listening, and we started to
laugh, but then I stopped laughing because it was a serious
thing, the way she talked about me to Joe, who goes, "Oh,
poor Ellie isn't going to get an A"—because of the trouble I
was having in history—and everyone knew I'd be disappointed not to make the grade. And Kerry said that she
didn't say anything bad, or anything private, they'd just been
talking, and it was Joe who made it into some big deal, and
she's never made fun of me like it seemed. And Joe's like
that, and Kerry reminded me of how he's done the same sort
of thing to this other girl, and everyone knows Joe'll just
tease you about anything, so no one really pays attention.

Ellie's first step during an argument is to air her complaint.
Kerry issues a counter-complaint: Ellie has decided Kerry is in the
wrong even before talking to her, and that's unfair. Ellie doesn't deny
that condemning a friend without talking it over first is unfair, but
she offers to talk and then Kerry seems to balk at taking her up on
the offer. Kerry walks off, refusing to talk. Ellie doesn't let her go, but
runs after her, and then Kerry explains why she walked away: Ellie
was shouting. Ellie's counter to that complaint ("I was shouting
because *she* wasn't listening") strikes both girls as funny. For a moment,
they seem to stand outside the dispute, amused by its format.
    The routine of complaint and counter-complaint is interrupted

by their laughter, which nearly ends the dispute. Ellie, however, insists that they shouldn't end it in this simple way; they should still talk it over, even if they no longer feel angry with each other. In arguing, they clarify the issues bothering them.

The two girls can argue because they agree on a lot of things. They share notions of what's fair and how friends should behave. They both recognize that they're responsible for what they say about a friend, but not for everything that other people do with what they say. And when they get to that point, they accept that a third person is to blame. They form an alliance against Joe, and as they focus on his faults, Ellie is reassured by Kerry that "no one pays attention" to what Joe says, so no real harm was done after all.

As Ellie argues with Kerry, she practices skills in self-assertion, but there is something more: She discovers she can express anger without destroying the relationship. Anger is not something she has to suppress in order to stay friends; it's something she can use to keep the friendship on an even keel. While she argues, she protects her "rights" to fair treatment by a friend. She also finds common ground and builds on that. She listens to Kerry (during the argument they endorse the importance of listening), and she uses their mutual understanding to resolve the conflict—to "make up."

For some time women's strong negotiating skills have been recognized. More and more, these skills are being put to use in the commercial and professional worlds. Often they are thought to come "naturally" to women, as though such finesse is inborn. From what we see when we follow girls' development through their friendships, though, it is clear that these negotiating skills are learned through hard experience.

Quinisha, Samantha, and Ellie have learned different modes of bringing conflict into the open and resolving it. They've learned that problems can be solved by talking them out. But girls know that this evenhanded structure where everyone will be heard, respected, and understood does not always come into play. In every argument, there is a range of possible outcomes, and in the heat of the conflict, panic and pathos govern the moves. And a girl's behavior in a conflict is always public, open to the scrutiny and judgment of others. One girl apologizes to another—and all the others in the group sit as judge and jury. Should this apology be accepted? Was she really sorry? Was the offense forgivable? The conflict becomes a topic of conversation, and girls take sides, perhaps using the argument to rearrange alliances between them, perhaps enjoying the power of seeing someone else squirm, but also to debate the rules for how people should be with one another.

Fear of Fighting

When our friends, whom we normally trust not to "judge" us, do sit in judgment upon us, we feel the awakening of terror. In adolescence, when girls depend upon their friends' approval as a protection against the self-doubt that strikes from every angle, confrontations take on a life-and-death aspect. Gloria, sixteen, has been president of her high-school sorority for the past year.

> I guess I've known for a while that some girls were grumbling about the way I did things. But it seemed all under control, and I'd ask people to speak out if they didn't like something, and that way we could change things. But then I see these girls charging toward me, and the ground was sinking away from me, so I sat down and said, "Okay, what is it?" and they eye each other, like "We know what's she's trying to pull."
>
> And one of them was Allie, and she's not just any friend—we've been really close. But here she is with those other two, and they don't surprise me so much because I know better

than to trust them. Anyway, Allie goes, "Butter wouldn't melt in her mouth." And my stomach's sinking, and I keep smiling, but I'm about to cry, and I sound like a frog when I say, "For Chrissake, what is it!" I was angry and ashamed, and I don't think I've ever been so frightened in my life.

It is through experiences like these that girls learn to fear confrontation. The blurring of boundaries and the trust that are part of close friendships between girls give conflict a special force. Conflict and competition are not seen to play a right and proper role in girls' friendships, as they are in boys'.[3] In no other relationship are there such high expectations of harmony: Mothers and children are expected to fight, partners' quarrels can end with romantic apologies, but girlfriends often feel unprepared for fights. Girls repeatedly described conflict as "coming out of the blue," taking them "by surprise," having a force "that takes your breath away."

Such experiences lead thirteen-year-old Silvia to conclude that a best friend is someone with whom one "never argues," for, as Silvia knows, as most girls know, a single argument can tear a valued friendship to shreds. Such experiences have formed nineteen-year-old Nina's admission that she would rather argue with anyone—a mother, a lover, whoever—than with a girlfriend. For Nina, the worry about "bad feelings" or "having a friend hate you" is far worse than anyone else's hostility. Part of the problem is that many girls do feel critical of a friend but suppress this criticism because it's not supposed to emerge in a friendship. When one friend expresses criticism, the other girl may panic: Once a dark side of feeling is opened, when will it stop? The imprint of these panic attacks is lasting. Gloria explains:

> There was this total lack of control. They were the ones calling the shots. My mind was full of their moves: What are

they going to say? How can I protect myself? I keep going over that time in my mind, and I'd give anything not to have sounded so . . . shaky. Even if I could just pretend not to care . . . In some ways I think I did the right thing. I kept telling them we should all talk about it. But what I hate about it all is how I felt—just powerless, just like a worm. I never want to be frightened in that way again. I think I have a harder front now, because I'm not going to let any friends get to me. If they've problems, we can talk, but if they're not going to talk, then I'm just going to stand and shoot as hard as they do.

For Gloria, the fear at the hands of her friends gives her a canny edge. She is not cynical; she is willing to talk things over when others are, but she'll be tough if they attack. She'll assess the situation: Will her own feelings be taken into account? Will she have a chance to put forth her views? Will she get a hearing? Or will others' anger seem more significant and powerful than her own? Her awareness that she can use different procedures for different cases of conflict helps manage her fear.

As difficult as these rites of passage are, girls who fail to develop from them feel something lacking in adulthood. Anthea, thirty-three, seems confident, and has a strong track record as an editor of a national magazine, but describes herself as isolated by her inability to connect to other women—which she attributes to her fear of arguing with them:

There are a lot of things going on in my life now which feel much better if I have the support of women friends. I'm thinking of changing things at work, and it would be good to discuss how I might go about things with a friend. And I've recently ended a love relationship, which was the right thing to do, and I'm pretty okay with it, but it would be nice to have people I could phone in the evenings, or someone to go to a movie with or have dinner—things you don't have to think twice about setting up with a friend. I see how much pleasure other women get from their friends, but I have trouble with that, and what is getting me down, and making me real angry with myself, is the way I know I've always had these problems but just haven't bothered with them. I guess for a long time I thought everyone was the same. After all, who likes to argue? But I hate hearing myself give in whenever a friend gets impatient. There's a woman I really like, but one time we were making plans about dinner and, out of the blue, she said, "Oh, I'm so fed up with all this. Why is everything so complicated with you!" I was speechless. I squeaked, "Sorry," and just left. I didn't know what to say, and I'm usually someone who knows just what to say, but here I felt struck dumb. I've been too hurt to call her, and sometimes I think I miss her, but most of the time when I think of her, I just feel hurt. This keeps happening—I have a friend and then she starts complaining about something I've done, and it all seems to be over.

In Anthea we can see the psychological time lapse in our formative experiences with friends. She doesn't seem able to "grow up"—at least in some areas. A friend's anger still overwhelms her, hitting her "like a tidal wave." Anthea is speechless because she hasn't learned—as Gloria and Ellie are learning—that arguments can mend rifts between friends, can help friends work toward negotiating changes in a friendship, and that such arguments are really maneuvers within a friendship rather than a threat to it. Terrified that a friend's anger signals the end to the relationship, she cannot ask for the complaints to be identified and discussed. Instead, she wonders, "Have I been annoying her all this time? Does she hate me? Does she hate being with me?" With her women friends, "it's like nothing's changed since junior high." Part of her is still stuck at age eleven, the victim of a friend's whimsical anger, which turned upon her and shut her out of a clique.

Flashback responses are extraordinarily common—when we feel right back in seventh or eighth grade, caught again in the machinations of girlfriends. Even as these psychological time warps shock us, and remind us that scars don't go away, we can manage these feelings well enough if we've learned that we have some power in negotiating our friendships. Yet if we don't learn the ropes, if we don't know how to "make up," or adjust the friendship to a close and equal footing, we can suffer a real snag in our development. If that's the case and something goes wrong, we will simply have to run away.

The fear that Gloria and Anthea describe so clearly and power-fully will be shaped, in part, by their experiences within the family. Do we feel in great danger when a parent shouts at us? Have we wor-ried that a physical assault will accompany a verbal one? Do we expect the verbal attacks to last for hours, or even days, or have we learned that they burn out quickly, and end with a hug or laughter? What we learn about anger and making up in our families will affect our tolerance for conflict and our confidence that we can improve the relationship. But these experiences, normally seen as the primary influences on us, are only some of many. When I see how anxious, distraught, and frightened my fourteen-year-old daughter is when any fights occur between her friends, I can, rather than berate myself for ever having shouted at her, for ever having let my anger make her cry, persuade her that friends can get angry and start arguments, but that these arguments are part of the friendship, that they can be used to preserve and improve the friendship, that they need not destroy it. I can listen to her make her case against her friend, let her practice having her say. Like Ellie, she can identify the issues, state her complaints, listen to a friend's complaints, find common ground, and reassert the attachment.

What seems to set some women back is not the number or intensity of these confrontations but how they feel they've handled them. Gloria would like to improve upon her response to that difficult encounter, and she struggles to work out what she might say "next time." Anthea is haunted by fear she couldn't handle in adolescence and doesn't feel she's learned to handle as an adult. Her friendships to this day are tenuous. She values them but cannot maintain them. When anger sounds within them, she tries to ignore it or leaves the relationship: She leaves because she assumes it is already dead, but it is her inability to put that anger to good use that really kills the friendship.

Many women, like Anthea, feel their relationships with other women grow brittle or shallow when they lack the skills to engage in conflicts. Many of us fear arguing with friends because we fail to see that these arguments are part of friendship. Girls, after all, are supposed to be "nice"—and both girls and women must continually struggle to integrate their "niceness" with authenticity when speaking honestly might involve conflict.

Some Things Are Better Left Unsaid

At the same time that girls are learning how to negotiate conflict, they are also learning that not every thought can be spoken, not every vision can be voiced. Some things are better left unsaid—in order, it seems, to preserve harmony. This is the process that Carol Gilligan has eloquently described as learning to take oneself out of relationship for the sake of relationship.[4] Buried conflict and evasion set boundaries to what a girl says—and often to what she acknowledges thinking or feeling. Girls learn to develop double vision, to participate in a friendship with part of themselves while guarding another part—the part that, if spoken truly, might wound their friend and drive her away.

Even as parents and schools try to broaden their sense of what's acceptable in girls, we are raised to the standard of "niceness" and quickly observe that it is the "nice" girls whom everyone seeks out, not the "bitchy" ones, the ones who are oversensitive, easily hurt or angered, or the ones who are ready to do battle over slights and insults. Therefore, a girl learns, she must choose her conflicts carefully and raise her anger in a controlled way, lest she be seen as "difficult." And as her friends follow the same social rules, she has no opportunity to experience ways in which anger can be safely and positively expressed.

Why, it is easy to wonder in any particular case, is a girl or woman having so much trouble speaking out? From the outside, such voicings seem innocent enough. Janet, forty, described in Chapter 3 how she saw Wendy, her best friend in the ninth grade, meet someone else after she'd made an excuse for not being able to spend the day with her. "Why," I asked, "did you not tell your friend you had seen her and were hurt by this? Why, nearly thirty years later, have you still never mentioned it?" Janet explained:

> I couldn't. Because I knew Wendy didn't want me to know what she had done. She wanted me to continue to think I was her best friend and that she'd always be loyal to me. It was important to us both that we think that, and so to tell her I had seen her would harm this image we had of our special friendship. It would have been like a crack in the mirror. Just like some women don't tell their husbands they know about their affairs. Sometimes if you both believe in some-

thing, it makes it real even if it isn't. And the fact is that the other girl didn't become a real threat to our friendship. Wendy went back to our Saturdays together. I don't know what happened. Maybe she felt guilty about it. Maybe she found out she didn't like Sandra as much as she thought she would. Maybe she felt guilty later and didn't want to risk our friendship. I'll never know that. All I know is that our friendship went on, and she never knew that I trusted her any less.

In the dilemmas of what to share and what to keep to oneself, girls wrestle with the enigmas of intimacy that will permeate their relationships forever. Always there will be the choice between harmony and authenticity, always the fear that conflict will rupture an otherwise reasonably satisfactory connection. Anna, forty-five, tells me:

Recently one of my closest friends, Kim, became friendly with Mariella, a woman I can't bear, who is still a good friend of my ex-husband. Mariella has continually gossiped about me over the years, seems to delight in having what she thinks of as "juicy news" about what I am doing. At first, Kim was a bit apologetic about seeing Mariella, but their husbands worked together and so she felt kind of forced into it. Then one day I was talking to her about some financial pressures I felt, and she said, "I heard that's not the whole story." I was stunned, because it was immediately clear that she'd heard a different story from Mariella. And she believed Mariella, not me. After that I didn't feel much like confiding in Kim, or talking to her about the things that are really important to me. Maybe—who knows?—if I had confronted her, she might have backed away from Mariella. But

I didn't want to put her in that position. It's up to her who she wants to be friends with.

Our experiences of friendship often bring us up against one of the most well-known principles of psychology, that it's better to show your feelings and speak your mind than to hold back. A problematic idealization of what a friendship is accompanies a problematic idealization of what we should be, so that we constrain our relationships by keeping them safe and keeping silent. In adolescence, girls learn to balance the tension between speaking to a problem and holding their tongue. "I really wish Shelley would call me more often, like every night, like some people's best friends do," fourteen-year-old Jasmine says, "but I'm afraid she'll think I'm clingy and I wouldn't want her to think that." How reminiscent this is of the later struggles girls will have with boyfriends, from whom they may want more but fear driving away. It mirrors the mother's struggle with when to complain about a child's behavior and when to hope it will simply change with time. Relationships always involve a thin line between painfully holding in what distresses us and taking a risk that we may irritate the other so much that they withdraw from us. "Kate annoys me when she is so aggressive," sixteen-year-old Melinda says, "but I can't think of a way to tell her without hurting her feelings. She wants me to love her just as she is."

Too often, pressure to feel what a friend wants us to feel ("She wants me to love her just as she is") takes shape in our adult lives. A few hours after seeing Melinda, I am having supper with a close friend, Lee, fifty, who has made an exhilarating start in a second career, switching from teaching to writing, but she is plagued by bouts of depression. She has mentioned this before and I nod, letting her know that I, too, know what depression is, but I also want more. "What's your depression like?" I ask. "What's its focus?" She describes her obsessive thoughts during these depressions:

In the middle of the night, I'll remember what I said to a friend and worry that I've been tactless. Can you imagine? I'm talking about things I said thirty-five years ago to a girl in boarding school, or to someone who asked me to write her a reference, when I was new and raw myself. But I hear this accusation shouting into the night: "You haven't been a good friend. You've been mean. You shouldn't have said that." I berate myself about how unkind I've been, and I feel totally worthless.

If we keep silent, then we don't learn how to voice our feelings and reactions to others. If we speak out, forgoing the fantasy of the perfect friendship and the perfect friend, then our outspokenness may haunt us in our midnights, long past adolescence. Only if we can shape our friendships to a realistic cut will our own feelings fit comfortably. And our friends need this, too: As Lee speaks, I think how often her efforts to be tactful have made me feel uneasy and distant with her. She'd be a much better friend, I tell her, if she spoke out more—not less. And she teasingly demands, "When did you last make a tactless remark to me?" And I take her point: I'm far more likely to gloss over difficulty between us than complain out loud. We all want a friend to be forthright, and yet we don't always overcome our own fears of speaking out.

Buried Conflict

At times, though, there may be an important rift in a friendship that cannot easily be given voice. Each friend is left with confusion, guilt, and anger. Amy and Rebecca had been best friends since elementary school, but in eleventh grade, when Amy moved to a new house in a middle-class neighborhood, things started to feel strained for both of them. But they never spoke about the increasing distance between them, hoping it would just go away. Rebecca seemed unresponsive and cold to Amy. One day Amy heard from another classmate that Rebecca had written a story for an English assignment which she called "The Fake Girl," and the main character bore a striking resemblance to Amy. The next day, Amy attempted to talk to Rebecca about it, but Rebecca just shrugged it off. They never spoke to each other again. When we talked to Rebecca about this, she was a sophomore in college, but she still felt troubled by what had happened. She told us:

> The thing is that something just didn't feel right anymore with Amy. Maybe it was that her life had changed after she moved. She seemed like a different person, someone I didn't know and didn't really like—just phony somehow. But how can you talk about that with someone? How can you explain something you don't understand yourself?

Often girls feel troubled in a friendship but have a hard time articulating just what is creating the distress. Primed not to speak their anger, but knowing it exists—both in themselves and in their friends—they watch others' behavior with a close-up lens: If she's not especially warm, does that mean she's cold? If she's not effusive, does that mean she's disappointed? Accustomed to indirect expression of negative feelings, they work hard to read between the lines. They may be vaguely aware of changes in one or the other that are too subtle to identify clearly. They may take a friend's lack of understanding of them as lack of love. "I didn't want to have to tell Allison she hurt my feelings," Tamara said. "I wanted her to know it by herself. She knew me well enough to know how I felt." Similarly, Anna wanted Kim to make the first move in rebuilding their friendship and, when she didn't, was willing to allow the friendship to grow distant and empty. As Rebecca reflects:

> You can't break up with a friend like you break up with a
> boyfriend. With a boyfriend, you can say, "I don't want to go
> out with you anymore." But with a girlfriend, you have to
> still be nice to her face. Maybe you're mean to her behind
> her back so she'll want to go away, or you act sort of distant,
> but eventually the friendship just ends without there being
> an actual ending. You just wake up one day and realize you're
> not friends anymore.

Most of the women we spoke to described the endings of their
friendships as being fade-outs rather than explosions.[5] Thinking
back, many thought there might have been buried conflicts, but it
was striking how many were unsure. A friendship ends and neither
friend may know just why. The failure to understand leaves a shadow
of self-doubt: What went wrong? Where did I fail? The fade-outs
may be triggered when conflict is covered up. Rather than admit and
integrate feelings of anger or competitiveness into the relationship,
the friends may kill the friendship. "If I'm angry with her, then she
can't be a friend," is the misguided assumption that we can be free of
when we understand the reality behind the ideal of friendship.

Silence and Depression

How can we protect friendships—which are supposed to be fun—
from the range of sorrows or disappointments or fears that dampen
our spirits? How can we be close to a friend while some of our feelings are too confused or painful to speak about? By not talking, we
may be trying to protect the friendship, or ourselves, but by not talking, by "forgetting it," we risk both the friendship and its benefits to
our self-understanding.

A refusal to talk does not always arise from the dynamics between
two friends; it can also arise from feelings that are too powerful to be

brought to another person. As they suffer the impact of a family crisis, teenage girls often refuse to discuss it with their friends, feeling a combination of shame, defeat, and confusion. Denise, sixteen, whose older sister was recently injured in a car accident, explains:

> People come rushing up to me—"How's your sister?"—and at first I was "God, I can't talk about this!" But now, I just give a few facts. This and this is okay, this not so good. And then I walk away. These guys aren't my friends. They're just curious.

Talking about her sister's accident is unacceptable, especially as Denise feels her sister's injuries are the subject of curiosity rather than genuine concern. People ask about her sister because—she believes—they take a gruesome interest in events, not because they really care. So she learns to relay the facts while hiding her feelings. The best way to hide her feelings is to freeze them, so that she barely feels them, too. Her friend Toshie picks up on this silence and complains that it threatens their friendship:

> She hasn't talked to me—not really talked—since her sister's accident. I really wanted to help her. The first time I saw her—afterwards—I wanted to know how she was, and all I got was "I'm fine. Why shouldn't I be fine?" And her eyes went . . . real wide, straight at me, nothing to hide, nothing to say. If she doesn't want to talk, what can I do? I still see her, but how can we be friends if she doesn't want to talk?

Talk is the currency of friendship. The route to sympathy, understanding and connection is through talk. As this sixteen-year-old sees her friend unwilling to talk, she feels helpless. Feeling helpless, she also feels rejected: "How can we be friends if she doesn't want to talk?" For Denise, putting on a brave face is a prerequisite of survival. But in Toshie's view, Denise shouldn't need such defenses with a friend. With a friend, you're supposed to let the barriers down. And when we can't let them down with a friend, we can't let them down with ourselves, either.

Edie, seventeen, knows her best friend, Olivia, has had a rough time over a breakup with her boyfriend. Olivia is "in trouble," Edie thinks, but won't talk to her:

> We used to talk every night. It was: Saul said something, so he still likes her, or Saul did something, so he doesn't. With this final breakup, though, she's turned mute. I asked her today why she didn't ring me last night, but what I really meant was "Why didn't you phone me last night or the night before or the night before that?" And you know what she said? She said, "There wasn't anything to tell you." Nothing to tell me! What an awful thing to say to a friend.

Edie notes with dismay that Olivia's new notion of what their conversations are about betrays their friendship. In the past, their conversations did not depend on having something to tell each other. They talked to explore their feelings, or other people's feelings. The information exchanged was not headline news, but the minute details of daily occurrences in their lives. Even the lives of television characters would provide a focus of friend interest:

> Sometimes we'd watch shows together. Once there was this special episode of *Ricki Lake* about interfering mothers who complained about their kids' friends, and we just hung on the phone the whole time and were like "Can you believe

that!" And we talked about what our moms would say, and whether they were worse or better than the mothers on the show.

Through conversations Edie could support, comfort, and distract Olivia from her love troubles. Without such conversations, Edie can make no sense of the structure of their friendship. "Talking is what we do," Edie reflects. "I don't know what we have if we don't talk."

When I speak to Olivia, and ask her how important friends are to her, the answer she gives explains her reticence with Edie: "My friends are annoying me right now, to tell the truth. They want to know how I'm feeling, and I don't want to talk about how I'm feeling. I feel like shit and I always feel the same, and I don't want to talk about it."

Closing the door on girl talk is a symptom of depression—a sign that a girl believes she is beyond help. As a girl withdraws because she's depressed, she has fewer routes out of depression—fewer chances to be comforted by a friend's understanding, fewer chances to explore her own feelings through "talking cures," and fewer chances to feel that her emotional dishabille is acceptable, that she doesn't have to hide it, at least from a friend.

Depression suppresses the very conversations that could lift us from it. Olivia's words echo in my mind: "I feel like shit and I always feel the same, and I don't want to talk about it." This seems the antithesis of what we may think of as typical of unhappy girls and women: They rush for the fridge and then they rush for the phone. As they weep into the Häagen-Dazs carton, they blurt out their sorrows to a friend, tears and melted ice cream dropping into the receiver. But perhaps that is true only of the good unhappy times. As I hear Olivia and Denise speak about their sense of the pointlessness of conversation, I think of my own battle with depression, and the toll it so often takes on my friendships. How can I phone a friend when I am so down that I've lost my sense of humor? Why should I bother meeting a friend when the news items of her life and those of people we know—the gossip that will keep the conversation rolling—will only drive me further into depression as I think, "She's happier than I am" and "She's doing better than I am" and that quintessential depressed thought, "Everyone else I know is something and I'm nothing"? I can keep my brave face on for my students and colleagues, but I avoid my friends.

This selective avoidance worsens as we mature into women and see our friends gaining in self-control and practicing a positive outlook on life. The sorrows we as women might like to pour out to our friends seem a throwback to adolescent relationships in which we could more easily complain and cry to our girlfriends. As women, our shame in unhappiness may increase. We should, we think, be independent; we should be able to "cope"; we should be striding forward. Then we see that our own blues can damage our image at work, or cloud our children's happiness, or infect a partner's spirits, so we learn to hide them. Our friends are busy: Why dump on them? They don't, we reason, want to hear us moan. The difference between what we feel and what we seem grows greater, and the greater this difference, the more miserable we feel.

When Froma, thirty-two, comes into therapy, she explains that she may be depressed, but she is not sure. I ask her whether she has a close friend. She says yes—then hesitates:

> I see one of my close friends several times a week, but I can't settle down to talk. I'm always distracted and just rush off. When we do talk, it's superficial stuff. She says, "You're avoiding me." But what can I tell her? When I have a specific problem, I can discuss it with her. When I'm worried about

something, or angry with someone, I can talk to her. But when I'm just down in the dumps, no conversation will do anything for me.

Depression is disturbingly common in girls and women, and often it seems to stem from an inability to bring our own wishes and needs into the series of interactions that shape our relationships.[6] It can arise from putting others' needs first, or being dominated by others' expectations. When women, for example, arrange their lives to accommodate the needs of their partner and children, and put their own on the "back burner," they may sink into depression without knowing why. When girls try to groom themselves into the best model image, or enact the nice, friendly, happy personality they think they need for others to like them, depression may result as they feel cut off from who they really are. As our spirits sink, we barely know what we ourselves feel. Olivia believes her awful feelings involve "nothing to tell her friend." She herself is distanced from her feelings. She feels miserable, but unable to speak about them. Froma is so distanced from her feelings that she isn't even sure whether she is depressed. Our inability to talk to a friend is emblematic of our inability to know—or bear—our own feelings.

One of the most frightening things about being unable to engage with friends because we are depressed is that such self-distancing increases depression. Our silence alienates us from others. Klara, at nineteen, is aware of her depression and how it paralyzes her ability to talk to friends, but she cannot overcome it:

I see what's happening, but I can't stop it. Maria comes up to me and I think of things I could ask her. How are you? How's your boyfriend? What happened at the party last night? Are you going to the movies this weekend? But they seem so stupid, not worth asking, but then she complains I never talk anymore. I want to talk about people who have died. I want to talk about what it would be like to die. I want to talk about how you commit suicide—like is there a painless way? Is there? But I get "Oh, you're so gruesome!" or "What an attitude!" So what's the point, anyway? I can see she's giving up on me, and I think, "You should do something about this." But I can't make the effort somehow.

Klara can think of things to say, but feels whatever she says will lack conviction or interest, and involve too much (useless) effort. Her real thoughts seem unacceptable, so conversation freezes over. She carefully registers a discrepancy between her friends' beliefs that she can tell them everything, that she can express her feelings, and the disapproval meted out to her "negative thoughts" or her "defeatist attitude."

Alongside the ideal of being able to tell a friend "everything" is a range of methods for flagging a topic as taboo. There are, of course, the direct protests about what's said, such as Klara expects to hear: "How can you say that!" or "What an attitude!" And though girlfriend talk often provides a wonderful arena in which normally unacceptable speech is greeted with laughter and pleasure ("Oh, you are wicked! I don't believe you said that. Say it again!"), rules of talk etiquette can still apply. Some things we say are ignored, or we get a scolding: "Stop thinking that way" or "Don't say that."[7] Or a friend minimizes our feelings. As Edie reflects, "Sometimes I get really hurt by something a friend does or says, and then when I try to explain why I'm hurt, I get 'That's nothing. You shouldn't be hurt by that.' How can it be nothing if I'm hurt?" When we're feeling strong, we can shrug off such lessons: "So she doesn't want to listen," we think, or "All right, I won't say such things to her," and then we move on. When we're feeling down, though, these reactions can make us feel even worse about what we feel and think.

Of course, the depressed girl soon learns that, in part, what she fears is true. If she is too depressed too much of the time, people will pull away from her. Ariel, seventeen, knowing that her friend Beth has been down lately, tries to get her to go with her to the class party that night.

"I'm really not in the mood," says Beth.

"Aw, come on," Ariel responds, "you never go out anymore. Sitting around feeling sorry for yourself isn't good for you. Come to the party. Have some fun. Maybe you'll start to feel better."

"Ari, I'd really like it if you'd just come over here and spend the evening with me. We could play some games, watch some TV. That would be fun for me."

But Ariel wants to go to the party. For a moment, she feels torn: Maybe Beth is asking for her help, but she's spent such evenings with Beth before—feeling bored, feeling she was missing "life." Ariel is in a tough place. She wants to "be there" for Beth, but she doesn't want to sacrifice her own needs in order to have a larger social life.

"Please come out with me, Beth," she pleads. But Beth says no, then wishes her a good time and gently hangs up the phone. The next morning, Ariel thinks about calling Beth to tell her about the party, but she feels that Beth won't really be interested in the goings-on, and so she calls her friend Ava instead. It will not take long for Beth, caught by her sadness and withdrawal, to feel herself bereft of Ariel as well.

Too Complicated to Talk About

Sometimes we refuse to talk to a friend because things are just too complicated and too painful for words. Disguising our bad feelings is a "skill" we may learn as children. "Cheer up" or "Can't you smile?" or "Can't you be more positive?" we hear, and so we learn that it is better to present ourselves to the world as happy. This "skill" plagues us. We learn to value being "cheerful," even with our friends, and therefore leave out of friendship's account the messy reckoning of our difficult feelings. The illness of Gail's father so confuses the sixteen-year-old that she glosses it over with a bright smile:

> I can talk about school and other girls and their boyfriends and anything under the sun, it seems, but when they ask about my mom and dad—it's like the whole conversation's changed and I don't know my way around, and I'll say something like "That's none of your business," but I'm so confused that it'll take me a week before I think, "God, I really blew it with her. Maybe I should apologize." But how can I apologize and explain that there are certain things I just can't talk about? You know people say talking helps, but when someone backs me into a corner and says, "How's your dad now?" and if I tell them the truth, I feel like something's been taken away from me.

With something so painful, Gail feels that others' interest is an intrusion on her privacy. Like Denise, when asked about her sister's injuries, Gail is skeptical about people's motives. Their "wanting to talk about it" does nothing for her, unless their interest is mixed with an anxiety and compassion that register her own.

Whether or not we can share our sufferings with a friend may be crucial to whether we can survive our unhappiness. In talking to a friend, we may gain the assurance that our "bad" feelings won't destroy the people close to us, that these feelings are acceptable, that they can be understood by someone else, and that someone else wants to help us weather them. The girl who most needs support and doesn't get it from a friend drifts further and further away from the relationships she needs—unless she finds another depressed girl. And this alliance between two depressed girls offers a dangerous comfort. As they support each other's bleak outlook, brooding upon death together, goaded by each other, neither knows just how serious she herself, or her friend, is. Sometimes one girl can help pull them both out of depression; at other times, the depression becomes the core of the friendship and neither girl can feel better or be better without risking losing the relationship.

How can we wrest a friend from this vicious cycle? How can we spot trouble or help our daughters when they seem in danger? We can keep talking to them, refuse to give up on them, stop the infection of silence from spreading. As we hear the gloominess we would like to swat (with responses such as "What an awful thing to say!" or "What an attitude!" or "Can't you look on the bright side for once?"), we can instead register their feelings and ask for more communication, rather than less. When a friend or a daughter says, "Forget it—I don't want to talk about it," then we know that she must remember, not forget, and talk till she feels whole.

Chapter Eight

"IF ONLY I COULD BE LIKE HER"

Cassandra, nineteen, tells us:

The first time I saw Chloe, she was sitting cross-legged on the floor of the dance studio. She was in my dance performance class, and I almost immediately decided I didn't like her. She was full of passion, wildly tearing around the dance floor, basking in the music. She was beautiful and strong and unafraid, throwing herself into her art with such imagination and energy. I was intimidated, envious, totally in love with her and hating her all at once. I was a college student feeling like I was in seventh grade again. Because I was afraid of her, I decided that she certainly must be conceited and snobby, someone I could never be friends with. But to my amazement, she not only became my friend, but she became one of my very closest friends. Now her passion inspires me rather than intimidates me. She takes me seriously, seems excited about what I have to say. In some ways, I couldn't believe that such an amazing woman could want to be my friend. She makes me feel so full of life. And we are different. We each need a lot of room to be alone, completely our-selves. But the fact that someone I adore and admire so much loves and admires me back—as I am—makes me feel like somehow I must be as amazing to her as she is to me. I don't envy her now, so I don't have to be afraid.

Admiration—and its close cousin, envy—is often what draws us to a potential friend. Often a girl "falls in love" with a friend—first admiring her from a distance, perhaps imitating her in manner or dress, and then managing to draw close to her as a friend. Although she may not be fully aware of it, in some part of her mind, the girl (or woman) may hope that closeness with her friend will enable her to become like her.

Many girls begin to idealize a friend and their love for her, just as they will later idealize a romantic partner and their romantic feelings. Joshri and Ellen, both nine, walk from school arm in arm. Ellen goes several blocks out of her way to walk Joshri home. Ellen loves Joshri's white teeth: "I keep hoping I'll make her smile, so I can see them." Joshri thinks Ellen's fingers, long and thin, are "interesting." "You keep doing that!" Ellen remarks as Joshri raises their clasped hands in front of her so she can see those fingers. They both laugh. Their mutual admiration is both playful and passionate.

As girls move into adolescence, these close, admiring friendships become survival networks. Leslie and Clare, both fifteen, work hard to look alike—their hair is cut the same and they wear similar clothes, which they exchange as tokens of their connection. As a team, they will never feel wrongly dressed or alone. They are special—not odd. Their admiration of each other is so strong that they feel sorry for—not scared of—the girls who don't appreciate them. But this intense admiration can lose its balance, and its fun.

When one girl idealizes another and strives to be like her, no amount of parental coercion can change her direction. This is sometimes labeled "peer pressure," but it is more like love. Kitty, age fourteen, was adoring of Tabitha. Something about her style, her manner, seemed to embody everything Kitty thought wonderful. When she discovered that Tabitha loved the band Metallica, Kitty began buying all their albums. When she heard Tabitha playing the electric guitar, she begged her parents relentlessly to arrange guitar lessons for her as well.

Admiring and imitating a girlfriend can lead a girl to expand and stretch herself, to study hard to be "smart" like Jill, to play lacrosse like Martha, to work at the soup kitchen like Hillary. Girls grow through such relationships, which serve to expand their horizons beyond the activities their families ordinarily pursue or the interests that are valued by their parents. Friendships provide the arena for new possibility, to try things that seemed out of reach—or, at least, out of a girl's usual field of vision.[1] Of course, this process can work in less positive directions as well. One girl starts dieting and her friend, admiring her thin body, follows after. Or a girl may admire the tough, rebellious girl who leads her into drugs and alcohol.

Longing to be like a friend, many girls will make themselves over, change their habits of speech, of dress, of response to others. There is a special joy in feeling like a twin with a friend. "Diana and I work out each night what we're going to wear to school tomorrow," thirteen-year-old Priscilla confides in us. "Then I see her the next day and she looks fabulous and I realize that I'm dressed like her, so I must look good, too. I love it when I feel like I look at her and it's like looking in a mirror."

Here, the issue is identification rather than acceptance, and identification is a much more powerful force. We need to feel that other people think we're okay, but, even more, we need to have some sense of who we are. But as girls grow more and reach their last years of high school, the need to differentiate themselves from their friends grows stronger. Just as they no longer wish to be "just like" their mothers as they did as very young girls, they no longer wish to be "just like" their best friends. Much of girl talk in late adolescence begins to revolve around noticing differences, still admiring qualities in each other, but accepting that each is a unique person who will have some wonderful attributes, but neither will have them all.

Sometimes this differentiation work is a deliberate attempt to mark boundaries. Christine and Lorin, both high-school seniors, had been best friends since childhood. They had moved apart, had other friends, but always found each other again. They were the two academic leaders in their large high-school class, but Lorin was also an outstanding athlete and musician. In junior high, Christine tried to excel at basketball and in music, but just didn't have the drive or skill that seemed to come so easily to Lorin. In ninth grade, Christine recounts, she decided she really didn't want to be like Lorin anyway and began a period of being the opposite of her. She even stopped studying, began letting her grades fall, and enjoyed defiantly showing Lorin her report card with all C's. Lorin remembers being confused by this. "I just don't understand you anymore," she said to her friend. Christine's mother was, of course, equally perplexed, took her to the school counselor, worried whether Christine was showing signs of disturbance, if she was unhappy at home. Neither parent nor counselor could see that the locus for understanding Christine's change was in friendship.

Christine's passionate interest in writing led her back to academic involvement in tenth grade, though she maintained her difference from Lorin by proclaiming that she studied out of interest in the material, not to "get the grades," implying, out of Lorin's hearing, that that was what Lorin was doing. By their senior year of high school, although Christine and Lorin were still best friends, Christine refused to apply to any college that Lorin was applying to. "I just need to be away from her," she explained. Now the qualities in Lorin that Christine had once so admired seemed less appealing. "She's a control freak," Christine said. "She's killing herself because she has to competition

be the best in everything. I don't care about competing anymore. I want to have time just to hang out with my friends, to enjoy life."

And from Lorin: "When we were little, Christine always did so much better than me—I always wanted to be like her. Then one day she just sort of gave up. If that's what she wants to do, that's okay. I still think she's really smart. We're just different, that's all." As she speaks, she casts a challenge not to probe further: She wants to focus on her difference, and not feel diminished.

Feminine Like Her

commodities

Girls look to one another, rather than to adult women, for models of ideal femininity. They daydream about the clothes they see in magazines, but they buy clothes like the ones the "popular girls" wear. They resolve their conflicts about sexuality by giving themselves permission to try what their friends have already done. They compare notes, check to see if they are feeling what other girls feel about their bodies, about boys, about sex. Sometimes there's a kind of competition: "I want to know as much as she does." And some girls make up stories of romantic adventures, partly to appear to keep up with their friends, and partly to test the plausibility of their fantasies.

Codes of acceptable femininity are established anew in each generation, and the power of friends to shape values is enormous. Why have we persisted so long in believing that girls learn femininity from identifying with their mothers? This belief burdens mothers with unnecessary guilt when a daughter grows dissatisfied with herself for not being pretty or thin or sexy like a friend is. Judy, a forty-year-old social worker and staunch feminist, felt helpless (and outraged) when her fifteen-year-old daughter began demanding slinky dresses and a pink bedroom because of her adoration of a friend who was feminine in a traditional way. Tamara, by contrast, at age sixteen, identified herself with strongly androgynous girls and refused ever to wear a dress. She and her friends were developing a code that resisted what they considered to play into "lookism."

Friends can pull a girl toward conventional femininity, but friends can also free a girl from conventional expectations and constraints. What is called "peer pressure" when parents don't like it is indeed an unstoppable force, but it is a force for great good as well as harm. Instead of countering head-on the influence of friends on her daughter, Judy could help her focus on other aspects of femininity within her daughter's culture: Parents can never control a daughter's response to each possible role model, but they can help widen a young girl's vision. There are—especially today—many ways to be feminine, and girls look around themselves for someone to emulate.

Beyond how one should look, girls test the waters of sexuality by tracking friends' experience. Katrina, at age twenty, felt desperate to lose her virginity when she found that she was the only one in her dorm suite at college who had not yet had sex. "I'm behind everyone else," she complained. "What's wrong with me?" She lived in fear that the other girls would find out and think her "a nerd or a baby."

The increasing efforts mothers are making to speak openly to their daughters about their sexuality is to be lauded, but there are limits to maternal influence. While it is extremely important that mothers gain skills at imparting useful, accurate, and positive information (thereby expressing comfort with adult sexuality), mothers must accept that girls will always turn to their friends for emotional and attitudinal information. It is with people at more or less the same stage of discovery, or at the same stage of comfort (or discomfort) with sex, that girls learn about the next small steps.

Identification with other girls and women is a powerful pull—"Oh, so that's how it is for you." Janet, at fifty, told about a moment that was an epiphany in her life:

I was twenty-five and had been married for four years. One day I was having lunch with my close friend Autumn, who was single and kind of a free spirit. She was telling me about being on vacation with her latest boyfriend, and she was describing how they were visiting some castle in France and she said, ". . . and we kept looking at each other, and then, you know, it became imperative and so we . . ." What they did doesn't matter so much. What got me was the "you know" because I realized I didn't know. I had never experienced sex as imperative. I had only had sex with the man I married, and it was kind of the thing we did on Saturday nights. I realized then that I had never known passion or intense desire, that I had married a man who was like a brother to me, and I wanted a taste of the experience Autumn had. In some strange way, I think that was the beginning of my path toward divorce. I thank Autumn for that.

The Specter of Envy

There is a thin line between admiration ("I think she's wonderful") and envy ("I want to be like her, but I'm not"). As we admire someone, we compare ourselves to her—and that comparison can hurt. Fourteen-year-old MaryBeth speaks of an admiration for Polly that cuts into her like a knife:

> She's so pretty, so together. When she walks into the school, everyone feels different. You know, clothes look different on her. And she always has a funny or clever thing to say. She just bubbles or something. And whatever she wants, she gets it. Who could say no to her? I try to talk to her every day,

just to find out what she's doing. Even if it makes me ache, I want to know.

MaryBeth creates a friendship with Polly to feed her fascination, but also to keep track of her, and to learn from her. The admired girl represents a code. "What makes her special?" or "What makes her different?" is the puzzle that MaryBeth wants to crack. As MaryBeth's classmate Rachel reflects, "I try to separate out what it is that makes her so special. Sometimes I get my thoughts together. She has this and that going for her, but I matter, too. Because, when you envy someone, it's as though there's nothing to you. So I try to sort things out, because envy—it really obliterates you." Mothers may protest against this "obliteration" in a daughter. Sheila, Rachel's mother, says:

> I'd think she was a natural mimic if I didn't know she was utterly serious. Now she has a fifteen-year-old friend—a year older than her—who wants to be a model, and there she is, wanting to be a model, too, and starting to dress and walk just like this other girl. But a few months back she was tuned into Jasmin. I swear, she began to look Indian. She talked like her and moved like her, and wanted me to cook all the things Jasmin ate.

But as Rachel mimics a friend in fine details of dress, food, speech, or career goals, she feels defeated by her inability to *be* someone else. Friendship does not fulfill her, it empties her.

Mothers frequently speak of the way a daughter's confidence can be destroyed by her admiration of other girls, whether these girls are friends or just girls her daughter works hard to befriend. MaryBeth's mother notes that her daughter seems "blasted by her belief that Polly has everything that's worth having—and there's nothing really special about *her*." The ideals embodied by an admired girl, against which a teenage girl measures herself, often seem strange or shallow to a mother: "She thinks Polly is wonderful because she has wide-set eyes—oh, yes, and they're gray. *Gray.* You should hear MaryBeth utter that word. That seems to add some essential something." As we talk to Rachel, however, we hear her efforts to hold on to her own self, even as she is wracked by her idealization and her envy: "Sometimes I just wish I could just be Polly, but then I realize she's not really perfect, but still I try to be like her in some ways." If Rachel's mother focused on this perspective, she would be in a better position to support her daughter's efforts. Rachel's mother means to protect her by mocking her daughter's friend fascination, but this mockery makes Rachel conclude, "She just doesn't understand."

When we asked teenage girls for a list of feelings they commonly have about their friends, "envy" was on every list. Yet girl culture condemns envy: "She just says that because she's envious," "Don't pay any attention to her—she's just jealous." Their own envy is shameful, and dangerous as well, for it leads others to condemn them. How can they make it go away? Lisa, sixteen, explains how she battles with the questions that envy raises for her:

> I wish I could see Yvonne the way other girls do—I mean girls who don't envy her like I do. She's really pretty. I used to look at her face and think, "Maybe if you really look at her, you'll see she's not pretty." But that doesn't work. She's pretty. And lots of pretty girls are smart, and it doesn't eat at me like it does with her. 'Cause it goes through me, like I'm—blah.

Hari, also sixteen, faces uncertainties about her grades and whether she will be able to go to the college her parents have set their sights on for her. She, too, experiences envy as a crushing blow:

My math teacher met me in the hall and goes, "I have some good news I want to share with you. Your classmate Deborah scored 1600 on her SATs. We're putting her through for National Scholar. Isn't that great?" Well, I hope I said something like "Great! Great!" but it was as though she punched me. And once you think someone knows how you feel, it's harder to pretend you feel something else. I made this cockeyed smile. I felt like crying. I mean, what a shit to want to scream when your friend does so well. But it was awful. I hurt for days, and everyone's talking about it as though it's good news for everyone and I should be so pleased.

The suffering incurred by envy is increased by guilt ("What a shit to want to scream when your friend does so well"), and questions about why she feels this way, and what it means about her, spin through Hari's mind. It's awful to envy a friend, not only because girls think they shouldn't, but also because it disrupts their relationships with others and their own sense of self. As Lisa explains:

It makes me feel like I'm nothing in the world. When someone does real well, or when Char got to be editor [of the school paper], I felt people were attacking me, hammering me into the ground. I couldn't talk to anyone on the paper for a while. Every time they looked at me, I thought they were thinking, "Not editorial standard."

Though we can express envy in a joking way—"You look great! I hate you!"—we aren't supposed to feel unsettled by admiration. We're supposed to *want* our friends to be successful and beautiful. When we don't, we feel ashamed and worthless, and wonder what our affection for our friends is really worth after all.

Although it is painful to experience and to watch, slogging

through the seas of envy mixed with admiration and admiration mixed with envy is a necessary process for girls to come to know who they are and what's possible for them. Other girls seem to be ideal, to be perfect, but with time, most girls discover that no one is really perfect. And no one can learn that unless they venerate a few idols along the way. "I always thought Anita was perfect, had everything anyone could want," Nikki, a sophomore in college, related. "I tried so hard to be like her and also spent so much time feeling terrible envy because everyone celebrated her, chose her. She was the homecoming queen, the class president, everything. Then one day I realized she was anorexic. She had to be hospitalized. I guess she has problems just like everyone else."

The fantasy of "the perfect girl," however, never completely goes away. She is usually someone who is like us in many ways, someone we feel we might be like if only we had a little more style, or brains, or confidence. We are more likely to envy a girl with whom we compete for our friends' or teachers' or neighbors' admiration than we are to envy someone outside our circle. Mara, forty-five, herself a psychologist, half laughs at herself as she reflects:

> I know that no one has it all figured out. I know that no one is completely confident. Yet there is a certain kind of woman who makes me wonder whether she isn't actually the one who's managed to get it all together. Such women are just like the girls who intimidated me in high school. They are superbly put together clotheswise, have the right kind of smile and the right kind of easy small talk. Charm, I guess. I know it's superficial, but they are like magnets. Everyone is drawn to them. And they still make me feel clumsy and awkward and a bit foolish. My friends aren't like this, but every once in a while I run into such people, like if I'm invited to speak at a charity function. And I know they are

probably intimidated by me—after all, I'm the "doctor" and the "expert"—but I'm just feeling like I did in tenth grade, wishing I could be so absolutely, perfectly got up.

Envy can, however, have positive effects as well on women. It can turn into admiration and open up a sense of possibility for oneself. Camilla, thirty-eight, tells us:

> I always envied my friend Pat the interesting life she seemed to be having. I'd just go to work, come home and take care of my family—and listen to Pat relate her adventures going interesting places and meeting interesting people. It was fun to listen to her, but I was jealous, too. My own life seemed so drab by comparison. Then one day I saw an ad for an "adventure vacation" which was really not very expensive, and I thought, "Why not try this instead of just going to the beach as usual this summer?" It took some work to persuade my family to try it, but we did and had a wonderful time, and now I've been taking scuba diving lessons at the Y and I feel I owe all this to Pat. If I hadn't envied her, I wouldn't have changed.

Many women whom we interviewed about their lives credit their friends with leading them into new regions of experience, whether career paths, relationships, interests, or worldviews. Feeling somewhat lost after disappointments in her marriage and her career, Nellie met Kathleen at her new job. "I've never admired a woman so much," she said. "She was very active, positive, and confident, and I dared to do things with her that I was afraid to do alone, both at work and outside. I helped her with her ill husband and she gave me courage." Idealizations, although they always tarnish, are nevertheless signs that there may be more to strive for; envy, although painful to experience, is a sign that we wish to expand ourselves—and the tension between idealization and envy is often a driving force in girls' and women's growth.

I Probably *Should* Want to Be Like Her

Often girls look at their friends and feel inspired: "I could be like that!" Or they learn from a friend's determination and skill. But we also look to our friends and wonder, "Should I want to be like that?" when we know we're not, and don't really want to be.

This was, in part, Christine's struggle with Lorin during her senior year in high school. Christine saw that others admired Lorin, with her bright smile, easy confidence, and power to please by working for good grades. The tension between her envy of such approval and her desire to forge her own personality and goals made her resist and demean her friend. As girls discover their differences from one another, they can be nagged by uncertainty: Mustn't one way be better than another? It's a hard-won emotional lesson that different is just that, *different*—but equally legitimate, equally valuable.

As a very young woman on a train journey going to college interviews, I listen to my friend Caroline's description of her ambitions: She is going to study medicine, become a cardiac surgeon. She tells me how she will combine her goals, and what changes she will effect in public health. I note how different we are, and how strange it is that I have felt close to her without realizing the precise quality and detail of her determination. My own far-more-diffuse goals start weighing my spirits down. I see we're different, but this difference fuels self-doubt. Maybe I should be what she is?

For modern women, adolescence and early adulthood present a series of questions and contradictions. We may have been socialized to please others—or, at least, to care about their approval and avoid their disapproval—and even to care for them when they are ill or sad or lonely. But we are also expected to be independent and ambitious. We now expect to work outside the home, but we also know we may have a special responsibility to our families. The contradictions within social expectations, and the echoes of past constraints, increase the inevitable strains of growing up. And when we are anxious about what we should be, a friend's security about who she is and who she will become can raise our anxiety.

Lucy, seventeen, describes how her confusion about what to aim for links in to her reactions to her friends:

> I've always gone around with Olga and Marta. We see each other most days, and we talk every day. And I'll know about Marta even if I just talk to Olga, because Olga will tell me what Marta's been doing. And it'll be the same with me: Whatever I'm doing—like if I had a fight with Mom, or I'm wearing my sister's sweater, or I got a detention—that'll be what they talk about. But ever since this fall, when we've started to think about college applications and stuff, I feel like I'm no longer with them. They're so excited about leaving home, and so full of doing well. They have everything all sorted out—and that's great. My sister thinks I'm jealous. And it sounds like that, but it's so complicated. I'm not a competitive person. And it's not that I want to compete with them. I know I can't compete with them. They've always been smarter than me. At least, looking back, I see that's true, but before it was never something we thought about.
>
> And I'm worried about leaving home. I'm worried about leaving my mom, 'cause my sister's leaving, too, and getting married. And I tried talking to Olga and Marta. Just this morning, at our lockers, I said, "Are you really all that pleased to be leaving?" and they looked at me like— Well, Marta's mouth was wide open, and Olga just laughed, so I

didn't say anything else. Nothing's more complicated than what I feel about them, and it makes me so confused about myself.

As Lucy confronts what is a serious problem for many young women, she seeks support from her friends: Through them, she might find allies against the social norms that confuse her. And yet not finding this support, she silences herself rather than leave herself open to ridicule or misunderstanding. Unable to express her desire to remain home and close to her mother, she feels that issues of independence come between her and her friends. But what seems to her sister like common jealousy is actually a reaction to self-doubt in the face of mixed social messages. Her friends are following new values, while Lucy feels the pull of the (devalued) traditional female values.

Idealization breeds in self-doubt. Lucy sees her friends as having "everything sorted out" because her own future seems tentative, and bound by others' needs. As she idealizes others who are so different from her, she loses respect for herself and her own values. But these social dilemmas are not played out in abstractions; instead, they are enacted in the very concrete arena among girlfriends as they together envision their lives and measure themselves against one another.

As grown women, we find these conflicts continue, and our friends support or undermine whatever delicate balance we achieve between our need for independence and our need for connection. Letitia, thirty-two, feels increasingly isolated as her close friends strike out for greater independence and, she feels, devalue her own wish to be home for her children:

> It's not that they're nasty or say bad things. Shelley and Nan are really good friends. They like me; they admire certain things about me, I know. But they come round and I tell them what I'm doing, and the conversation is just polite,

bland. But then they start talking about what they're doing, and their eyes light up. The last thing I want is to be jealous of them—my best friends. I really want things to work out for them, and they're in the thick of setting up this business now. At first I was all excited: "Can you really do that? How did you manage that?" I was impressed, and it was fun. But now their buzz confuses me. "I'm doing something real, too," I want to tell them, but that's pathetic. And I'd really think less of myself if I just had housewives for friends. But I can't help feeling defensive.

Letitia came into therapy because her defensiveness was infiltrating her marriage. She needed extra reassurance from her husband, who would try to offer what she needed, but because it wasn't reassurance from him that she really did need, his efforts were unsatisfactory, and he felt let down. "How many times and in how many ways do I have to tell her and show her how much we value her?" he asked. "If she's going to be so down on herself at home, she should work outside." But Letitia claimed she didn't want to leave her children for hours at a time—not yet. What she needed was to feel valued by her girl-friends. She explains: "Only my women friends know what this dilemma feels like. You need to live in a woman's skin to understand. My husband's too rational: 'If you're not happy doing this, then do that.' I do want to stay with the kids. This is my job. But I also want to feel I'm someone with my high-flying friends." Letitia wishes her friends would be interested in her and admire her balancing acts, how she creatively does so many unusual things for and with her children. She needs to find ways of expressing and satisfying her need for her friends' understanding and approval. What she needs is not marital therapy but something that isn't really recognized—friend therapy.

Thank God I'm Not Like *Her*

We learn a great deal about ourselves through the friends we like and the friends we admire—but we also learn who we are through connection with girls we in some sense hate. Often, as young girls, we are thrown together with someone whose mother our mother likes, or feels sorry for. We sit next to a girl in school and find she walks home our route. We collect a common history with someone, and yet we see her as unappealing—and discover a desire to scratch her skin, to kick her shins. We stay "friends" and discover in ourselves a desire to damage her or to get away from her as though she were contagious.

On the other side of idealization is denigration. "I can never be what she is" may mean we can never be as perfect as we think she is, or it can mean we deny we could ever be as pathetic, excluded, and vulnerable as we think another girl is. When we idealize who we should be, and what other girls are, we may refuse to register our own imperfections. When we see such imperfections in someone else, we cannot admit that we are like this other girl, who wears on her sleeve the awkwardness and vulnerability that we deny in ourselves and work so hard to hide. Such a girl must be punished for displaying what we don't want discovered in ourselves.

This (wishful) denial of any possible similarity lies at the center of that distinctive cruelty girls can inflict on one another. When I ask Fiona what she has learned this year about herself through her friendships, a series of emotions ripple her ten-year-old face, and she looks at me, brazen, harsh, anxious, as she announces: "I learned it was fun to be mean."

Immediately, I understand. She is talking about a kind of meanness that girls excel in, that all girls and women learn to fear. They fear being the victim of such cruelty—and they also fear being its perpetrator. They suffer a sickly horror as they join with their friends to attack an especially vulnerable, awkward girl—a girl who isn't like them. And yet deep down they know that girl *is* just like them. We are, after all, most critical of others for what we dislike in ourselves.

"Boys will be boys," we say when they play cruel tricks on younger brothers, stray cats, and new teachers, but in fact girls have a special talent for cruelty. This talent is linked to their verbal strengths and their quick understanding. It is easier to be cruel with words when you know just what taunt or criticism will hurt most. This is the fun, the skill, the dare in girls' cruelty. Why throw sticks and stones when, with acute psychology, you can hurt far more with words?

The target of girls' cruelty is invariably another girl—a girl who can be marked as different, a girl who makes others squeamish or angry, a girl no one else wants to be like. She is "weird and shy," with a "funny voice" or "irritating laugh," usually "overweight, and doesn't know how to dress." She is needy, hopeful, trusting. Other girls will bend over in side-splitting laughter when you utter her name. Mockery bonds girls as they tease this girl about things any teenage girl is sensitive about—her complexion, her periods, the shape of her ears or nose or breasts. It's fun to set her up for a fall by pretending to like her, raising her hopes, only to dash them; or by pretending to offer comfort, only to terrify her more effectively afterward. Cruel rituals can go on for days or weeks. The victim remembers these trials all her life. The girls who inflict such torture are in turn haunted by recognition of their own cruelty, which they may try to bury—sometimes by being extra nice to girls or women they really don't like.

When adults discover such betrayals of common decency, we are angry, but our shock—our claim "I don't believe a girl like you could do such a thing"—is a sham. When my red-faced teacher looked at the hideous drawing I as a ten-year-old had made of another girl's big ears and big breasts, I felt superior to her surprise, because I sensed she was only pretending to be appalled by my behavior. Instead, she was remembering her own.

In the early stages of writing this book, we collected stories from girls and women about their friendships. One, entitled "Cruelty," by Rosa, a woman now in her thirties, tells of lost innocence at summer camp when, as an eleven-year-old, she experienced her own capacity for humiliating another girl, Christy, who "was probably somewhat disturbed, but was being mainstreamed before the term was even invented. Marginally functional, she was especially unattractive." In short, Christy was someone Rosa looked at and thought, "Thank God I'll never be what she is." At first it is only Rosa's bunk mates who act upon their cruel impulses:

> During the first summer, Christy has her period. None of us has begun to menstruate. . . . Distressed and confused creature that she is, she doesn't dispose of her used pads in the trash; instead, she hides them in odd places around the bunk—under her pillow, beneath a bureau, wedged between her mattress and cot frame. The other girls are both delighted and disgusted with this habit. . . . It gives them good reason to torment her.
>
> "I smell something funny. Does anyone else smell something funny?" says one girl. A coconspirator slowly circles Christy's bed, where she lays with her face buried in her pillow. She dangles a used pad by its end and twirls it in lazy figure eights above Christy's head. "Could it possibly be this?"
>
> "Well," sings a third, "I don't know. That looks like a used pad to me. Now, who in the world would put a used pad under her mattress and hope no one would notice?"
>
> "Somebody awfully stupid," counters the first one again. "Do we know anyone *that* dumb in *this* bunk? . . . Do we,

Christy?" When Christy sobs her second or third muffled plea to leave her alone, they leave off and move on to more engaging rest hour activities. The game loses its allure once the victim ceases to squirm.

Here is an awful counterpart to those lessons in hygiene and grooming that constantly take place among girlfriends. Together they experiment with lipsticks, instruct one another in the application of eyeliner and mascara, offer advice on hair-remover and deodorant. I see them in the rest rooms just after the lunch hour. They observe one another's reflections in the wall mirror, and study one another's faces with the same hopeful criticism they would their own. "Try this color—that's a bit heavy for you." "Don't put mascara on that way—it'll smudge." They educate and support one another. But at summer camp Rosa learns that these girl bonds can group them into a hunting pack that attacks someone who doesn't know the basic "laws" of hygiene.

The worst lesson Rosa learns, however, is that she, too, is capable of cruelty. At first she feels protective of Christy. Acknowledging her own revulsion, she wants to make "restitution": She wants to cover up her bad feelings and make up for them by being the girl who will befriend this other girl no one wants to be friends with. But her own cruelty wells up, fueled by Christy's hungry response to her friendly gestures:

> It wasn't enough that I talked to her during rest hour or walked next to her to tennis so she wouldn't have to be alone all the time. Then she wanted more. She wanted to sit with me at meals, to confide in me. She watches me all the time. It's almost like she wants to be me. She wants to be my friend, but I don't want any of this. I felt like she was stalking me, just because I showed her a little kindness.

Something in Christy—her neediness, her awkwardness, her lack of social "knowledge"—infects Rosa with an urge to denigrate her further. Knowing Christy is afraid of heights, Rosa organizes her bunk mates in a ruse to terrify Christy under the pretense of helping to "cure" her. They circle Christy's bed and lift it up while she's in it. Chanting "You will never be afraid of heights again," they raise the bed higher and higher, and catapult her through the air. Afterward she is dazed and sad and only cries softly, "That wasn't right. You didn't cure me. You hurt me."

Many of us have such stories to tell—stories about our unfair and uncontrollable revulsion, and our delight in making another girl suffer. When we organize a clique to attack someone, we feel safe from exclusion and ridicule ourselves. When we torment someone for not knowing how to accommodate physical womanhood, we deny the self-doubt and self-consciousness about our bodies that plague us, too—at least throughout adolescence. When we mock someone who is "just not cool," we disguise our own insecurities and fears of lacking whatever ineffable quality it is that divides those who are "cool" from those condemned to scorn and derision. The girls and women whom we dislike, whom we tease, who represent the shadow side of our existence, can provide a disturbing window onto our soul—and a means to self-knowledge.

Avoiding Others' Envy

Girls and women tend to forge their strongest bonds when they share vulnerability and anxiety, commiserating together about common problems. Some, in fact, have suggested that what appears to be the greater relational capacity among women derives from their historically subordinate social status.[2] Girls and women are less likely to bond together in triumph and success, in part because the envy is so difficult to manage.

Knowing the power of the envy they feel for others, girls are often frightened of the envy they might *arouse* in others, and to protect themselves, they learn to make light of their accomplishments or admirable qualities. It becomes, therefore, a social ritual among women to respond to a compliment with a self-criticism. "You look terrific." "How can you say that? I feel like a mess!"

Being the ideal girl, as we saw in Chapter 5, can seem rewarding, but in truth it is frightening and alienating. As Nadine sees how others idealize her, she feels unrecognized as her real self. "I'm not who you think I am," idealized girls would love to shout to the world. But while some teenage girls feel divided—unwilling to give up this special status, however uncomfortable the pedestal is—many make deliberate moves to avoid having others idealize them. They want to placate, not arouse their friends' envy.

Self-denigration begins in the forms of girl talk that are learned early on: "Oh, this old thing," in response to a compliment on a dress, or "If you think *I'm* pretty, *you* should look in the mirror," or "I only got the English prize because Mr. Connors doesn't realize how brilliant Sue's work is." These are tactics girls learn for assuaging other girls' envy. However much girls want to be admired, they want more to be liked. They know in themselves the impulse to "take down" someone who seems too successful, too sure of herself, and they fear arousing the same wishes in others.

Girls also learn to control envy with their friends by making an unspoken "bargain" that admiration will be reciprocated. Compliments pass in plenty between girlfriends: "Everyone likes you," "You always know what to say," "I wish I had skin like yours." Such compliments are returned very quickly: The reciprocating compliment, I found in observing adolescent girls together, usually followed within three minutes of the first one.[3] The deal is: I admire you and you admire me. As thirteen-year-old Jeanne explains:

I love talking about our future—how things will be for me, and what sort of things Gwen'll probably do. Gwen really admires me. And I admire her. I mean, if she wasn't a friend, I'd envy her. So when I see her doing well, I guess I can think I might do well, too, that things might turn out well for me.

One friend reflects back the appreciation of the other: Jeanne feels her value confirmed because someone she would envy if she weren't such a close friend admires her. Becky feels that Carol is so smart and funny—she'll never be like that—but then Carol laughs at what Becky says, or is struck by her acuteness, and Becky feels, "Well, maybe I am worthy of that." The comfort comes as we think along these lines:

> She's so wonderful/funny/smart.
> I'll never be like that.
> She think's I'm wonderful/funny/smart.
> Therefore maybe I am like that!

When there is no possibility of reciprocal admiration, women may downplay their achievements or try to restrict their friendships to people who are less likely to envy them. Margo, an administrative aide in the mayor's office, has made a new friend at her gym. They have being walking together regularly, enjoying their talks about life, men, children, finding that they have the same quirky sense of humor. But Margo, who is very wealthy, is afraid to invite her new friend to her home because "I'm just afraid that if she sees the opulence, she won't want to be friends with me anymore. I'm afraid of her envy—I don't know, maybe this is stupid, but it scares me."

Recently I read in the newspaper that a close friend of mine had received an important civic award. I called to congratulate her, genuinely pleased for her, not at all envious. We are in different fields, and anyway, I've had my own awards. "How come you didn't tell me?" I demand to know. "Oh, well," she answers, "it wasn't such a big deal." While I am deliciously relieved by my absence of envy, I'm hurt by her reticence, which is driven, I know, by her expectation of others' envy. Even when neither friend actually feels envious, envy shapes their interactions.

Beyond Envy

Many women, aware of past difficulty with envy for their girlfriends, count the ability to admire other women and take pleasure in other women's positive qualities as an achievement to be proud of. Donna, twenty-three, describes important advances in her capacity for friendship:

> I've grown up with my girlfriends. I've always found it diffi-cult to be with girls who are clearly better than me—either smarter or prettier or more popular. And I could really miss out on a good friendship, because I'd just assume that being with someone I really admired a lot was a putdown. If there's any indication that I'm more confident than I was, it's that I really enjoy having really great friends. A few years ago I wouldn't have been able to have Jane as a friend. You've seen her—she's gorgeous. And she charms everybody because she gets so involved in what you're saying, and will always say something that shows she's right there with you, and she's always right on target. She's wonderful—and I'll never be like that.

Donna's double vision—of what she once felt and what she feels now—is a common experience in friendship. As we make friends and work to keep them, we act and respond within the context of our memories of past relationships. I become aware of this myself as Beth walks into the meeting room. There's the rustle of her nearly late entrance, which speaks of her overbusy high-profile life. She takes us all in with her eyes and greets us individually with her characteristic eagerness. Even as the dreary meeting begins, I feel happier because she is there: She will pick up on things I may miss, but she will also respond to some things as I do. The room becomes a place of significance because she is there. Later we will talk about what transpired, discuss who said what and why, analyze the politics and prejudices of the other people there. Together we will construct an account of what went on, enjoying our own and each other's views. I enjoy her now, and I realize how her presence would have irked me, diminished me, in my teenage years. My admiration would have been overpowered by envy; her attractive, space-filling presence once would have been a burden rather than a pleasure.

Yet I cannot claim to have left such feelings behind. They slip behind other feelings, but remain in my repertoire of responses. It doesn't take much more than a scratch on the surface to reveal raw "adolescent" feelings. However mature we become, we are always susceptible to that feeling Lisa describes, that of having our admiration for someone else twist into the conclusion "I'm—blah." The issue of who is more or most admirable can still sting. While planning a college function, I review the dinner seating plan with Patricia, a senior professor and longtime friend. She reminds me that Marina Warner is coming, a woman generally recognized as multi-talented, who sails to success with every book, novel, play, libretto she writes. Sluggish from a recent virus, not feeling too bountiful in ego strength, I wonder whether I really want to sit near her. I ask whether she is intimidating, but Patricia assures me, "She's lovely— witty, attractive, warm—intelligent, of course, marvelously intelligent, but not at all frightening. She's attractive, too, very stylish. I

find her utterly charming. In fact," she says, raising her chin in tri-
umphant conclusion to this accolade, "I think she's the nicest
woman I know."

Floundering amid this barrage of praise, pushing away my
protest that a close friend should say to me of someone else, "She's
the nicest woman I know," I mutter, "Oh well, perhaps I wouldn't
mind sitting at her table," but am assured, "Oh, but you can't. I've
already picked people for our table."

The friendship that is usually warm and enabling suddenly
speaks of boundaries and status, declaring, "You will never be what I
am, or what my real friends are." What stuns me is the ease with
which we are cast back to schoolgirl roles. Though the professor is
over sixty and I am close to fifty, a silent pirouette can turn her into
the head girl telling me I don't matter in the way another girl does.
She can say, looking blandly through me, that Marina is "the nicest
woman she knows" because I am not even a competitor: I am outside
the arena of true significance. And how can I protest? I have to take
this with a smile. I cannot object to her praise of someone else. Any
objection would show me up as grudging, as envious. The more
unhappy I become, the more I am to blame.

My only comfort—and revenge—will come later when I tell
another friend what's happened, what's been said. As I describe the
scene, I watch her widening eyes and find her amazed condemnation
so satisfying: "Patricia is *so* full of herself! She can't help reminding
us all how grand she's become." I am assured that the envy I feel was
deliberately induced: "She meant to make you feel bad." I am
assured that the fault is with Patricia, not me: "She's offending so
many people these days." These interchanges rest on our mutual
knowledge of the dynamics of envy. My friend Patricia can use my
(normal and predictable) envy against me: She uses it to make me
suffer. The friend I confide in assures me that my envy or discomfort
is normal and predictable and that Patricia is being nasty. Both

friends interact with me on the basis of their knowledge of friends' potential cruelty.

These moves constantly create breaches and alliances. When we don't understand them, we can be outraged. When we don't get the kind of friend support we need, we can shy away from all friendships. When we understand them as part of the tricky moves in which our relationships dance, we can shrug them off and move on. But I never learn the reason for Patricia's skillful blow. Have I offended her, neglected her, shown some ingratitude? If I could understand her behavior, I could correct my fault or revise my interpretation of what passed between us. But because I never understand why she makes this declaration of status, the contours of our friendship are changed forever.

For most adult women, these stinging reminders of hidden antagonisms come and go without too much disruption. We know where to seek comfort, and we know how to offer it. The balance in our self-image is tipped but soon regained. Or sometimes it is just one woman who sounds this awful chord—one woman we refuse to admire because if we did, we'd feel like jumping into a pit. There may always be one woman whom we want to strangle because her children are "perfect," or because she's "gorgeous," or because she so easily gains successes we labor toward uncertainly. Most of us just tough out these bad feelings and move on. For some women, however, the dynamics of envy skew their lives. Ashamed and anxious, they cannot seek that comfort another woman friend might offer.

Roberta, in her forties, believes she has failed, badly, to realize her potential. She manages her husband's marquee business and acts as his design scout, constantly modifying and improving the structure of the marquees he sets up for weddings, plays, parties, conferences. But she is nagged by disappointments, both large and vague. When she works toward identifying her frustration, she talks about getting older, but also about being outside the warm rush of excitement that emanates from her women "friends"—or women she knows, but whom she can't quite connect to. She struggles like fourteen-year-old MaryBeth with her idealization of others:

> Something about another woman will just spark it off, and I'm burning with fury, asking "Why *her* and not *me?*" These feelings leave scars, and you never know when they'll open up again. I get so angry, and think and say such awful things. But it makes me ache, just feeling what it's like . . . for a minute you think what being her is like. And getting older—facing fifty!—well, that's me locked out, isn't it? I feel trapped in my own life. I just don't see a way out. My friends will ring up and tell me their good news—phew. It's like being battered, one slap after another, and they just keep on. Especially this one woman—she's been doing this and that on the *Tribune,* and suddenly she's become real big, traveling all over the place and covering everything. On and on she goes about what new thing she's going to do. It's a nightmare—she just won't stop, and I want to say, "Give me a break; can't you just give me a break from all your fucking triumphs?"

Unlike so many women who, in their forties and fifties, enjoy release from the lingering envies and anxieties of adolescence, Roberta experiences a resurgence of that raw adolescent sensitivity whereby others' qualities seem to dwarf one's own. The women who are pleased with their own lives seem to Roberta to be mocking her. While her friends try to break the feminine code "Never boast" by sharing with her their pleasure in their activities and successes, she feels they are attacking her.

Roberta's inability to grow into a more relaxed admiration of other women prevents her from learning from them. Instead of watching and gaining knowledge and confidence through what they do (for example, thinking "That's a good idea! I could try that"), she observes other women and thinks, with anger and resentment, "I'll never be what she is." Her envy renders her powerless: She cannot learn from them, she is not inspired by them, she can only envy them. Friend therapy—learning how to express her needs to her friends, recognizing and containing her envy—would ease her despair. By allowing her to see how other women enjoyed and admired her, Roberta could believe in her own value among her peers.

Competition

Men and boys are much more skilled in and comfortable with competition than girls and women are. Girls are taught it's not "nice" to be competitive, and they therefore learn to mask these urges, to compete without seeming to do so. It's terrible either to win or to lose. Either way you end up feeling alone, so it's better to pretend there is no competition at all. There is no way, for example, for me to point out to Patricia her competitiveness in the account I related above. She would just deny it ("But I didn't mean that at all. I was just . . ."). Women are skilled at giving themselves an out—they learn to do this as girls. But this leaves girls uncertain about where their own or others' competitive feelings are. If we can't ever be sure that another woman is trying to get the best of us, how can we trust her if she says she isn't?

That women have little opportunity to openly acknowledge and learn to deal with competitive feelings colors and distorts their relationships with other women—in the workplace particularly. At work, women cannot choose whom they will relate to as they can socially. The dilemmas of competition among women at work are further compounded by the fact that what experience most women have in competing with other women is in the sexual arena—competition for men. Growing up as girls, we learn the rules about "getting" guys, and when it's okay to "take a guy away" from another girl, and when it's not, and how to do it if is permissible. But girls learn very little about besting one another in other ways. In our interviews we were repeatedly told, for example, about how girls on the soccer team persist in apologizing when they bump into one another. Observing girls playing basketball, we saw how they could be ostracized by others for "hogging the ball," even though they thereby scored goals and helped the team win.

But while girls and women do need to learn from boys and men how to compete without guilt and rancor, girls and women don't generally want to compete in the fierce hierarchical way that boys and men do. They know that only one person can get to the top, and being alone at the top doesn't seem so much like a prize.[4] Therefore, girls must learn to negotiate competition within collaboration, striving to compete while maintaining relationships, moving ahead but moving their friends with them instead of leaving them behind.

Miye, a research biologist in her forties, was invited to a very selective professional meeting while her best friend and work partner was not. She was honored and tempted by the invitation, but troubled that her friend was excluded. "I didn't go," she explained. "If they want me, they'll have to invite her as well. The meeting isn't important enough for me to want to create bad feelings between us. I think that our contributions in microbiology have been pretty equal. I have no wish to show her up. We're a team. I want it to stay that way. I'm not going to let anyone split us."

Miye is someone who has learned to compete and to collaborate and to choose which will take precedence at a given time. Most women who have been successful in their work report to us that they no longer feel plagued by feelings of envy or wishes to compete. They laud the value of women's networking groups, where women can put into play their wishes to help one another rather than get ahead at one another's expense.

Having "arrived" in a professional niche, most women experience a long period of respite from the "Why am I not more like her?" pains—a respite until the arrival of a much younger woman. This ushers in one of the most painful of the envy/competition dynamics among women, a scenario encountered with increasing frequency in work environments.

Kendra's story is one we heard again and again from women who, with both pain and shame, spoke of a resurgence of old adolescent feelings. Kendra is a forty-eight-year-old lawyer, well respected among her colleagues, known for her helpfulness and willingness to mentor younger women just entering the field:

> I had a wonderful mentor, a judge who was also a woman who really took me under her wing and helped me launch my career. And I remember even in high school I had a really good friend who was a couple years older than me, and how I loved to hang out at her house and watch her do things and think, "In a few years I'll be doing these things, too." So I know how important it is to have a woman to look up to and try to emulate. But when Lynley came into the firm, right away I sensed there was going to be a problem here. She's my associate and I know she adores me. She wants me to take her everywhere with me. But I can't, and if I'm honest with myself—I can't bear it that I feel this—I can't because she grabs all the attention. We go to a negotiating meeting and all the guys are checking her out. She's gorgeous. And part of me is furious because I feel they are

objectifying her, no matter how surreptitiously—treating her like a sex object instead of the competent lawyer that she is—and part of me is envious because they aren't looking at me—at least not anymore. I used to be like Lynley, but now I'm middle-aged, not likely anymore to draw those looks. And I hate her for it and I can't bring myself to praise her at partner meetings even though she does very good work—and what I hate the most in this process is myself.

Professional women in midlife are often in positions to help younger women, but old competitive, envious feelings often intrude. They then find themselves reverting to long-discarded adolescent tactics, using devious means to deflate the women they envy, recognizing its irrationality yet finding it hard to resist the temptation.

Even when Kendra made this statement, thought, she was closer to resolution than she thought. When we spoke to her two months later, she reported:

You know, just realizing what was going on and saying it out loud helped a lot. I told one of my friends about it and she said she has exactly the same feelings about a woman in her office. This led us to realize that the problem isn't Lynley—or her rival—but our own misery about aging, about giving up sexual power. That's going to be true whether we kill off the Lynleys of this world or not. There will always be another to take her place. Since then, I've been more able to deal with Lynley as the budding lawyer she is there to be, someone I can nurture and help; to see my own former self in her flirting with guys to get what she wants and somehow to be more tolerant of the whole thing. But first I had to do that "brutally honest with myself" bit—that was the hardest part.

When women can acknowledge their envy and competitiveness, their capacity to work and play and be together is usually improved. It's out in the open then; everyone can call it by name, and the possibility of true cooperation and collaboration is enhanced rather than diminished. It was always hard to know what to say if a friend said to me, "I really envy you. . . ." I'd want, first of all, to tell her there was no reason for envy. Then I'd go on to devalue whatever it was she felt I had, or to tell her she should think about all there was about me *not* to envy, or to scold her for feeling envy at all ("Don't envy me—that's silly"). But now I merely thank her for letting me know how she feels. Or I tell her that I regard envy as a close cousin to admiration.

The Pleasures of Admiration

My college is interviewing high-school students for admission. I ask seventeen-year-old Miri whom she most admires. We are trying to gauge her goals, ideals, and values. Since she is planning on studying science, we expect to hear about great inventors or Nobel laureates. Instead, she looks at me, and in her eyes I see a familiar hesitation: Will she try to impress me or will she speak her mind?

"The people I admire most are my friends," she says, and I see she has opted for honesty. "I admire them because I know them best, and what I admire most are personal qualities." As she speaks, resisting the expectations she knows we have of how she should answer this, I feel the strength her friends have given her—strength to speak her mind and strength to be herself.

Admiration of our friends is essential to our well-being. It gives us a sense of hope and breadth, and our world becomes richer. At its best, envy for a friend brings a sharper focus on that person's character. Envy is often not the green-eyed monster but the focused appreciator. As journalist Sue Limb notes, with a nimbly realistic sense of what goes on in day-to-day friendships, "I envy one friend her youthful looks; another, her freedom from the need to work; another, her single, footloose status and the travels she enjoys. But I assume that they in turn probably envy me what good fortune has brought me. I too have blessings to count."[5] Envy is not a fixed item separating girl from girl or woman from woman (or woman from girl), but something that comes and goes, often easing into appreciation. As Dorothy, who at fifty achieved remarkable success as a television presenter, said:

> What's been so much fun about my success is the way my friends enjoy it. You have a stunning photo in the paper, and it could mean nothing, but my friends—a few close ones— have made it last: "See how gorgeous you are." And with this new high profile, I knew I might be torn down: "She thinks so much of herself," or some variation of it. So I kept playing it down. "This is a one-off series, and it's airing at an awful time," I kept saying. But what Pam and Tess and a few others seem to think is that I deserve this, that this is what they knew I could be, and they're pleased it's happened. And that's made me feel far more proud of my success than I could have otherwise. It's convinced me that this is right for me.

But it's not only mature women who learn how to admire their friends and ensure that admiration is a source of pride, not envy. Amy, eleven, wrote the following poem for her best friend, Laura:

> *She is a calm Mediterranean sea*
> *and a bottle-nosed dolphin, friendly and trustworthy*
> *Placed by Mount Everest, she would be a determined piece of*
> * climbing rope.*

If she were sweet she would be a delicious toffee cream
   which sticks to you.
Set in the middle of a sports field
She would be a ball dying to get into the goal.
She is a wild red strawberry
and a pair of Doc Martens
She is a sleek black BMW
and the color purple, bright and vibrant.
Placed in the night sky, she would be like the Pole Star,
   leading the way.
She's a JCB, strong and in control.
If she were a Shakespearean actor, she would be Lady Macbeth.
And if she were a person, she would be the best friend in the
   world.

Admiration is one of the great pleasures of our friendships. Laura, in Amy's eyes, has everything: calmness and strength, determination and glamour. Amy plays with her idealization of Laura—who is really too good to be a real person. But "if she were a person," she would be "the best friend in the world." This exquisite vision in which a friend's virtues instill a stunned admiration, without envy, may be too good to be true very often, but its image enlivens and strengthens every one of our friendships.

Chapter Nine

"I NEVER THOUGHT THIS WOULD COME BETWEEN US"

MollyAnn was my friend from—forever, I think. And we stayed friends for a long time. And we'd watch other girls fight or drift apart, and shake our heads and say, "Nothing like that will ever come between *us*." Then there was a real change when we were sixteen and started dating. Suddenly there always seemed to be something behind things she said. "Did you go out with him again?" she'd ask, and I'd think, "Why does she want to know?" There was this suspicion. We started picking on each other and just grew wary. We couldn't share things like we used to. The thing is, when girls get interested in boys, everything changes.

Angie, now twenty-two, reflects on her girlhood and sees a breach between a time when things were simple and straightforward with her girlfriends and a time when a "real change" occurred, making it no longer possible to keep the promise that "nothing will ever come between us." Angie found that interest in boys pulled a valued friendship apart. The wariness that began in adolescence hasn't yet left her:

Now, whenever I'm sure I really like a guy, I keep him at a distance from my girlfriends. Not that I hide him or anything, but I don't talk about him too much, and I don't go out with him and them. It's a terrible feeling—a split deep down inside me. Because I'd really love to talk about all sorts of love stuff. But if I do, then maybe she'll think my guy's appealing. Or maybe she'll just want to see if she can stir things up. You never know when a guy's going to come between you. That trust just goes. Maybe someday when I'm old and married I won't worry about that anymore and I can be friends with anyone I want.

Angie deals with an age-old image of girls and women divided by their interest in men. In this young woman's experience, the trust goes out of her friendships when issues about romantic love arise. She finds that when she becomes interested in or attached to a man, her friendship with a woman then forms a triangle: Her woman friend will compete with her for the man.

This triangle configures a powerful fear: Someone I trust, someone I confide in, someone who knows my man through me, will then abuse that trust and confidence. Someone uses her connection with me to forge a relationship in which I am the loser. "I feel like an animal that's been hunted by one creature and eaten by another," Cheri tells me. "My best friend and my boyfriend. I can't believe it. I just can't get a fix on this one." In Jane Austen's novel *Emma*, one character extols the pleasures women take in their women friends, insisting that "no man can be a good judge of the comfort a woman feels in the society of one of her own sex," but this novel also tells the story of a young woman who is taught a lesson for making another girl her friend, teaching her everything she knows, and sharing her life with her: As a result, her new friend comes to love the man she loves. (This plot recurs in the film *Clueless,* which many teenage girls know by heart, and which is a modern rendition of *Emma.*) Teaching a new girl the secret to female success may be fun, the thinking goes, but it's dangerous because she'll go for your man.

Yet such commonly portrayed and commonly feared triangles aren't, in fact, common. On the whole, we want our man to like our friends. Most women who have been jealous of another woman were not friends with her first. Among girlfriends, jealousy tends to be over another girl. The question a girl asks when she experiences a triangle is far more likely to be "Whose friend are you?" than "Who's going to get the man?" Yet the image of two women friends focused on one man, and divided from each other by their love for one man, strikes our imagination because of the fear that such a double betrayal inspires. When things go wrong with a boyfriend, we run to a friend. When a friend runs off with our boyfriend, we don't know where to turn.

It is the fear, not the frequency, of such betrayals that makes them a common theme in novels and films. The image of a girlfriend taking what we want from us registers our continuing sense of how dangerous these usually comfortable and comforting attachments can be. We hear a boyfriend compliment one of our girlfriends, or tell her something he hasn't told us first, or laugh loudly at her jokes—and there's a hesitation, a moment of blank panic: "The bitch inside me," as the novelist Kate Pullinger calls it, rises up.[1] The question that is then posed is "What happens to the women's friendship?"

In Louise Bagshawe's novel *Career Girls,* two college friends, Topaz and Rowena, generously admire each other's talents, brains, and beauty: no envy here, just pure admiration. Their friendship begins in college, when their talents and ambitions, rather than their background, create a bond. They see themselves as soul mates, as friends for life—but a man comes between them. Rowena "betrays" Topaz by taking her boyfriend as a lover, and Topaz, editor of the university newspaper, slams Rowena's reputation in print. The broken shards of friendship shape their futures. Each is set upon outdoing and undoing the other. But though their feud seems to be about a man, the issue is not who gets him, but whether the young women could trust one another. As Topaz says to Rowena, "You see, Peter doesn't matter. . . . He was nothing. He was good in bed, he was charming. I'd have found out what he really was soon enough. It's you that matters, Rowena. Because I was your friend. Because we trusted each other."

This theme is repeated in an episode of the comedy series *Home Improvement* that centers on Jill's twentieth high-school reunion. Jill has to face Joni, who "stole" her boyfriend. The betrayal remains fresh and fierce in her memory, however well things turned out for her (she married a better man), for the greatest betrayal involved the breakdown of the *girlfriend* relationship. At the reunion, the breach is repaired as Joni admits that she was pregnant—and miserable and frightened—when they graduated from high school. Aghast at learning of this lost opportunity to support her friend, Jill cries, "Why didn't you tell me?" Any outrage she may have suffered at the loss of a boyfriend would have been superseded by her wish to stand by her "first real friend. I would have been there for you. I loved you," Jill insists. What hurt her the most, she realizes, was not losing Jack, but losing Joni.

Often the betrayals of a girlfriend outlast any concern for the man who comes between them. As the women we interviewed who had lost a man to a best friend told us, "You expect men to betray you. But not a girlfriend."

Comforting Irreverence

At around age thirteen, a new subject is introduced into girls' friendship talk. "Isn't Hugh cute?" "I think he likes you." "I don't like him.

I just think he's cute." And once this subject is introduced, it stays. Throughout their lives, females offer one another love advice. Together they plot strategies to interest a romantic partner and scheme revenge on unfaithful lovers. Attraction to a boy can act as cement in girls' friendships: It is something to talk about, something to plot and plan, to analyze, to exult in or despair over. Boys—and the tumultuous feelings they arouse—are a frequent topic of discussion. We learn about sex and love through our girlfriends. Throughout girls' and women's lives, girlfriends provide a reality check ("Do you think he's handsome?" "He's nice, isn't he?" "Does this mean he's right for me?"), and provide comfort when love goes wrong.[2]

Girl's and women's interest in men is more likely to make them allies than enemies.[3] Men, and the special kind of interest we have in them, become important points of contact, significant conversation themes, as girls and women share their observations and descriptions of men, analyze their character and their value. They watch a friend's love life intently, learning from her trials, experimenting with life and expanding through a friend's experience. In some respects, they learn to love and to idealize men in one another's company. Girls see their personalities as "interesting" or "cute." They find "depth" in even the most brutally abrupt young man. They guess at—or create—a wonderful inner life on his behalf: "He's sweet. And he's really sensitive. *I* can tell."

Often, the first forays into dating are emotionally more meaningful to the girl as material to chew on with her girlfriends than in terms of what is happening between her and the boy. Out on one of her first dates, the girl may be more engaged in memorizing details to replay for her girlfriend the next morning (if she can wait that long) than in the experience itself. There is more fun in the telling—the analyzing, the squeals of giggles ("He really did that? Tell me all the details—every one. Don't leave a single thing out")—than in the actual date.

Girls' insights into a girlfriend's experience with a boy can be perfectly serious, yet they provide a point of sharp amusement. Though girl talk often reinforces the value of men, and idealizes them, and aids and abets romantic liaisons, it also has a profound capacity for irreverence. Girlfriends provide a close, sharp lens on the male world. Through this lens girls learn about the power men can have over women, but through their alliances, women also resist male power. Girlfriends have been confidantes and wits for centuries, criticizing men, mocking them, even plotting against them—and, above all, not taking them too seriously. A friend can quash another girl's love interest: With the right word, the right gesture, a romance can be diffused by ridicule.

Girls' verbal facility—their constant conversation, their sharp tongues and quick minds—offer a formidable defense against boys and men. Olivia, Karina, and Sue, at seventeen, make "mincemeat" of any boy who dares parade his self-importance in class. Olivia explains:

> These guys are so easy to put down. It's just irresistible. Jed keeps telling the same awful jokes and laughing at them as though he's never heard them before. He swaggers up to us and starts playing cool, talking to me like he's really going to impress me, and I say, "Yeah, yeah," not bothered by a thing, because Karina and Sue and me—we'll just have a laugh over it later. Most of the real nerds know better than to waste our time, but a few still keep trying.

In Renaissance England, Ann and Meg, those "Merry Wives of Windsor," compared the love letters Falstaff wrote to each of them, and their pleasure at being admired by a Knight of the Realm gracefully gave way to a female alliance against male pretension. "Who does he think he's kidding?" they ask, and then decide, "We'll show *him*." Meg and Ann don't fight each other for the knight's attentions;

they protect themselves and revenge themselves by joining forces to ridicule him. And today, in the halls of a city high school, male "lines" are compared, and even their relative kissing is assessed. Jaqui, twenty, says she and her friend Ruth have compared notes on boys for years:

> It sounds real strange, but this is what we'd do. Some guy would ask Ruth out, and then she'd tell me about it, and she'd describe his moves—you know, how he put his arm around her, how he'd kiss, and how long it took him to try other things as well. If she liked him, she'd ask me to flirt with him. Things like "Tell him you need help on that history project." And if he'd hit on me, well, we'd laugh about it and compare notes, and we'd know him for what he was. And she'd do the same for me—though she's prettier, and I always felt she was a better tester than I was. When she'd flirt and the guy didn't react, I'd be real impressed. I don't know how I would have sussed out guys without her.

Men understand all too well the radical nature of female friendship. Their fear that women friends are laughing at them can be heard in the way woman talk is demeaned as "natter" or "gossip." Female friendship provides a wonderful space for solidarity and irreverence. Through it, friends can construct new norms. The social control of gossip can turn to liberation, as friends, sharing girls' worlds, look and assess and decide with the strength of a shared female perspective.

And so it is that women's friendships are often endangered by the larger social order in which values are set by men who have learned that if they manage to keep women divided, they will maintain their power over them.[4] This is especially apparent in the workplace. Men can easily pit women, who have little power to share, against one another, thus reinforcing the circuits of patriarchal power. In the brilliant English television series *Yes, Minister,* Sir Humphrey, who does not want more women in the civil service, tries to make the minister's wife jealous of a woman whom the minister, Jim Hackett, wants to promote. Initially, Mrs. Hackett is behind the promotion and "for women." Sir Humphrey pretends to agree with her and then extols the candidate's beauty. How nice it will be, he muses, for Mr. Hackett to see such a lovely woman on a day-to-day basis and work closely with her. Sir Humphrey reflects aloud at how noble Mrs. Hackett is to allow her husband such privilege, how trusting she must be to encourage this appointment. As Mrs. Hackett takes these risks on board, her support for the woman withers. Sir Humphrey's message is loud and clear: Support other women at the risk of losing what you have. And without Mrs. Hackett's support, the woman candidate will not be successful. The lesson is: Keep women divided and men will maintain their power over them.

As long as some men continue to regard women's bonds as threatening, they will refuse to acknowledge their existence except in skeptical, condescending terms. This means that women have to work hard—and sometimes secretly—to preserve their ties to other women. If men and success do not divide women from their female friends, these friendships will make them strong.

The Stronger Bond

Once women have worked through "girl triangles" and are less worried about abandonment by their female friends, they find their friends provide a safety net against fears of abandonment by men. The first response of any woman or girl abandoned by her lover is to call her best friend. "The only thing that got me through my separation and divorce," said Dorothy, "was calling my best friend—about every hour—to tell her the latest outrage. I guess in some way, even though I knew he was leaving and that my heart would be broken, still I knew I wouldn't be completely alone. My friends would still be there for me. And they were."

While men can divide women, they also bring them together. Janet told us that one of her closest friends was the former live-in lover of her ex-husband. "We just got to know each other while we moved the kids from one household to another, and I could sort of tell when she started having problems with him. Then after they broke up, she called me to commiserate and we discovered we had lots in common. I guess he's consistent in his taste in women. So we've become really good friends ever since."

Some women will be intrigued by a potential rival and bond with her rather than compete with her. Dorothy told about meeting Tess at a convention she attended:

> I went to this meeting sort of to be with a man who was interested in me, but I wasn't that sure I really liked him. Anyway, when he met me at the train station, he was with Tess, and I sort of thought, "So who is *she?*" By the time we got back to the hotel, I had really made a connection with Tess, and actually spent most of my time at the meeting with her. She was really much more interesting than that guy. She asked me if I was interested in him and I said, "Not really." But I truly felt from the way she asked the question that it was clear that if I was, she would clear out. I liked this kind of honesty in her. She's since become one of my closest friends—for years now. And I don't know what ever happened to the guy. But you know, when I think about it, I'm proud to say that I've never betrayed a friend. I've cheated on guys, I've had affairs with married men. But with men who are attached to my friends, strictly off-limits for me. I couldn't bear to hurt a woman I care about, who trusts me.

Cecile, a fifty-year-old therapist in her second marriage, was amused at our question about whether a man had ever disrupted a friendship with a woman:

> On the contrary. I've sort of needed my two closest women friends—and we've been friends for years—to be able to be with a guy. During the times when they were less available, I'd get too absorbed in the latest guy, sort of lose myself. And then I'd get scared and break off the relationship. They are like a safety net for me, keep me in balance. I really think it was they that made it possible for me to get married again.

How Men Come Between Us

Yet any close relationship *is* changed by another close relationship. When we have a child, our relationship with a partner changes. When we have a second child, our relationship with the first child changes. We still love as much, and may feel that we love the same, but our time and attention are limited. Della, sixteen, feels confused, and threatened with loss, as her friend Robin becomes "all wrapped up by this big boyfriend of hers":

> We'd decided to go to this prom together—me, Robin, and two other girls. We felt so excited—so brave. We wanted to go, so why not just go? Then Robin phones and says, "Joel asked me to go with him!" And it was "Well, he asked me, so I'm going." "But I asked you first." And she just laughed. Like what's a date with me, after all? And it's not only being dropped, it's also taking second place. I mean, second place and no apology. *Of course* he matters more. Right? But that doesn't feel right. It makes me angry.

Della wrestles with the assumption that a boyfriend comes first. While Robin buys into the assumption that friendships with girls will no longer play such a large role in her life once she has a man, Della registers the continuing importance of friendship.

Many girls, like Della, feel humiliated by this shift: Why, if they are really valued, should they suddenly take second place? Della hears the message: "You're not as important as a boy." What's more, as Robin's involvement with Joel grows, Robin sees more of *his* friends than of her. For Della, this raises questions about her friend's ability to sustain power or have her "say" when she is with her boyfriend:

> Robin will go out with him, hang out with him, and they do nothing special—just walk around or go for a pizza—but it's now with Joel's friends. It's odd—she sees Ralf more than she sees me, and Ralf doesn't mean anything to her, but he's a friend of Joel's. My mom says, "Well, you have to expect that." And I think, "What do I have to expect?" What's all this nonsense about us being equal, when even my best friend doesn't think I'm equal to some stupid guy?

Della puzzles out notions of equality and sees the inconsistency: Girls are supposed to be equal to boys, but her friend's boyfriend sets the social agenda, so her best friend sees more of his best friend than of her. Because Robin is so deeply affected by exposure to traditional female roles, she doesn't see that Della has any grounds for complaint. And Della's mother endorses this: "You have to expect that." Della tries to ask "Why?" Why does she have to expect that when her girlfriend goes out with her boyfriend, that she will *follow* him? Why does she have to assume that arrangements with him are fixed, and those with her can be broken? But neither her friend nor her mother gives her a satisfactory answer. Instead, she is left with her sense of betrayal, which puts her in a subordinate place on her friend's emotional map.

Girls engage in constant and often painful negotiations of their own importance to their girlfriends. Messages parents and teachers mean to give girls about gender equality or personal significance can be undermined or contradicted by their experience of important relationships. Boys and men can "come between" girls and women as they are given greater significance by a girlfriend. "She says she's 'still there for me,'" Della muses. "She says we're still friends. And we are still friends. We still talk on the phone. She still tells me things. But it's not the same and, apparently, I'm supposed just to accept it."

Where men really "come between us" is through the time they take away from our friends and the relative importance they expect—or are granted. And this split can come at any time. "You know what really hurt the most?" seventeen-year-old Jeanine asks. She hesitates while she watches me to make sure I see how serious this is. "It was when Mandy came back after having won the tennis tournament and called her boyfriend, Bill, to tell him first. Maybe it's silly, but all these years, she's always called me first with any news. Now I come after Bill."

But the girl who forges ahead into relationships with boys also feels her share of confusion about the changes in her friendships. Thinking back to when she was sixteen, twenty-two-year-old Liza remembers:

> I sort of fell in love with this boy and we would go to his house when his parents weren't home and I started to discover sex with him, and I felt that it was all very sinful and exciting, but not something that my best friend, Anita, would want to know about or even that I wanted to tell her about. It was somehow too personal—and special and delicious, not for talking about. I told her a little about what was

happening, but I felt it creating a distance between us because she didn't approve and she didn't have a boyfriend. I felt so torn. Like she was more important for my soul and he was more important for my body and for growing up. I felt between these people but not fully with either of them— and just so torn.

As adults, single women can enjoy the companionship of a single friend so profoundly that they feel abandoned when this singles bond is disrupted, however strongly each has acknowledged the importance of finding a partner. Enid, who as a college junior felt beholden to Veronica, her roommate and best friend, for seeing her through the first years of college, enjoyed meeting up with her friend four years later, as they both had jobs in Cleveland. "We were no longer suited as roommates," Enid explains, "but we were close as ever, and together the downsides of our lives were such fun. I'd describe impossible dates, and she'd hoot with laughter, or sometimes top my stories of the worst date ever." She laughs as she speaks, but her face suddenly grows tense:

> If I'd thought about it, I guess I would've known it couldn't last. I mean, there were things I could really count on, like she'd never make plans when it was my birthday until she knew I was set up to have dinner with someone else, even if that someone else was only my dad. And when I'd phone, even if I knew she was working, she'd talk. But then she met a guy she was serious about, and the relationship really worked out, and that seemed to leave me high and dry. First, her plans were now his plans, and second, she wanted to talk about him, not me. So there it is. I'd never been pathetic before. Whatever I went through was simply funny, you know, not pathetic. But now I'm not sure. Now I feel

pathetic with her, and when she listens to me, it's as though she's making an effort, not really interested, her mind is somewhere else, and the worst thing is, I think she sometimes feels smug. You know, "I have a man and she doesn't." It's just not the same anymore.

Enid's responses focus a number of friend problems. When the fortunes of a friend seem to shine more than our own, what happens to the friendship, and what happens to our own equilibrium? Even women who like being single are aware that there's a fine line between appearing strong and independent on the one hand, and, on the other, pathetic and lonely. If my friend no longer needs me for comfort, will she still value me? If we no longer act as witnesses of each other's romantic comedies, then what will happen to our relationship? And in the midst of these questions about status and attachment is the more simple and straightforward one: Who can I depend on to be with me when I don't want to be alone?

Men can come between girlfriends because they take up time and take priority, but they can also come between us when we lose the power to protect our friend from what we see as a bad relationship. Della watches Robin "get sucked into another world," and despairs at the power of love:

Robin's always been sensible. I really have a lot of respect for her. She's helped me be strong. "Don't let them push you around," she says, and helps me walk by the other kids who are teasing me. "Keep your head right up," she says. There were times when I was afraid of some other kids, and I'd feel safe with her. Now she's different. She asks Joel, "Are you coming over?" and he says, "I don't know. I'll see. I don't know what I'm doing." If he doesn't know what he's doing, he can decide to come over, can't he? I try saying to her what she's said to me: "Don't let him push you around." And she says, "I'm not letting him push me around." I might as well be talking to a zombie. But sometimes we start to talk and she'll say something so I know she registers what he's doing, but then she'll say, "Oh, he's all right as long as you know how to handle him," and I say, "I know how to handle him—give him the old heave-ho," but then she goes all quiet, like she's frozen.

In her frustration, Della mocks her friend's moony impasse, but this is far more than an observation of a friend's weakness. She learns about suffering and subordination through her friend. Her knowledge is stretched by her friend's experience of love and desire. She herself learns about the limits of care. She suffers from her own helplessness: Though together they have laughed at the foibles of teachers, parents, and peers, she cannot—at this point—protect her friend from love's blindness. However much we learn about love between men and women by observing our parents, we also learn about love and power from our girlfriends. When we see them "sucked into another world," a world in which they don't count as much as they count with us, a world in which we don't matter with them as much as we know we should, then we touch the edge of our power to protect others, and we feel the reverberations of constraints that we thought society was leaving behind. A girl's best friend's first love can, indeed, be her own rite of passage.

Conflicting Loyalties

Throughout their lives women struggle with balancing their loyalties to their men with their loyalties to their friends. What to do if their husband doesn't "like" one of their close friends? What to do if they don't like their friend's husband? What about a husband's suspicion

of the long phone conversations, the late nights out with a friend—
he is convinced, after all, that all they are doing is dissecting him!
And when Natalie's husband retired, she felt torn between his needs
and those of her friends:

> I hate leaving him alone. It was all right when he had his
> work. Then an evening out was no big thing. But now I
> worry he'll feel lonely or useless. But it doesn't make sense
> for me, at my age, to give something up and pussyfoot
> around a partner. I'm over fifty now. There's this urge to just
> do what I want. Yes! But I worry about him. Even a half
> hour's phone conversation with a friend seems to rattle him.
> I feel all up afterward, and he says, "What's made you so
> happy?"

For Natalie, then, the question seems to be: Will my husband
come between me and my friends, or will my friends come between
me and my husband?

We asked the women we interviewed to tell us about times that a
valued friendship was threatened, when something seemed to "come
between" them and a friend. Dorothy, fifty, related the following
story:

> It was about fifteen years ago. Alyssa had been my college
> roommate and we were so close, like sisters. We knew we
> were going to stay friends forever. We supported each other
> in our twenties, even after she had moved to Japan with her
> husband, John. I hadn't seen her in two years until Alyssa
> and John were going to be in L.A. for a few days. I could tell
> right away that something was wrong between her and
> John—and John was acting really strangely toward me, sort
> of hitting on me. I was horrified. After all, I had known him

for years—he was like a brother to me. That night after we had all turned out the lights, I became aware of John crouching next to my cot whispering to me. I also knew that he was naked. I panicked and didn't know what to do, so I pretended to be asleep, which is not easy to do when you are about to burst out crying. How could he do this to her? And with me? I wanted to kill him—for hurting Alyssa and for trying to drive a wedge between us. I didn't move. Eventually, Alyssa ordered him back to bed. The next day, I said to Alyssa, "Something strange happened last night. What's going on?" Alyssa then told me that their marriage was falling apart, but she was still trying to save it. "Please believe me, Alyssa—I didn't do anything to invite this." And, thank God, she said she knew that. I just kept praying, "Please don't let this come between us."

Then a year later John abruptly left Alyssa, ran off with another woman. She came back to the U.S. hurt and confused, with nowhere particular to go. "You're coming here—next plane," I said. And that led to the first real argument I ever had with my [then] husband. See, he thought I should have asked him first before I invited her to come and stay with us. But I thought I didn't have to ask him—after all, I would not have accepted a "no." It wouldn't have been a real question. If Alyssa needed me, of course I'd be there. Of course she could stay as long as she needed to. She was my friend—but he didn't understand what that meant. So that's two men who have tried to come between us. Husbands come and go, but Alyssa and I will be friends for life.

The entry of men into a woman's life sets up inevitable loyalty conflicts. The love a woman has for her husband is different, of course, from the love she has for a friend, but the rules of loyalty in a friendship continue despite marriage and children. Sometimes, though, the relative closeness in a friendship is affected by who is where in their relationships with men. Gwen, forty-three, structures the history of her friendship with Edna, a friendship that dates back to high school, in an interesting and revealing way: "We have had a very cyclical relationship. When I got married and she wasn't, we kind of strayed, and then when we both were married, we came back together. Then she got divorced and we kind of separated, didn't have things in common; then when I was divorced we did a lot together. But now that I'm engaged I don't see her as much."

Men often affect friendships among women, but seldom as part of a romantic triangle. Men alter the structure of a woman's life, and it is within that structure that a woman has to make space for her women friends.

Sex and the Girls

Girls who mature sexually at different times may find the gap too much to bridge in their friendship. A girl who feels she "can't talk" to her best friend about the new physical sensations, sexual fantasies, or wishes that she has—because her friend is not at the same developmental place—will likely go in search of a new friend. Silvia at thirteen is meticulous at preserving a precious friendship, but at fourteen she becomes attached to a nineteen-year-old boy. "When that was over," Silvia tells us, "I felt a lot older and wiser than Helen." Robin finds Della's anxiety over her involvement with Joel an irritating sign that her friend doesn't understand her feelings: "She's upset with me because I've changed. What upsets me is that she doesn't want to talk about how I've changed. It's awful to tell her how I feel and have her laugh at me." Silvia and Robin, like many junior-high-school girls, told about leaving a friendship because they thought the old friend "immature," which seemed to be a coded way of saying that they had moved on to pondering the mysteries of sex and romance while a friend had not. As their sexual awakenings get out of sync with those of their friends, there isn't the closeness there used to be.

Some adult women, similarly, indicate that they could never be "really close" to another woman who was reluctant to trade confidences about sexual experience. Differences in how sexuality is integrated and expressed can "come between" girls and women by damping mutuality in a place where it is most needed—whether it's as children wondering whether the people they know actually engage in sex, or as teenagers musing over the emotional depths sexual feeling arouses, or as overstretched young women laughing about needing sex "too much" or being "too tired for it," or as middle-aged women supporting one another's sense of their own sexuality in opposition to a young daughter's assumption that sex belongs only to youth. It is the failure to laugh or cry together, rather than rivalry over a particular boy, that may lead sex and romance to threaten girls' friendships.

Rules about what's an acceptable expression of sexuality can also come between us. Girls together construct femininity and the norms that will guide their generation.[5] As Lorraine listens to her friends talking about another girl, she picks up on what behavior is called "flirtatious." Stories that filter into the gossip network about what another girl has done with her boyfriend warn her how she might be spoken of if she, too, were to "let a guy take off my blouse." As the hormonal shifts of puberty in concert with cultural pressures open the gates of sexuality, girls must learn to manage their impulses and regulate their behavior. They hear messages about the importance of restraint and saying no from parents and teachers, but nothing controls them as much as the policing of friends. Breaches in the "rules" about expression of femininity and sexuality are grounds for the most severe condemnation—because this is a realm of experience where girls are least sure of themselves. Getting labeled a "slut" or "whore" (or some variation) is a terrible fate. If a girl hears herself called such names, she'll either run away in shame or fight tooth and nail to clear her name.

Although different groups of girls have very different criteria for what warrants a bad reputation, each girl is careful to learn what lines she cannot cross. Literature is filled with women—from Anna Karenina to Hester Prynne—who lose their friends because of sexual transgressions. The girl "caught" in some sexual misadventure worries about what her parents will think, but worries more about how her friends will treat her.

Similarly, as Janet ranks the closeness of her friends, she divides them into those she can talk to about the affair she is having and those she can't confide in for fear of their disapproval or outright rejection of her. "But it's hard to stay friends with those I can't talk about it with," she says. "After all, this is what I worry about and think about most of the time." As adults, we may worry less about being called "bad names" behind our backs, but we still are careful to scout out another's sense of what's acceptable or forgivable before we trust her with our romantic woes.

Loving Women

There is a special dilemma for girls who find their romantic interest within female friendships. Arlie, twenty-one, explains how "bereft" she felt when her friends first "got interested in boys":

> I think that was when I first realized I was different from my friends. At twelve and thirteen I couldn't have been happier. We were close—a whole bunch of us were real close, and we'd do everything together and laugh at the older girls when they went all moody over boys. It never occurred to me that this wouldn't go on forever. It just seemed so complete.

And then at about fourteen my friends started talking about boys, and I thought they were just making fun of themselves, or of other girls. I couldn't believe they were serious, but they were. So I started going out with guys, too, because that's what we'd do. But one day my best friend took me up to her room. It was one of those perfect evenings, when it was just us, with bags of some kind of junk food, and I didn't have to be home till late, and she said, "I really want to talk to you," and I thought, "Okay, sure, I'm here." But she says, "I really love this guy. I mean, I really love him." And for the first time I thought, "I can't let her know what I'm thinking." Because I wanted to cry.

From then on I knew that she didn't look at me in the same way I looked at her. She didn't want to be with me in the same way I wanted to be with her. You know, how you just like being with a person and looking at her, and getting a kick out of the way she moves in a chair or rubs her feet together? Instead, she was enjoying all those things in some guy. I felt I didn't know what she wanted from me, or where I fit into her life. I felt so left out. Even today I'm still realizing how left out I can be. Even when a friend knows what I feel, and knows my drift, I still feel that kick in the stomach when she starts going out with a guy. Maybe it's not so bad if I get to know them and they already have a partner or a boyfriend, but when a girl's single she can be a special kind of friend, and then suddenly she's not because she has a guy. I never thought I'd limit myself to being friends with gay women, but I can see why some do. They get in with a guy, and everything changes, and they don't even see it.

The stories of girls whose sexual orientation to women is felt early, and experienced as immutable, reveal a poignant realization that they often misread the codes of affection. Arlie's response on discovering that her friend is sexually attracted to a boy confuses her. What shape does a close female friendship have for someone who is sexually attracted to women? Arlie wonders. It is difficult for Della to understand her place in her friend's "emotional map" when a boy becomes her primary focus. How much more difficult for Arlie, who senses that her sexual orientation might make all female friendships different for her.

Carmel, twenty, is often confused by the displays of love between women, which in most cases don't involve sexuality. We have talked about many things, and she is calm, gracefully confrontational in her declaration of herself as gay, her confident Ivy League senior's manner well intact. But when we speak about specific problems with some of her close friends, her composure is overpowered by a flush that creeps from her cheeks down to her neck, and she shakes her hands nervously in front of her as she speaks. How can she read another woman's feelings? she asks:

> Jill touches me, looks at me closely, compliments me just like a lover—but no way would she ever be my lover. There's a code I'm trying to crack. Most women have it pat because they don't need it. They feel this love for a woman friend, and everyone knows it's not sexual. So how do you go about reading desire in another woman? That's what I'm trying to figure out each time I feel drawn to someone.

The views of gay women focus an important aspect of women's feelings for their female friends—that it is love, but it does not seek sexual expression.[6] Carmel works hard to understand this:

> I've asked Jill, "Do you love me?" And she says yes, and says that she loves several women—maybe ten or eleven—and

she even described something that I would call "falling in love." She meets a woman, and there's something about her—maybe something strong, like the ways she stands up to a colleague, or it can be some show of weakness, like being self-conscious about her hips, or it can be physical: "I like her voice. I like her gestures. I like the way she looks." And then Jill says, "But I'd never even think of going to bed with her or developing that kind of relationship with her." And that's where I get confused. Because it's so very different for me.

Social mores about expression of feeling are deeply ingrained and form a social code that most people can clearly decipher. Women, for example, may kiss their female friends whenever they meet without the risk of being misunderstood, but must be more circumspect about kissing male friends. But for girls who are sexually drawn to other girls, the code may become inscrutable as they struggle to understand how to read declarations of love, especially because gay girls (and women) have both sexual and nonsexual relationships with other girls (and women). Lesbians insist that many of their friendships with women are precisely what other women's friendships with women are.[7] Now thirty-seven, Barbara, having experienced herself as gay since her late teens, describes her anger when other women assume she's offering a different style of friendship:

I like lots of women. I love some women. And some of the women I like I may want sex with—but mostly not. And some of the women I love I may want sex with. You know, I'm explaining this, and I'm feeling angry, because I don't see why I have to explain something as basic as this—something everyone who's straight knows, and then you have to explain it all over because you're seen as different. What about how much the same we are? Look, I know women who have all sorts of different responses to men. Some women like lots of men and some women are for-one-man-only. And do you go around asking them, "Well, how does your love life affect your friendships?" I bet you don't. So why should mine? And when a woman who's a friend suddenly goes cold and clammy when I touch her like a friend, I feel sad, but mostly I feel mad, because I can't see why the gestures that are fine for straight people are forbidden to me.

Here is a forceful reminder of similarity in the face of difference. While Arlie and Carmel focus on the ways in which their sexual orientation toward women creates painful and uncertain border emotions with some women, Barbara shifts the focus, declaring that sexual attraction and choice of partner are not relevant to most of her relationships with women. The structure of friendship is the same, she insists, however difficult some particular relationships can be when conventions of love talk and affectionate gestures have to be overridden.

The first sexual experiments even among heterosexual girls are often with their girlfriends. Twelve-year-olds Anna, Erica, and Iris sit in a row on Erica's bed and giggle as they jostle for talk time. Who's going to shock me the most? they seem to be asking.

> "I'm going to tell her," Anna announces, and while Iris shrugs ("Big deal!"), Erica groans ("You're not!").
>
> "See, we play these games," she continues, "and we'll pretend that I'm a real come-on guy and another one is a really loose girl."
>
> "Yeah, we don't waste time on small talk," Erica adds.
>
> "And we just wonder what it is they do and how it's done. And we really feel each other up."

"And we play strip poker," Erica whispers, "so we see everything, too."

"Well, if I was shaped like you, I'd always lose, too," Iris says.

"Shh," Erica insists. (We're at her house, and she's afraid someone will hear.)

"So now you know," Anna says. "We're really loose women, but no one knows because it's just between friends."

Sexual curiosity is played out in the protected sphere of friendships. Here girls can ask questions about how sex actually takes place (Who does what? What goes where?) and discover how their changing bodies are both like and unlike one another's. There are few dangers of exposure here: The games they don't want anyone else to know about are mutually played, and because Erica can't tell me without implicating herself as well as the others, the others can feel safe in their secret. These girls feel safe, too, from any real sexual implications: They're just playing games; their reputations and sense of shame are untouched. They don't see themselves, really, as acting sexually toward one another, because the game is framed by heterosexual presumptions ("We'll pretend that I'm a real come-on guy and another one is a really loose girl").

Within this safe frame, they observe one another's sexuality—sometimes assessing a friend's attractiveness from a man's point of view, and sometimes learning about the many ways women appreciate other women. Iris compliments Erica on her breasts, even though talking to me, she's her female self, not the come-on guy of the game. Like all adolescents, she is curious about other people's bodies and wants to know the range of what's normal.

Girls—and women—continue to scrutinize one another, quick to enjoy one another's looks. They dress up for one another, knowing a girlfriend is far more likely to admire a stylish outfit and haircut than is a man. The intense grooming sessions involving what color lipstick suits which girl, and which sweater is right for whom, that we observed in school rest rooms and store changing rooms subside in adulthood, but the connection between looking, admiring, and caring never goes away. As Kirsten, in her thirties, remarked, "A compliment from a friend about how I look can cheer me up as much as any compliment from a man. She's more likely to be honest, and less likely to have some agenda to charm me. Anyway," she laughs, "a girlfriend tends to have better taste in clothes."

Are You Leaving Me Behind?

If sex is one potential division between girlfriends (as well as a common bond), another two-sided issue in friendship is success. Our good friends support our dreams and boost our confidence, yet may be unsettled when those dreams are realized.

Throughout life, we need friends to keep our dreams in motion. Only those who understand us now can help us imagine where we might go. Michiko, at sixteen, reflects on why Lia has been her best friend since they were both twelve:

> I get along well with most of the girls at my school, but Lia is the one I can talk to about all the things I want to do and all the things I want to be. The others—well, they might show respect, because I think they respect me, but they don't take my seriousness seriously. I found this out the hard way. I spent the whole lunch hour talking to one girl about my plans—from graduate school into the Senate—and she nodded, very interested and polite, like a true friend, and then later her best friend passes me in the hall and says, "Hi,

Senator," and a group of them giggle. Lia, I know, understands it the way I feel it, so when I talk to her about what I
want to do, it all seems possible.

As a young girl draws her future on the shifting background of adolescent hopes and fears, a friend can stabilize the picture. With so
much potentially undermining her confidence at this point in her
life, a close friend can keep that confidence afloat. Michiko's friends
both sustain and diminish her: The girls who are not really her
friends ridicule her pride, whereas her true friend Lia affirms her.

Sometimes, though, when dreams are realized, one friend feels
"outdone" or "outclassed." However glad we are for a friend, we
often feel threatened by her success if we worry that she may move
into worlds beyond the one we have shared, that she will outgrow us
in some way. The wedge is not so much jealousy as fear of loss.
Eileen, twenty-eight, felt Jessica's support during their mid-twenties,
when they were learning the ropes of job-hunting and negotiating
promotions, but she feels jolted by Jessica's sudden career leap:

I've shared an apartment with Jessica for nearly four years.
We met my first year in Chicago, and she helped me get my
first job, and when that was too awful, my second. I convinced her to try for a job at the firm where I'm now in Per-
sonnel, and she got it, and I felt we were friends for life.
Yesterday she announced that she's just been appointed
managing director of the Evanston branch. She rushed in to
tell me. She was waiting for me to be pleased for her, but I
wasn't. I was just surprised and confused. It never occurred
to me that she'd move up so quickly. I never thought of her
this way, and never thought I'd be jealous of her for *this*. But
there you are: Success has come between us. She thinks I'm a

rotten friend not to be happy for her. She's insulted that I'm surprised. And she just doesn't see that I feel she's leaving me behind.

In Eileen's eyes, her friend's success threatens their attachment. In Jessica's eyes, Eileen is threatening their relationship with her jealousy. The young women, both in their late twenties, are appalled by the growing split. Jessica describes her disappointment:

> We've been through everything together in the last few years. We've had awful bosses, awful colleagues, disastrous boyfriends. And Eileen's always been great. I couldn't imagine a better friend. She knows just what to say when I come home after an awful day. She has a great way of making me see the funny side of things. And now I've had this promotion, I expected we could be happy together. But we're not. There's this awful tension. It doesn't help to say, "She's just jealous." Her being jealous makes things worse, and hurts more. It never occurred to me that this would come between us.

Eileen and Jessica have had a close, supportive friendship. They provide comfort and company for each other. Together they see the comic side of their problems and so feel less daunted by them. But when their problems ebb, what will keep them together? Eileen hears of her friend's promotion and wonders, Will she still need me? Will she still care about me? Will she still be my friend?

Eileen's less-than-satisfactory job is bearable because it seems inevitable. When she and her friend are "in the same boat," they can support each other's self-esteem when others humiliate, constrain, or harass them. Comforting skills are built into the commonplace structures of girls' and women's friendships. We know how to cheer a friend up, keep the big bad world at bay, and make a cozy private space within friendship. When these skills are not needed, then some women panic: "How do I keep a friend who's happy, strong, and successful?" we may ask, feeling as Eileen does that such a friend has no need of her. Eileen struggles with the implications of her own reactions:

> I realize this has happened before. I have a friend and then something makes the friendship go sour. I think, "She's not such a good friend after all." And I stop seeing so much of her, stop talking to her. But I can't do that with Jessica. I see her every day. And I don't want this to go sour. We often complained about our positions at work, but somehow it was okay to complain. We were in it together. But now we're not.

Eileen is negotiating a difficult change in her friendship. Someone who is close to her, someone who—she thought—was "in the same boat," now sails away. Eileen appreciates the message that her friend is trying to send—"Nothing's changed between us"—but Eileen knows something has changed because she experiences the relationship differently. She realizes that they will have to reestablish their friendship on somewhat different grounds, and she worries that Jessica will meet more interesting people and will be bored by hearing Eileen relate the "same old stories."

What's complicated for Eileen are her own feelings, as well as her fears about what those feelings say about who she is and what implications Jessica's success has for her own stalled ambition. She tries to explain that it's not "just jealousy," but she can't quite get into words all the contradictory feelings raging inside of her. Why? girls and women ask. Why at twenty-eight are we feeling what we felt at thirteen? Why hasn't this gotten any better?

Shoshanna, forty, tells a similar story:

> I yearn for friendship with other women and I miss my
> friend Marcia. We had such a close relationship and we
> wanted to be equal at all costs, so we pretended that there
> wasn't any competition, but there was. She helped me a lot
> at the beginning, but I moved past her and I tried really hard
> not to make her jealous, but I had all this success and money
> and eventually she rejected me. She was having a hard time,
> and it was just too unbalanced I guess.

Even the perception that one of the friends has broken an
unwritten rule about competition in friendship can endanger the
relationship. Shereen, forty-five, an office manager, told about a crisis in her friendship with Joy:

> We met years ago—she had been my boss. Then I got a pro-
> motion to a different office and we became close friends.
> One day I mentioned to her that I had applied for another
> job, which she had also applied for, but I didn't know that.
> And she wouldn't speak to me after that. I felt it was no big
> deal, but she was so angry. I remember that her face just
> dropped and she looked so upset. She really felt I had done
> her dirty. And for nine months we didn't talk. Neither one
> of us got the job, as it turned out. Finally, at a friend's wed-
> ding, I said, "This is ridiculous," and we became friends
> again. If I had gotten the job, I suppose she would never
> have talked to me. We still see each other a lot, but we never
> talked about it again.

Immersed in the dramas of inclusion and exclusion on the girls'
playground, girls do not learn to compete the way boys do. To be

included, you have to be the same, and most women find it easier to bond with one another around shared problems and vulnerabilities. As a result, they remain uncomfortable with their competitiveness and with their success—and fear its damaging effects on relationships. Men can say proudly, "I win," and go out for a drink. A woman who says, "I win," all too often goes home alone.

Remembering her high-school best friend, Cynthia laughs. "We were together all the time. We were the two smartest girls, the class leaders. Maybe we were keeping an eye on each other, I don't know, but after we graduated, we never had any more contact. I realized years later that I really hated her. I don't know why I spent all of high school in her company." As Cynthia, a successful lawyer, observes, her very closest friends ever since have been men. With them, somehow, competition is out in the open and brings them close. "You don't have to work so hard at looking out for the other person. If he knows something I don't, he doesn't have to apologize for making me look bad. It's okay. And if I beat him at chess, he isn't going to die or hate me. It's just so much easier."

And so some women seek reprieve from the pressures and tensions of female friendships in the company of men, whose style of competition seems more straightforward to them. Any person has a right to choose her own friends, yet many women took note of those women who didn't link closely with other women. As Shoshanna reflects:

> I understood when Harriet said, "Most of my friends are men." She's a high flyer, works mostly with men, and is very comfortable in high-finance circles. I admire lots of things about her, but when she said that, I thought, "That's how we're different." I know having women friends is difficult, but I couldn't give them up.

One of the great challenges for women remains integrating competition into their relationships, recognizing it and embracing it.

Most women will fight hard to maintain a valued friendship, but sometimes they find themselves swept away on the currents of other needs and interests, and a friendship just seems to lapse. Many women say that if their friendships ended, it was through attrition rather than a big argument, and yet looking back, they usually can identify a "something" that "came between us." Sometimes it was a something they couldn't even see clearly at the time. Men, success, and distance are the biggest threats to women's friendships, followed by time—the sense that there isn't enough time, with all the emotional demands, to stay loyal to friends. "How do I make enough time for my children?" is a familiar enough question, and the ways a woman answers this question structure her life. Less well known but just as common is the question, "How do I make time for my friends?" and the ways a woman answers this question may change her life.[8]

Chapter Ten

"WILL WE ALWAYS BE FRIENDS?"

Friends are what have enriched my life. Oh, I have loved my family, but it's not the same. Friends have brought me more of the world; they've added spice and variety. My oldest friend, my friend from grade school, just died. We really were friends for life. How I miss her.

The deep and urgent need for female friends may be felt throughout life, as eighty-year-old Joyce explains. Throughout their lives, girls and women develop through their friends, and throughout our lives, friends offer comfort and cheer. They make us "feel better." A child's friendships open to her the social world beyond that of the family. They provide a girl with irreplaceable channels of creative communication and awareness of herself as a social being— as a person among peers. In the playground she learns hard lessons in both inclusion and exclusion. She experiences friends' kindness and protection alongside their cruelty and neglect. Out of school, she learns about companionship and the flexible structure of play, mutually created. In adolescence, friends help her with the self-questioning, self-doubt, and self-discovery that are essential to further development. Friends inspire her as models, filling her with hope—or they make her despair because she can never be like them.

As adults, we grow and change and are maintained by relationships with people who matter to us. Friends remain what Lillian Rubin calls "central actors in the continuing developmental drama of our adulthood."[1] We discover new parts of ourselves with our friends, who see us in different ways, touch aspects of ourselves we didn't realize existed, and encourage the changing identities our families may resist. While a partner may feel threatened by our restless ambition or growing independence, and while a child may have a vested interest in seeing us as familiar and unchanging, a friend will simply help us be what we want to become. With our friends, we can change or resist our existing sense of who we are. "How do you see me?" we continue to ask. "What do you think I might become?" As adults, when we are poised for change, we are most likely to seek out our women friends in the old, psychologically compelling manner of adolescence.[2] Our friends' views give us new ways of knowing ourselves and our world.

Friends validate both our larger ambitions and hopes as well as the more minor details of our lives: how we handled ourselves on the phone to a bank manager or electrician, what we said to a partner who wasn't doing a fair share of housework, how we went about returning a faulty pair of shoes. They provide a space for talking in which we're allowed to say things we ordinarily don't say. In friend talk, we can be unlikable without being disliked. "There's always a sassy thrill in being brutally honest with a girlfriend," Glory, fifty, declares. We feel both excited and warmed by our delicious impertinence.

Maturing Friendships

In the very busy phase of early adulthood, the typically overworked and overstretched races we run in our twenties and thirties, there often seems to be less time for friends—less time to hang out, fewer evenings to fill in, too much exhaustion for late-night phone fests. But from midlife onward, friendships reprise the joyous companionship of adolescent friendships—with a twist.[3] Midlife women's descriptions of how their friendships with women have changed commonly involve the word *relief.* They describe their relief at being "unhampered by self-doubt and envy," or from "worrying what she's thinking about me," or in being "no longer hemmed in by what she's going to say about me to others." The "feminine fronts" many women describe—the image they project of being happy, in control, having it all, and inhabiting dust-free homes—is now set aside. The messy room, the cluttered bookshelves, the sometimes scruffy hair, the imperfect mothering, the cracked marriage, the stalled career— these do not have to be hidden. Beth, having gone through a difficult transition—a "midlife career crisis"—reflects:

> I hate to think what the past few years would have been like without my close friends. I was having all this trouble at work. I felt *embattled.* I could see the hard edges that others were drawing around me. It was good, of course, to go home and be just "old Mom"—nothing special, nothing awful. But what amazed me—like a gift out of the blue—was the way my friends rallied round me. I started doing things like having lunch with them, meeting them in the evening—not just one, not a best friend like it used to be, but a whole river of them, women who are willing to talk like I can't remember talking since my pajama party days. And they had so much to offer, more than I ever knew they had in them. What I got was not just "Ooh, how beastly"—the sort of easy sympathy you can get when you trade horror stories about work. There was a real listening, so that makes it better than a family. And what surprised me about myself was what I said—how freely I spoke. And I realized how guarded

I used to be with women friends, as though they might do something with the negative information I gave them—even if it was only feeling better because I was having such trouble at work.

Beth touches on a number of issues that emerged repeatedly as women reassessed the importance of friendship and noticed how it had changed since early adulthood. It is as much fun in midlife as it was during adolescence (her "pajama party days"), but it is more fluid: Friendships are no longer ruled by a clique, wherein one alliance can threaten another; instead she has a "whole river" of friends. The significant friend is now someone who listens and gives back "more than I ever realized was there."

This startled realization is echoed by Monica, who finds "buried treasures in women I thought I knew for years." Having gotten "off track" with an early pregnancy and "nonstart marriage," she feels inadequate compared to her friends who have thrived in early adulthood. They didn't make the "mistakes" that, in her eyes, are humiliating because they are "so typical of a black girl who just couldn't escape her fate." For many years, she felt that her pride depended upon keeping her distance from them:

I was always so defensive—like they'd got their acts together when I'd really messed up mine. So maybe that's why for so long I didn't really talk to them, just presented this brave face. Even to good friends, who'd done a lot to help me, I don't think I came clean with . . . you know, about how down I could feel about myself and sometimes my daughter. So to hear how they were really feeling their way, too, in this mess we're handed when we try to make a good life while we're stuck with being a woman—like the good life is somehow cleansed from womanly things . . . So to hear how they were often down, too, on themselves, on their kids and their husbands, and to see how they were dealing with these things—I don't know, it was just an eye-opener, and such a relief, to feel that they were feeling some of things I felt, that they could understand, not because they were "lady bountifuls," but because they were in the same boat. So now I can begin to talk to them without thinking that they're going to think they're superior.

Whereas Beth finds friends supportive in her crisis at work, as the actual conditions of her job jolt her against the constraints of her ideal as a career woman, Monica finds friendship important in edging her away from the ideal that has haunted her—the ideal woman who had not "messed up" her life, who never felt "down on herself, on her kids and her husband." As her friends unearth their "buried treasures" of struggle and empathy, Monica realizes that her own struggles are not isolated instances, worthy of shame and derision, but part of that tricky task of constructing a "good life" that still honors "womanly things." In seeing that other women do not adhere to the ideal that shadows her, she is able to feel less "down" on herself and more able to increase her communication with them. Hence, Monica increases her sense of "belonging to a whole group of women who are really great and not fundamentally different from me." Her renewed appreciation of other women goes hand in hand with self-acceptance. This handclasp spreads: As more women silence the ghostly chattering of the ideal to hear their own voices, the more directly they can speak to one another and inspire in others the assurance of belonging to a stream of life deeply shared with other women.[4]

Going into midlife, we continue to construct the social world that matters, protecting one another from the marginalization that all women experience—at least to some degree—simply as a result of being older, being no longer young. Glory explains that with her friends she exults in being "too loud, too bawdy, and too sexy." Friendship develops into a form of resistance—against feeling marginal, against a machinelike dedication, against self-doubt, against stereotypes of what it is to be middle-aged.

Old Friends, Situational Friends

Some women, thinking back over a lifetime of friendships, remember ruefully friendships they thought would last forever but vanished through disuse. Friendships forged through shared challenge, in a particular job, during the child-raising years, through a spouse's professional circles, may have seemed intense at the time but could not withstand moves beyond the life circumstances that gave rise to them. These friendships are often remembered fondly, with a spontaneous "I wonder what ever happened to . . . ?" Or they are minimally maintained with yearly greeting cards. Sometimes they are even reawakened by a new shared interest.

For some women, friendship has a somewhat interchangeable quality. Hazel, sixty, for example, says, "I guess I always needed some friends to do things with and some friends to talk to, but that was different people over the years. I never really made any lifelong friends."

Maria, fifty-five, remembers fondly her three women friends during one particular period in her life:

> We were discovering together our sense of being women, feminism, being angry at men together, seeing that our careers were affected because we were women. It was a time I was intensely close to women. One of these friends was writing poetry, and we were all getting into deeper and deeper levels of our lives together. But after these early years

of self-discovery, it got less intense. They are still friends, but I don't see them very often.

Over time, women's needs of friendship change.

Most women say that as they get older they make fewer friends but feel closer to the ones they do make. "I have so little time now to devote to friendship," says Eileen, forty. "If I'm going to go out to lunch with a friend, I want it to be someone I really enjoy being with, someone I can really talk to."

On the basis of the interviews we conducted, it seems that the women who have maintained lifelong friendships are those who can keep trusting a friend, even when they've been disappointed by her, who can talk openly with a friend and allow her to see the low points in her circumstances and in her self. These women also came to value the shared experiences, the long-term knowledge they had of each other. Asked what had kept her in contact with her best friend of thirty years, Dorothy grinned and said, "Alyssa is the only person in the world who has known all my husbands and all my lovers— and seen every apartment or house I've ever lived in. Alyssa is my continuity in life. Men come and men go. My children think I was born when they were. Alyssa is the record of my life and I am the same for her."

A friend for life knows one's story—firsthand. To a lifelong friend, you don't have to explain much of anything about yourself.

Working at Friendship

For all their importance and for all the pleasure they offer, friend-ships with women are never simple. Time and again, we get "burned"—rejected, disappointed, betrayed. Don't these problems end when we "grow up"? we ask ourselves, knowing the answer is no. While we learn as we mature to deal more realistically with our needs for romantic love, while we learn to adjust our expectations of our parents and our children, we too often fail to learn how to address the clash between desire and reality in the world of friendship. As a result, these important attachments have an underlying fragility. However long-term, however apparently robust, they can nose-dive, taking our spirits down, too, when the ideals of closeness, understanding, and confidentiality are not met.

As we mature, the longing persists for a friend who understands, but the enigmas of maintaining a friendship don't go away just because we gain some wisdom with age. They are modified as we gain a bit in security and self-confidence, so we are no longer quite so badly crushed to hear that someone has said something unkind about us. But we still ask, "Whose friend are you, anyway?" when a friend spends far more time with someone other than us. I still worry that my good friend will come to like and admire a woman who has competed with me and undermined me in the past. "You can't like her too much," I jokingly declare. "You can't become her friend. After all, she's been mean to me." And I laugh, pretending to mock myself, implying, "I can't possibly be so silly as to mean what I say," but everyone who hears me knows I do.

Though we may belittle the impact of our daughter's friendship quarrels, if we are honest with ourselves, we see that we know well this anguish ourselves. Even as mature women, we say, with the intonation of a fifteen-year-old, "As a friend I would expect you'd understand." As "grown-ups," we still feel that a friend can become too possessive, accusing us of slighting her at the conference or the party. We still feel claustrophobic if a friend gets angry when we have to cancel our routine meeting. We can feel stifled by a friend who won't "get on with her life" after a divorce and instead wearies us with the same old complaints. And then we still feel guilty because she is a friend, and we want, really, to offer support. We still feel the power of gossip: What do my friends say about me "behind my back"? I wonder. What annoys them? Do they ever make fun of me? What do they admire? I still feel that to know who I really am, I need to know how my friends really see me.

As we understand our friendships, we can see how persistent is the adolescent within us. This gives us a new pathway to our daughters. Instead of trying to control their friendships, we can talk with them about common difficulties. How many times does a mother's advice prove to her daughter that she "just doesn't understand"? Has any mother been able to separate a daughter from a friend the mother doesn't like? We can be far more effective in helping a daughter through adolescence by talking to her about the ways we do understand, because we are still there, too.

In addition to many enduring tensions, women's friendships are now undergoing change—part of the changing female culture. At one time, the support women offered one another was based upon the similarity of their lives. Left alone during the day to get on with essential jobs in the home, women bonded with other women to form their own networks. Often they protected one another from loneliness, or from feeling marginalized.

Some women, looking back on the changing patterns of their lives, mourn the loss of a community built up by traditional women. Patty, in her late forties, remembers the friendships in her early twenties that worked well for her. They helped provide support and establish an environment in which children could be safe. Women in her neighborhood were friends because their lives were pegged to the same routines, the same troubles, and the same constraints: "Our friendships grew from the other things that were important to us— our children, our neighborhood, and our homes. We were friends with women who had children the ages of our children. We compared our kids. We worried about them together, and we reassured each other. We felt safe with each other." In Patty's view, friendship is based on shared life patterns and life events. She and her friends could look at one another and gain a sense of being right—or not; together they tracked the development of their children. The stability and security they felt with one another was based upon the stability and security of their lives.

As women's lives cease to have that stable commonality, communication and continuity can become more difficult. What is shared? What isn't? What has to be explained? What is understood? Who is critical of whose lifestyle? How can friendships be established on ground that isn't shared? The new variation in women's lives weakens the thrust of all easy comparisons friends might make with one another. "I know exactly how you feel" or "I know just what you're going through" can seldom be uttered with easy confidence. Moreover, time, in which friendships are made and maintained, is now a scarce resource, driving some of us into a loneliness of our own making. "I treasure my women friends," says forty-three-year-old Millie. "I just don't have time for them. I see my friends—rarely—as I'm flying from one thing to another." Clara, also forty-three, is nostalgic for a time when women had time for one another. "Imagine—in our mothers' day, you could just invite a woman friend in for tea in the afternoon. Maybe when I retire in twenty-two years, I'll have time for tea in the afternoon. But by then, who knows if I'll have any friends left?"

The diversity of women's lives creates an essential privacy that often makes contact among women more difficult, more reserved, more scarce. Friendship requires work. "It isn't easy now. There's a new feeling of separate worlds," Patty muses.

Kay, in her mid-forties, notices that she enforces this separation. For her, there is an emptiness in her friendships, as she (implicitly) insults her friends with the assumption that they couldn't really understand her world. Her friendships are friendly but superficial—she chats about inconsequential things with her tennis partner in the locker room, but it's been years since she really "opened up" to a friend. Her life is outwardly directed and she makes no space for the soul-searching she used to associate with friendship.

As women get older and their lives diverge into different configurations, it is harder to make new intimate friends, even though women easily fall into ready companionship at professional meetings or public gatherings. From midlife on, women's friendships begin to involve a dance in which sympathies are tested gingerly, like steaming bathwater. "One word can shut me up," Glory admits, "and I give up—just start to go through the hoops of social talk." At fifty, with many of her previous friendships "flat," she feels a new urge to connect with women: "It can happen quickly—just like it did when I was fourteen, and on a school bus someone becomes your friend. It's like that—but it's more than a few words. You have to be sure she's going to listen, and not judge, and not tell me what I should do. But understand."

The diversity of women's lives and of their values and of their communication styles means that meeting many women doesn't ensure making any friends. There is, then, a new sense of how precious and unpredictable making a friend is. For Patty, friendship is established by an unexpected "exchange of rhythms." With some people, she notes, her conversation is "stilted" and "doesn't flow." She discovers potential friends by the ways they key into her sometimes halting, searching conversation. That eager keying in to what she says, which is such a clear mark of women friends' talk, helps her formulate her own thoughts and vision:

> What I say sometimes just rolls over someone. It's an awful feeling, when you're trying to talk and nothing happens. I may barely know whether something makes sense, and just try it out. And then sometimes it's picked up—you see the flash in the eyes; it's taken in and it means something. The feeling that ideas matter—which is difficult when you're

talking about difficult things. Who is it who understands? Not someone who just thinks they know what you mean, but someone who sees it and wants to see it more.

For Glory, the friendship she yearns for is that intense adolescent connection of listening intently and not judging—just experiencing a resonant flow of mutual exchange. Glory prizes these moments, but they are rare. At fifty, she's aware that no one has had just the same life experiences, so she has to content herself with sharing different bits of herself with different friends:

> In high school, it was so different. You knew all the same people, made fun of the same teachers, went to the same parties, applied to the same colleges. Now it's not so much fun to listen to a friend's stories about people I've never met, and I feel she'd be equally bored by my stories. I mean, you want to talk about things your friend can relate to. You want to have things in common. So I come back from a really stimulating meeting and my friend may ask, "How was it?" and I just say, "Fine," because it would be too complicated to explain all the new ideas and the political intrigue and she wouldn't want to listen that long.

When life is stable in midlife, the growing edges of friendship are sometimes dulled and friendship devolves into steady harmony and companionship. But when a woman is in a phase of change and growth, the passion of friendship returns. Decisions must be made and dreams brought to light, and she needs women friends in the old ways—for validation and support. For Patty, understanding means caring about her experience, rather than sharing it. She wants to explore different meanings, things she "barely knows" and is unsure of. She seeks again the pleasures of adolescent friendship in which her experiences are put on the table to discover their meaning, where she can explore her inner self in the company of a trusted friend.

Just as some women continue to seek the ideal romantic hero, some women continue their adolescent quest for an ideal friend. But most women content themselves with the company of imperfect women they have grown with over time. Although some women get so absorbed in their work and families that they let friendship slip away, a woman without woman friends is a fundamentally lonely woman. And she is missing an important structure through which she can continue to grow.

The Importance of Being Friends

Women differ enormously in whether or not they have maintained long-term intimate friendships. For some, friendship among equally busy friends has a lot of staying power. No one gets insulted by how much time may pass between meetings. Many women spoke with pleasure about the joys of reconnecting with friends after a long period of separation and finding the relationship still intact. More and more, friends are separated by geographical distance as well. "Our friendship is in short, intimate bursts when we see each other," said fifty-five-year-old Belinda.

> We talk nonstop to catch up. And I feel so . . . well, warmed and happy with these hours together. I feel like we've recon- nected and I'm still with her and she with me. But we might not even speak by phone for another six months. It's not a daily kind of friendship. It's a life friendship. We've known each other since junior high. Our lives are very different. But I know we'll always be there for one another.

But maintaining a friend for life takes work, particularly in a highly mobile culture that publicly overlooks the importance of friendship. Our society gives little weight to the emotional and psychological significance of "girlfriends." Friendship among women continues to exist at the margins of our public social order.

Women can now take time off work to care for a sick child or ailing parent, but what company will give time off to take a friend for radiation therapy? When Clara's best friend got cancer, Clara reduced her work schedule to part time so she could take her each day for her radiation treatments and help her look after her four-year-old daughter. This occurred just as Clara was beginning to work in the Rare Books Collection of the Yale Library and was trying to balance her increased professional investment with the needs of her own two young children. "It just seemed like the sort of thing you'd do for a good friend," Clara said.

> One of the things that troubles me about the way the world has evolved is that women have so little time anymore to give to their friends, and I have these moments of having nostalgia for the fifties, when women had time. I can't even think of anyone to put down as an emergency backup person on my children's school cards. I was lucky at the time to have a job that was flexible. I'm a fiercely loyal person and it's very hard for me not to be there if my friends need me.

We have achieved family leave policies in this society, but we are a long way from extending that to friendship leave.

When my best friend of twenty years moved across the country, following her husband's career, there was no marked time or ritual for mourning (although if my husband goes out of the country for a month, everyone around me imagines me to be lonely and seems very sympathetic). Why are there no sympathy cards for losing a friend?

The special bond that is women's friendship grows in soil that provides few nutrients. Our society regards women's friendship as somehow trivial—or a footnote to the depiction of women as wives and mothers—despite the fact that women tell us again and again that it is closeness to other women that oils their lives.

Friends mark our expectations of relationships—of their safe points and areas of danger. Friends pick us up when we fall down and help us reclaim who we are. But even more, friendships keep us warm. Each bond, or repertoire of interactions, is special to each friend, so that after an interval of separation, we catch up so quickly that we exclaim in amazement: "This is just where we left off!" The excitement, tension, fun, and pain of these relationships key us to the mysteries of human connection. They are a special form of love.

Friend Therapy

Throughout this book we have described girls and women who have suffered through longing and conflict in their friend relationships. There is Nadine, who cannot negotiate her position away from being the "perfect girl" everyone likes to know and wants to be with, and the sense of shame in "the real Nadine" that comes back to haunt her in adulthood. There is Janet, who sees Wendy's "protective" lie about what she's doing on a Saturday afternoon as a sign of human limitation in trust and attachment, whose sense of the enormity of this "minor" betrayal remains one of her big secrets even as we speak to her in her forties. There is Tamara, whose first great disillusionment in love comes from seeing her cherished best friend grow away from her. There is Madelyn, who strikes an awkward compromise with her compulsion to charm others, based on her experiences as "the popular girl," and her desire for authenticity. There is Connie, who risks shame with every fantastic lie she tells to gain even a moment's glory with her friends. There is Rosa, who experiences her own cruel impulses toward a dependent and unpopular friend, and carries this knowledge as her secret burden. There is Angie, now ever-cautious of her friends when she forms a romantic alliance: once burned, twice shy—forever after, if one has been burned by a girlfriend.

We have also heard girls and women speak of the liberation and comfort of their friendships, such as how Emma sees that with her friend she's interesting and different, whereas with her family she's a "known quantity." We have seen girls discover their talents, their beauty, their uniqueness through a friend. They experience their interpersonal power: They can comfort, amuse, and instruct. In the wake of current research that shows how girls and women can silence their thoughts, desires, and visions, we see friendship as a relationship offering special opportunities for self-discovery and self-realization. But we also see friendship as an area fraught with danger, and where these dangers are met, but not overcome, they compound the problems girls and women are likely to confront elsewhere. As Enid, while a college junior, muses on a problem she has with Veronica, she notes, "I can't tell Veronica that she's upsetting me by bringing someone else on her vacation. And the fact that I can't speak about that makes it harder to talk to her about other things. In fact, it's getting harder to talk to anyone about anything. It's so easy for them to take something the wrong way, or make you feel bad for what you've said. It's easier just to keep quiet." What's said and not said between girls and between women influences what we can speak to ourselves.

There is no substitute for this double-edged relationship, any more than a substitute can be found for the essential, enabling—and dangerous—liaison between child and parent. How can we help a girl, a woman—ourselves—to maintain authenticity when a close friendship threatens it? How can we help a girl withstand the disappointment or humiliation when a girlfriend turns away from her, or teases her, or betrays her? How can we help girls, and coach ourselves, to speak our minds? How can we teach our daughters, and remind ourselves, to accept differences? How can we learn better strategies for competing comfortably with other women without guilt and without rancor?

As a society, we have come recently to recognize the way girls have been tyrannized by social expectations to be the "perfect girl," and the image of perfection often extends to her friendships as well. In early adolescence, as the growing girl comes to recognize the failings of love in her family, she often turns to another girl in hopes of finding the perfect love. Silvia, at thirteen, believes she has found it, but knows the perfection is fragile, so keeps her best friend separate from her day-to-day school friends. When we speak to her again at fifteen, she admits she often feels annoyed with Helen, but shies away from her when she feels a quarrel coming. This avoidance clashes with her desire "just to say what you mean." Her goal is to develop the art of tact, "the way to say what you mean without hurting feelings." One year later, at sixteen, Silvia still feels anchored by the friendship. She and Helen have quarreled and parted and come back together several times. Silvia didn't like this pattern, but it helped both her and her friend discover that they "can talk about things going wrong." Though she has lots of friends, and no "best friend," she has a special attunement to Helen:

> We hadn't spoken for a while and I realized that we'd lost some ground, and a few weeks ago I went to find her. She had noticed, too, and said, "I could feel you drifting," and I thought, 'No, Silv, don't drift, this is when I need you most.' It is honesty that keeps us going. Our loyalty has stayed from when we were children, and also our admiration for each other, but we no longer idealize each other.

We hope that all girls will learn what Silvia has worked hard with her friend to learn: that honesty will keep them together, and that loyalty and admiration can remain strong, even when friends no longer idealize each other, and even when they've experienced being annoyed by each other.

There will never be rules for making any relationship perfect or without strife, or formulas for speaking one's mind without hurting a friend's feelings. Good friendships are complex and never easy. Therapy for friendship, like all other kinds of therapy, involves increasing communication so that we become more able to speak our experience and recognize and contain the thoughts and feelings of our friend. Always, the edge of growth in relationships is learning deeply that other people experience from their own center, a center that is different from our own.

We need to learn, as women, to stop idealizing friendship, expecting it to be without its bumps and disappointments. As mothers, we can help our daughters learn to live with "good-enough" friends, friends who allow them their authenticity and claim their own. If we stop being "nice" and say who we are, we potentially gain in honest mutuality but risk conflict. If girls' friendship is the testing ground for expectations in later relationships, let us try to do whatever we can to ensure that they are relationships in which girls can discover their "true" selves.

As adults trying to guide girls through the stormy places in adolescent friendships, we can help them by recognizing the pain, sadness, and danger in these friendships without being overwhelmed by them. We do this by allowing ourselves to acknowledge that, yes, this is how relationships are—imperfect and conflict-ridden. But we also know that it is in the journey through these perils and disruptions that lie the experiences of joy and authenticity that are the "pure gold" of girls' and women's friendships.

ENDNOTES

1. "What Are Friends For?"

1. Pat O'Connor (1992) points out that the study of women's friendship has been largely ignored in the social sciences. Generally, the scientific community, when it has dealt with the topic at all, either idealizes or trivializes women's friendships. Recently there has been renewed interest in the topic largely because of a recognition of the relationship between friendship and psychological health. O'Connor provides a careful and thoughtful review of the work on women's friendships in the 1970s and '80s. Her overview concludes that "women have various kinds of friends; that these friendships are no longer exclusively dyadic; that friendship has some similarities with kin relationships; that friendships tend to be positively associated with various indicators of psychological well-being; that social class position, age, life stage and marital status are amongst the factors which need to be taken into account in understanding them; that friendship plays an important part in creating and/or maintaining women's social worlds and the moral discourses within them" (p. 174). The 1990s have seen an increase in ethnographic studies of girls' friendships, particularly in England; see Griffiths (1995), Hey (1997), and Thorne (1993). In the United States, even work that makes an effort to look carefully at girls' adolescent experience gives scant attention to girls' friendships (Gilligan, Lyons, and Hammer, 1990; Brown and Gilligan, 1992).

2. Belenky, Clinchy, Goldberger, and Tarule (1986); Gilligan (1982); Tannen (1990).

3. See, for example, Berry and Traeder (1995). Speaking of the problem of the idealization of friendship, Helen Gouldner and Mary Strong (1987)

say that "not only is friendship idealized, but the disparities between ideal and actual behavior tend to make some friendships fragile" (p. 8).

4. See Rubin (1985) and Pogrebin (1986) for an exploration of the varieties of friendship among both women and men.

2. "If Only I Had a Real Friend"

1. Dan McAdams (1988) identifies two styles of friendship: one more focused on power, the other on intimacy. The latter, which characterizes women's style of friendship, is associated with the need to merge by surrendering the self in open, cooperative contact. Studies of women show that they say they can "talk" to other women in a way they cannot talk to most men, who seem uninterested in speculating about the happenings of the day or analyzing other people's actions or character. Thus, there appears to be a "universe of discourse" unique to the female world. In addition, in woman/man pairs, women tend to be the listeners, while woman/woman pairs afford equal talk time to both (Gouldner and Strong, 1987).

2. Nancy Chodorow (1978) has given a brilliant and influential account of the reproduction within each generation of certain general and nearly universal differences that characterize masculine and feminine personality roles. She attributes these differences not to anatomy but rather to the fact that women, universally, are largely responsible for early child care. Because this early social environment differs for and is experienced differently by male and female children, basic sex differences recur in personality development. As a result, in any given society, feminine personality comes to define itself in relation and connection to other people more than masculine personality does.

   In her analysis Chodorow relies on Robert Stoller's studies that indicate that gender identity—the unchanging core of personality formation—is with rare exception firmly and irreversibly established for both sexes by the age of three. Given that for both sexes the primary caretaker in the first three years of life is typically female, the interpersonal dynamics of gender identity formation for girls and boys are different. Female identity formation takes place in a context of ongoing relationship, since mothers, Chodorow writes, "tend to experience their daughters as more like, and continuous themselves." Correspondingly, girls, in identifying with themselves as female, experience themselves as like their mothers, thus fusing the experience of attachment with the process of identity formation. In contrast, "mothers experience their sons as a male opposite, and boys, in defining themselves as masculine, separate their mothers from themselves." As boys separate themselves from their mothers, Chodorow suggests, they curtail their primary love and sense of empathic tie. Consequently, male development entails a more emphatic individuation and a more defensive firming of experienced ego boundaries.

Chodorow argues that the existence of sex differences in the early experiences of individuation and relationship does not mean that women have *weaker* ego boundaries than men, or are more prone to psychosis. It means instead that girls emerge from this period with a basis for empathy built into their primary definition of self in a way that boys do not.

3. Tamplin (1989).

4. Nielsen and Rudberg (1994).

5. Thorne (1993).

6. Ibid.

7. Youniss and Smollar (1985).

8. Research has shown that, in contrast to boys, girls expect more of their friends, feel more attached to them, and experience greater intimacy with their best friend; see Sharabany, Gershoni, and Hofman (1981) and Claes (1992). In a study of college students, Robert Barth and Bill Kinder (1988) found that women were more likely to have friends to whom they could relate on a variety of levels while men were more likely to develop different friendships for different needs.

9. Rubin (1985), p. 175.

10. "Best friends" may not see each other for years due to external factors such as geographical distance. What is important to the friendship is the perception that there is a reservoir of affection and responsiveness (O'Connor, 1992; Duck, 1986).

11. In a study of middle-class women, Helen Gouldner and Mary Strong (1987) found that many of their participants were not sure whether their closest friend was close enough to be called a "best friend." In part, the women were often puzzled about how the other woman felt.

Gouldner and Strong point out that, unlike being able to ask a lover, "Do you love me?" it is considered uncouth to ask a woman friend, "May I call you my best friend?" Degrees of intimacy in friendship are often hard to calibrate.

3. "Whose Friend Are You, Anyway?"

1. Friendship among girls (and women) also invokes a mutually understood moral order pertaining to caring, trust, and loyalty. Girls must prove that they can "do" the moral work of friendship correctly or risk exclusion (Nilan, 1991).

2. Miell and Duck (1986) have done some research trying to track the subtle processes by which people negotiate how close a friendship they would like to have.

3. Thorne (1993).

4. Lever (1976) considered the peer group to be the agent of socialization during the elementary-school years. She set out to discover whether there were sex differences in the games that children play. She studied 181 white middle-class children, ages ten and eleven, observing the organization and structure of their playtime activities. She watched the children as they played at school during recess and in physical education class, and in addition kept diaries of their accounts as to how they spent their time outside of school. From this study, Lever reported many sex differences. Boys play outdoors more often than girls do. Boys play more often in large and age-heterogenous groups. Boys play competitive games more often, and their games last longer than girls' games. This last finding came to be of particular interest, because what she found was that boys' games tended to last longer partly because they required a higher level of skill and so were less prone to become boring, but also because when disputes arose in the course of the game, boys were able to resolve the disputes more effectively than girls. "During the course of this study," Lever wrote, "boys were seen quarrelling all the time, but not once was a game terminated because of a quarrel and no game was interrupted for more than seven minutes. In the gravest debates, the final word was always to repeat the play, generally followed by a chorus of cheater's proof." In fact, it seemed that boys enjoyed the legal debates as much as they did the game itself, and even marginal players of lesser size or skill participated in these recurrent squabbles. In contrast, the

eruption of disputes among girls tended to end the game. Girls would stop playing rather than fight about the play. Lever believed they kept their games simple (and boring) so that they could play harmoniously. This view of girls' play as essentially noncompetitive has been modified many times (see, for example, Goodwin, 1991, and Eckert, 1990), but it remains a widely held bias.

5. Eder (1990).

6. Sheldon (1990) videotaped three- and four-year-old boys and girls playing in threesomes at a day-care center. She compared two groups of three—one of boys and one of girls—that got into fights about the same toy. Though both groups fought over the same thing, the dynamics by which they negotiated their conflicts were different. The girls referred to others' needs to justify their desire to control the toy, whereas boys appealed to their own needs.

7. Girls learn to find and take a place among the multiple regimes of power that exist among them. Standards of beauty have been well explored as conferring higher prestige, but there are other aspects of the political world that girls create to differentiate among themselves which have not been well understood (Hey, 1997).

4. "I Knew You'd Understand!"

1. In her study of adolescent girls' friendship, Griffiths (1995) found that girls had an intense need to identify themselves as the same as their friends and that the fact of sameness often preceded mention of the specific aspects of themselves that were the same.

2. The ethos of women's friendship is for the friends to stay the same. Luise Eichenbaum and Susie Orbach (1987) go so far as to say "difference cannot be allowed and it is experienced as dangerous and threatening and invokes feelings of abandonment" (p. 89). They see this as resulting from the merged attachment girls feel as infants with their mothers, an attachment they try to replicate in their friendships with other females. Other writers, however, stress the ways in which the experience of sameness in relationship actually promotes self-differentiation (Berzoff, 1989; Miller, 1984). From the point of view of psychoanalytic object relations theory, the experience of fusion with the mother in

infancy is the soil in which the self grows (Winnicott, 1958; Guntrip, 1969). Moments of experience of unity between girls and between women can lead to a psychological restructuring that allows for expansion and increased awareness and differentiation of the self. When too much of the friendship is bound by the requirement of inflexible sameness, however, either partner may experience the relationship as suffocating.

3. There is an art to commiserating talk, which involves reciprocal self-deprication and may, at times, necessitate camouflaging one's true reactions (Fillion, 1996). Over time, girls learn—often painfully—which responses to a friend in distress enhance closeness and which are viewed as competitive or insensitive. Adult women, however, still struggle with these issues, and one aspect of "women talk" is figuring out what one might have said to another or whether what one did say was the "wrong" thing. Like any art, responsiveness is a creative process. In this case, it requires exquisite balance between one's own needs and one's friend's needs.

4. Gouldner and Strong (1987), whose research demonstrated the centrality of talk to women's friendship, point out that woman talk is also a form of entertainment.

5. Brumberg (1997).

6. Stern (1991) describes the child's concern with stories other people tell of her as she constructs her own narrative of herself.

7. Among women, talk is central to the relationship (O'Connor, 1992; Gouldner and Strong, 1987). While talk is inherently satisfying as a form of mutuality (Josselson, 1992), it has the effect of creating social discourses and shared understandings, thereby structuring the social world (Duck, 1986).

8. See Moore (1994) for a description of a similar relationship.

9. O'Connor (1971), p. 236.

10. "For the girl, the erotic is diffuse, remote, ambiguous and complex. She also has the task of controlling and gratifying impulses, but at the same time she must learn their nature . . . she does so through intimate friendship" (Douvan and Adelson, 1966, p. 193).

5. "I'm Not Who You Think I Am"

1. Barker (1991), p. 242.

2. Music becomes a central way for adolescents (who live in homogeneous groupings) to differentiate themselves. Groups of friends may feel bonded by liking certain music groups and not others. Changes in a girl's music tastes usually signify changes in identification with certain friends and therefore changes in a girl's sense of identity.

3. Coates (1996); Tannen (1990).

4. Many gifted women and strong girls were socially isolated and lonely in adolescence, but emerged from this experience more independent and self-sufficient (Pipher, 1994). See also Kerr (1985).

5. Cited in Brown and Gilligan (1992).

6. See Winnicott (1965) for a discussion of the early development of true and false selves.

6. "Promise You Won't Tell"

1. Lakoff also observed this in 1990, Chapter 4.

2. Coates (1996) calls this "exchanged vulnerable talking."

3. Goodwin (1991) noted in her study of adolescent girls elaborate procedures during which girls instigated storytelling about who said what about whom. She describes how this gossip becomes a way by which girls can confront others and defend themselves against others' unfairness.

4. Henry (1965).

5. Many researchers have noticed how exhausting this precious balance is for women and how difficult it is for them to retain contentment with their own choices. See, for example, Apter (1995) and Hochschild (1997).

7. "Forget It—I Don't Want to Talk About It"

1. Goodwin (1991); Tannen (1990).

2. Griffiths (1995).

3. Sheldon (1990) videotaped groups of preschool children playing and arguing, and her study showed that even by the age of three, children have internalized certain norms: Boys are supposed to be openly competitive and girls are supposed to be openly cooperative. However, as Deborah Tannen argued (1990), girls do compete, but they do so indirectly.

4. Brown and Gilligan (1992) describe a process whereby some girls silence their own feelings and thoughts in order to accommodate others' values. A common effect of this suppression is dissociation, whereby some girls subsequently fail to acknowledge their own experience. This process (an extreme version of being nice in order to be liked) is then described as the paradox of taking oneself out of relationship in order to preserve it.

5. Research also demonstrates that the ending of a friendship among women rarely involves confrontation. Rather, the friends gradually or suddenly curtail their involvement (O'Connor, 1992).

6. Jack (1991) builds a theory of depression on this process. In her research she found that women who were depressed believed that it was dangerous to express their own thoughts and feelings to someone they loved. Women were often controlled by a sense of who they should be, and felt worthless insofar as they did not meet these internalized cultural norms of "the good woman."

7. Coates (1996) records a conversation in which women friends refuse to pick up on certain kinds of critical remarks. One woman refers to another woman's body hair, and her friends act as if they haven't heard her, thus signaling that certain types of criticism are unacceptable.

8. "If Only I Could Be Like Her"

1. The encounter with difference in friendship can both enlarge and enrich the self. Our Western notions of the self construct it as endlessly transformable—one can be anything one wants. Thus, girls may use the experience of difference to demarcate the self, but they are more likely, particularly when they admire someone, to feel that if only they do the right things, they can have her valued qualities.

2. Spender (1985).

3. This finding was reported in Apter (1991).

4. Horner (1972) showed that some young women exhibit marked fear of success because they believe that success will lead to social isolation. Her studies have been reassessed and reinterpreted many times (for example, see Georgia Sassen [1980]).

5. Limb (1989).

9. "I Never Thought This Would Come Between Us"

1. Kate Pullinger's novel *The Last Time I Saw Jane* deals with the cruelty toward a friend that can arise in the face of a friend's betrayal.

2. Stacey Oliker's (1989) research shows that friendship among women works to stabilize a marriage and mitigate its disappointments by providing personal space and validation of identity. Women support and learn from one another in regard to men, using one another to smooth the rough spots (O'Connor, 1992).

3. For most of this century, the accepted canon of psychology taught that girls gave up their close emotional relationships with other girls when they became interested in boys. Helene Deutsch, the great psychoanalyst of women's development in the middle of the twentieth century, taught that it was regressive and therefore pathological for adult women to maintain close friendships with other women. Research, however, has demonstrated that girls do not give up their friendships with other girls when they become involved with boys (Griffiths, 1995).

4. Men frequently fear what may happen when women get together, fearful that they may no longer have a place in their lives. Pat O'Connor (1992) points out that public recognition of the ways in which women enjoy themselves with one another undermines patriarchal ideology with its stress on romantic love with a man as the focal point of pleasure. In pointing out that part of what bonds women is working through romantic love ideology and experience, we don't mean to suggest that this is *central* to what bonds them. As we point out in other chapters, women certainly do enjoy themselves together without talking about or thinking about men. Yet being in a shared place in the patriarchal order does necessarily influence their relationships with one another. Women's friendship can be seen as a means of both preserving the patriarchal order and undermining it.

5. Hey (1997).

6. Girls are relatively free to express affection physically with one another. Some writers regard this as practice for later heterosexual pairings; others speculate about the possible latent homosexual meanings this behavior may have. See Griffiths (1995).

7. Jacqueline Weinstock and Esther Rothblum (1996) have edited an excellent volume on lesbian friendship. In their introduction, however, they acknowledge their dilemma in drawing a clear line between lesbian friendships and lesbian sexual/romantic relationships. There are nonphysical lesbian friendships that are nevertheless construed by the participants as sexual and lesbian lover relationships that do not include genital sex. Women may engage in passionate and intense relationships with each other without the relationship being "lesbian." The distinction lies in how the participants define the relationship rather than in how they act or feel toward each other. Jeanne Stanley (1996) says that friendships for lesbians are very much like those of heterosexual women when homophobia and heterosexism do not impede the relationship. Lesbians are also more likely to live in and value the importance of community, building networks that define their lesbian existence in contrast to the expectations of their families and society.

8. See Apter (1995).

10. "Will We Always Be Friends?"

1. Rubin (1985).

2. Josselson (1996). In the elderly, old friends maintain identity, preserving a woman's image of herself (O'Connor, 1992; Crohan and Antonucci, 1989).

3. As women age, they turn even more toward one another for emotional support (Block and Greenberg, 1985). Most older women report getting together with friends "just to talk," emotional exchange being more important than any practical, logistical helping that may be involved (Roberto, 1996).

4. Dana Jack (1991) finds that friendship is an important factor in helping women overcome depression.

BIBLIOGRAPHY

Adair, Catherine Steiner. 1991. "When the Body Speaks: Girls, Eating Disorders and Psychotherapy." *Women and Therapy* 11, no. 3/4 (1991): 253–66.

Apter, Terri. *Altered Loves: Mothers and Daughters During Adolescence.* New York: Fawcett, 1991.

———. *The Confident Child.* New York: W. W. Norton, 1997.

———. *Secret Paths: Women in the New Midlife.* New York: W. W. Norton, 1995.

Atwood, Margaret. *Cat's Eye.* New York: Bantam Books, 1988.

Bagshaw, Louise. *Career Girls.* London: Orion, 1995.

Barker, Pat. *Regeneration.* New York: Plume, 1991.

Barth, Robert J., and Bill N. Kinder. "A Theoretical Analysis of Sex Differences in Same-Sex Friendships." *Sex Roles* 19, no. 5/6 (1988): 349–63.

Beauvoir, Simone de. *The Second Sex.* Trans. and ed. by H. M. Parshley. Hammondsworth: Penguin, 1972.

Belenky, Mary F., Blythe M. Clinchy, Nancy R. Goldberger, and Jill M. Tarule. *Women's Ways of Knowing.* New York: Basic Books, 1986.

Bell, Robert. *Worlds of Friendship.* Beverly Hills, Calif.: Sage, 1981.

Berry, Carmen Renee, and Tamara Traeder. *Girlfriends.* Berkeley: Wildcat Canyon Press, 1995.

Berzoff, Joan. "Fusion and Heterosexual Women's Friendships: Implications for Expanding Our Adult Developmental Theories." *Women and Therapy* 8, no. 4 (1989): 91–107.

Block, Joel, and Diane Greenberg. *Women and Friendship.* New York: Franklin Watts, 1985.

Brown, Lyn Mikel. *Stones in the Road: Anger, Class and White Adolescent Girls* (forthcoming).

Brown, Lyn Mikel, and Carol Gilligan. *Meeting at the Crossroads.* Cambridge, Mass.: Harvard University Press, 1992.

Brumberg, Joan Jacobs. *The Body Project: An Intimate History of American Girls.* New York: Random House, 1997.

Campbell, Anne. *The Girls in the Gang.* New York: Basil Blackwood, 1984.

Chodorow, Nancy. *The Reproduction of Mothering.* Berkeley: University of California Press, 1978.

Claes, Michael. "Friendship and Personal Adjustment During Adolescence." *Journal of Adolescence* 15 (1992): 39–55.

Coates, Jennifer. *Women Talk.* Cambridge, Mass.: Blackwell Publishers, 1996.

Crohan, S. E., and T. Antonucci. "Friends as a Source of Support in Old Age." In R. G. Adams and R. Blieszner, eds., *Older Adult Friendship.* Newbury Park, Calif.: Sage, 1989.

Davies, Bronwyen. *Life in the Classroom and Playground: The Accounts of Primary School Children.* London: Routledge, 1982.

Douvan, Elizabeth, and Joseph B. Adelson. *The Adolescent Experience.* New York: John Wiley & Sons, 1966.

Duck, Steve. *Human Relationships.* Newbury Park, Calif.: Sage, 1986.

Dunn, Susannah. *Venus Flaring.* London: Flamingo, 1996.

Eckert, Penelope. "Cooperative Competition in Adolescent 'Girl Talk.'" *Discourse Processes* 13 (1990):1.

Eder, Donna. "Serious and Playful Disputes: Variations in Conflict Talk Among Female Adolescents." In *Conflict Talk,* ed. by Allen Grimshaw, 67–84. Cambridge: Cambridge University Press, 1990.

Eichenbaum, Luise, and Susie Orbach. *Between Women.* New York: Penguin, 1987.

Fillion, Kate. *Lip Service.* New York: HarperCollins, 1996.

Gilligan, Carol. *In a Different Voice.* Cambridge, Mass.: Harvard University Press, 1982.

Gilligan, Carol, Nona Lyons, and Trudy J. Hammer. *Making Connections.* Cambridge, Mass.: Harvard University Press, 1990.

Goodwin, Marjorie Harness. *He-Said-She-Said: Talk as Social Organization Among Black Children.* Bloomington: Indiana University Press, 1991.

Gouldner, Helen, and Mary Symons Strong. *Speaking of Friends: Middle-Class Women and Their Friends.* New York: Greenwood Press, 1987.

Griffiths, Vivienne. *Adolescent Girls and Their Friends.* Avebury, England: Aldershot, Hants, 1995.

Guntrip, Harry. *Schizoid Phenomena, Object Relations and the Self.* New York: International Universities Press, 1969.

Henry, Jules. *Culture Against Man.* New York: Vintage, 1965.

Hey, Valerie. *The Company She Keeps: An Ethnography of Girls' Friendship.* Buckingham, England: Open University Press, 1997.

Hochschild, Arlie. *The Time Bind: When Work Becomes Home and Home Becomes Work.* New York: Henry Holt and Co., 1997.

Horner, Matina. "Towards an Understanding of Achievement-Related Conflicts in Women," *Journal of Social Issues* 28 (1972): 157–76.

Jack, Dana. *Silencing the Self: Women and Depression.* Cambridge, Mass.: Harvard University Press, 1991.

Josselson, Ruthellen. *Finding Herself: Pathways to Identity Development in Women.* San Francisco: Jossey-Bass, 1987.

———. *Revising Herself: The Story of Women's Identity from College to Midlife.* New York: Oxford University Press, 1996.

———. *The Space Between Us: Exploring the Dimensions of Human Relationships.* San Francisco: Jossey-Bass, 1992.

Kerr, Barbara. *Smart Girls, Gifted Women.* Columbus, Ohio: Ohio Psychology Publishing, 1985.

Lakoff, Robin. *Talking Power: The Politics of Language.* New York: Basic Books, 1990.

Lever, Janet. "Sex Differences in the Games Children Play." *Social Problems* 23 (1976): 478–87.

Limb, Sue. "Female Friendship." In *The Dialectics of Friendship,* ed. by Roy Porter and Sylvana Tomaselli. London: Routledge, 1989.

Mantel, Hilary. *An Experiment in Love.* New York: Viking, 1995.

McAdams, Dan. "Personal Needs and Personal Relationships." In Steve Duck et al., eds., *Handbook of Personal Relationships.* Chichester, England: Wiley, 1988.

Miell, Dorothy, and Steve Duck. "Strategies in Developing Friendships." In *Friendship and Social Interaction,* ed. by V. J. Derlega and B. A. Winstead. New York: Springer, 1986.

Miller, Jean Baker. "The Development of Women's Sense of Self." *Work in Progress,* no. 12. Wellesley, Mass.: Stone Center Working Papers Series, 1984.

Moore, Lorrie. *Who Will Run the Frog Hospital?* New York: Alfred A. Knopf, 1994.

Nielsen, Harriet Bjerrum, and Monica Rudberg. *Psychological Gender and Modernity.* New York: Oxford University Press, 1994.

Nilan, P. "Exclusion, Inclusion and Moral Ordering in Two Girls' Friendship Groups." *Gender and Education* 3, no. 1 (1991): 163–82.

Oates, Joyce Carol. *Foxfire.* New York: E. P. Dutton, 1993.

O'Connor, Flannery. *The Complete Stories.* New York: Farrar, Straus & Giroux, 1971.

O'Connor, Pat. *Friendships Between Women: A Critical Review.* New York: Guilford Press, 1992.

Oliker, Stacey J. *Best Friends and Marriage: Exchange Among Women.* Berkeley: University of California Press, 1989.

Orenstein, Peggy, in association with the American Association of University Women. *Schoolgirls.* New York: Doubleday, 1994.

Pipher, Mary. *Reviving Ophelia.* New York: Ballantine, 1994.

Pogrebin, Letty. *Among Friends: Who We Like, Why We Like Them and What We Can Do About Them.* New York: McGraw-Hill, 1986.

Roberto, Karen A. "Friendships Between Older Women: Interactions and Reactions." In Karen A. Roberto, ed., *Relationships Between Women in Later Life.* New York: Haworth, 1996.

Rubin, Lillian. *Just Friends: The Role of Friendship in Our Lives.* New York: Harper and Row, 1985.

Sassen, Georgia. "Success Anxiety in Women: A Constructivist Interpretation of Its Source and Its Significance." *Harvard Educational Review* 50 (1980): 1.

Seiden, Anne, and Pauline Bart. "Woman to Woman: Is Sisterhood Powerful?" In N. Glazer-Malbin, ed., *Old Family/New Family.* New York: Van Nostrand, 1975.

Sharabany, Ruth, R. Gershoni, and J. E. Hofman. "Girlfriend, Boyfriend: Age and Sex Differences in Intimate Friendship." *Developmental Psychology* 5 (1981): 800–808.

Sheldon, Amy. "Conflict Talk: Sociolinguistic Challenges to Self-Assertion and How Young Girls Meet Them." *Merril Palmer Quarterly* 38 (1992): 95–117.

———. "Pickle Fights: Gendered Talk in Preschool Disputes." *Discourse Processes* 13 (1990): 1.

Spender, Dale. *Man-Made Language,* 2d ed. London: Routledge, 1985.

Stanley, Jeanne L. "The Lesbian's Experience of Friendship." In Jacqueline S. Weinstock and Esther D. Rothblum, eds., *Lesbian Friendships.* New York: New York University Press, 1996.

Stern, Daniel. *Diary of a Baby.* London: Fontana, 1991.

———. *The Interpersonal World of the Infant: A View from Psychoanalysis and Developmental Psychology.* New York: Basic Books, 1985.

Stoller, Robert. "The 'Bedrock' of Masculinity and Femininity: Bisexuality." *Archives of General Psychiatry* 26 (1972).

Syal, Meera. *Anita and Me.* London: Flamingo, 1997.

Tamplin, Alison. *Six-Year-Olds in the School Playground.* Cambridge, England: University of Cambridge, unpublished doctoral thesis, 1989.

Tannen, Deborah. *You Just Don't Understand.* New York: Morrow, 1990.

Thorne, Barrie. *Gender Play: Girls and Boys at School.* Buckingham, England: Open University Press, 1993.

Trapido, Barbara. *Temples of Delight.* London: Michael Joseph, 1990.

Weinstock, Jacqueline S., and Esther D. Rothblum, eds. *Lesbian Friendships.* New York: New York University Press, 1996.

Winnicott, Donald W. "The Capacity to Be Alone." *International Journal of Psychoanalysis* 39 (1958): 416–20.

———. "Ego Distortion in Terms of True and False Self." In *The Maturational Process and the Facilitating Environment.* New York: International Universities Press, 1965.

Youniss, James, and Jacqueline Smollar. "Adolescents' Interpersonal Relationships in Social Context." In *Peer Relationships in Child Development,* ed. by T. J. Berndt and G. W. Ladd. New York: Wiley, 1985.

INDEX